SHAKESPEARE ON SCREEN

SHAKESPEARE

O N   S C R E E N

DANIEL ROSENTHAL

hamlyn

Commissioning Editor Julian Brown
Project Editor Tarda Davison-Aitkins
Creative Director Keith Martin
Executive Art Director Mark Winwood
Designer Peter Gerrish
Picture Research Zoë Holtermann
Production Controller Louise Hall

First published in Great Britain in 2000
by Hamlyn, an imprint of
Octopus Publishing Group Limited
2–4 Heron Quays, London E14 4JP

Copyright © 2000 Octopus Publishing Group Limited

Distributed in the United States and Canada by
Sterling Publishing Co., Inc.
387 Park Avenue South
New York, NY 10016-8810

ISBN 0 600 60115 3

A catalogue record for this book is available from the
British Library

Produced by Toppan
Printed in China

CONTENTS

INTRODUCTION

Above: William Shakespeare
(1564–1616) – would the Bard
have enjoyed cinema's
treatment of his plays?

Cinema's love affair with Shakespeare has lasted for more than 100 years. It began in September 1899 with a silent film showing brief extracts from a West End stage production of *King John*. It is still thriving in 2000 with Ethan Hawke appearing at American multiplexes as the first screen Hamlet of the 21st century and new versions of *King Lear* and *A Midsummer Night's Dream* in the pipeline.

Films based on Shakespeare's plays have emerged from as far afield as Brazil and Ghana, Finland and Japan. British and American contributions have generated more than 20 Oscar victories and a handful of box-office smashes as well as some woeful flops.

This book sets out to illustrate the extraordinary breadth of screen Shakespeare, by assessing in detail more than 50 films based on his plays and by tracing their production history and critical and commercial fortunes.

Most of the films covered are English-language adaptations of the tragedies, histories and comedies, which use Shakespeare's text as their screenplays. Also included, however, are numerous Shakespeare 'variants' – movies such as *West Side Story*, *Joe Macbeth* and *Tempest*, which retain the Bard's plots and characters without using his poetry or settings. The variants reveal the extent to which the plays have been customized to fit almost every conceivable screen genre: Westerns, melodramas, gangster thrillers, musicals, horror and even science fiction.

Thirteen chapters are assigned to the plays that have been most frequently adapted. Each chapter begins with an introduction, comprising a synopsis of the play, a discussion of its suitability for screen treatment and a summary of its film history. This is followed by sections devoted to individual films.

An additional chapter, 'Other Plays', deals with five Shakespeare dramas, each of which has been turned into an English-language feature film on only one occasion, and briefly summarizes other screen treatments of the remaining plays, whether originally made for cinema or for television. 'Shakespeare on TV' rounds up five outstanding examples of the Bard's treatment on the small screen (all of plays that feature in the main section or in 'Other Plays').

A chapter on 'Shakespeare in Other Movies' looks at how material from the plays has been incorporated into original screenplays, most of them set backstage in the acting world.

Academy Award wins and nominations are not always given in full in the text; compete details are in 'Shakespeare at the Oscars' on pages 188–189.

Throughout, I have concentrated on each production as a film in its own right and as a work of adaptation, looking at how 'faithfully' it has treated its source play.

Actor-directors Laurence Olivier, Orson Welles and Kenneth Branagh, directors Akira Kurosawa and Franco Zeffirelli and John Gielgud – arguably *the* voice of Shakespeare in the movies – have all had an immense impact on the history of

Shakespeare on screen. I have profiled each of them, setting their Shakespeare work in the context of their wider careers.

The Bard v the box office

'The value of Shakespeare to the screen is more strictly in the creation of prestige for the individual production company than in the accumulation of receipts.' That was *Variety*'s conclusion in 1936, after the first three Shakespeare movies produced by Hollywood in the sound era (1929's *The Taming of the Shrew*, 1935's *A Midsummer Night's Dream* and 1936's *Romeo and Juliet*) had all underperformed at the box office. As a general rule, that assessment remains true to this day.

With the exception of occasional hits, such as Zeffirelli and Baz Luhrmann's versions of *Romeo and Juliet*, or Branagh's *Much Ado About Nothing*, Shakespeare films rarely leave an impression on the box-office charts. Millions of cinemagoers are automatically put off by the plays' rarefied language, something they are more likely to associate with the classroom than an enjoyable night out at the movies. Miramax Films boss Harvey Weinstein even wanted to change the title of 1998's *Shakespeare in Love* because he believed, incorrectly as it turned out, that the Bard's name alone would make audiences stay away in droves. Similar concerns have been expressed by studio executives for generations and directors have usually faced an uphill battle to raise the millions of dollars necessary to film a Shakespeare play.

Dozens have succeeded, allowing those cinemagoers not dissuaded by the poetry to enjoy movies which can be viewed as the ultimate remakes. The opportunity to watch three or more versions of one Shakespeare play gives rise to unique comparisons between some of the most celebrated names in film history. You can find out what playing Petruchio in *The Taming of the Shrew* says about the charisma of Douglas Fairbanks and Richard Burton or what playing Richard III reveals about the screen presence of Laurence Olivier and Al Pacino. You can

decide who was best-suited to playing Ophelia: Jean Simmons, Helena Bonham Carter or Kate Winslet.

It's easy to see why so many stars have been drawn, not always wisely, to Shakespeare. Because of their poetry and depth of characterization, roles such as Richard III and Ophelia undoubtedly offer a greater test and, if actors' comments in interviews are to be believed, greater rewards than even the finest modern prose screenplay.

An appearance in Shakespeare cannot fail to add prestige to the CV of stars who lack experience of classical stage roles, particularly Hollywood superstars determined to alter the critical consensus that they can only play tough guys in modern-day pictures. This book relates how this particular manoeuvre was made by James Cagney in *A Midsummer Night's Dream*, Marlon Brando in *Julius Caesar* and Mel Gibson in *Hamlet*; it may work again for another typecast leading man in 2030.

Comparisons between Shakespeare films also reflect how cinema itself has evolved. The contrast between MGM's stiflingly reverent, bland *Romeo and Juliet* of 1936 and 1996's electrifying *William Shakespeare's Romeo + Juliet* speaks volumes about how much Hollywood changed in the intervening 60 years in areas such as camerawork, editing, music and sexual explicitness.

Yet the fundamental challenge for film-makers approaching Shakespeare has not changed: how do you transfer a 400-year-old play written in blank verse for fairly primitive theatres to film, a medium more dependent on moving images than words and necessarily restricted action?

How have directors dealt with the problem of soliloquies? An integral element of Shakespeare's craft, readily accepted by theatregoers, soliloquies are an oddity in cinema, where it is always shocking to find characters talking to themselves let alone acknowledging our presence. Nicol Williamson's Hamlet and Ian McKellen's Richard III both break this convention magnificently.

Should directors depict key events that Shakespeare only described by report? Should they show the violent acts that Shakespeare sometimes kept off-stage? To obtain a commercially viable running time of, for instance, 150 minutes, which characters and scenes should be cut from those plays that run for three or four hours on stage? The films in *Shakespeare on Screen* offer some very distinctive answers to these questions.

From stage to screen

In the 1590s and 1600s, when Shakespeare's plays were performed at the Rose and Globe theatres in London, his language was all important. Scenery was almost non-existent, and the Bard relied on his poetic genius to conjure foreign settings – Verona, Elsinore, Rome, Alexandria – hoping that, as the chorus in *Henry V* says, his audiences' 'imaginary forces' would do the rest. With cinema the only restrictions are imposed by the size of the budget and viewers do not expect to have to exercise their imaginations.

By transporting us to spectacular locations and using magnificently detailed sets, films such as Grigori Kozintsev's Soviet *King Lear*, set in the barren landscapes of Estonia, establish more successfully than any stage production could the sense of a *real* world in which Shakespeare's characters live and die.

This effect is most powerful in cinema's response to a simple stage direction that appears many times in Shakespeare: 'The field of battle. Alarum.' Those five words have inspired some of the screen's most memorable battles, in Welles's *Chimes at Midnight*, or *Ran*, Akira Kurosawa's version of *King Lear*. The graphic carnage in those sequences is a devastating complement to the humanity of Shakespeare's verse when it deals with violence.

Despite cinema's advantages over the stage, gaining in scale and realism what it loses from theatre's intimacy and shared physical experience, a constant thread in this book is the influence of theatre on filmed Shakespeare. From Max Reinhardt's *A Midsummer Night's Dream* in 1935, to *Chimes at Midnight* in 1966 and Julie Taymor's *Titus* in 1999, Shakespeare movies have frequently been developed from the directors' earlier stage production of the play, and it's no coincidence that these are often the best adaptations. These directors began shooting when they had worked through their ideas about the play on stage and had already gauged the responses of cast, critics and audiences, something that would be impossible when diving straight into the production of an original screenplay.

This, perhaps, is the aspect of Shakespeare on screen that would give the Bard the greatest pleasure if he were alive today; to know that cinema, the medium which has embraced his plays, was benefiting from theatre, the medium for which he wrote, and in which his works still flourish.

As to the question of where the artists responsible for even the finest of these films should rank when set against Shakespeare's genius, let Orson Welles answer that one. 'I really can't make a comparison between a movie-maker and Shakespeare', he once remarked. 'No movie that will ever be made is worthy of being discussed in the same breath.'

Unless otherwise indicated in the text, the date given for each film, for example *Henry V* (1944), is the year of its first theatrical release in its country of origin. To give an idea of how much the older films would cost at today's prices, their original production budgets are given with approximate present-day equivalents in parentheses. The present-day values have been calculated according to inflation-adjustment tables from Britain's Office for National Statistics.

Within sections devoted to a single film, its title is given in bold throughout the text, and other titles (films, plays, television programmes, books etc.) are given in italic. Within the introductions to each play, the featured films are indicated in bold and other films in italics.

Readers who have not seen Shakespeare variants such as *Forbidden Planet* and *A Thousand Acres*, or the films discussed in the 'Shakespeare in Other Movies' chapter, should be aware that these films' endings are revealed in the text.

Acknowledgements

I would like to express my thanks to the following for their help in the research and writing of this book. For supplying Shakespeare films on video: Buena Vista International Home Entertainment, Connoisseur Video, Merchant Ivory Productions, Tartan Video, Universal Home Video, Video Collection International and Warner Home Video.

For research assistance and advice: Adrian Berrill-Cox, Kathleen Dickson at the British Film Institute (BFI), Professor Peter Holland, Tony Howard, Mary Ann Hult at Fox Searchlight Pictures, Milly Marmur, Sylvia Morris at the Royal Shakespeare Company, Sarah Reynolds at Miramax Films, Jim Shaw and Kate Welch at the Shakespeare Institute Library in Stratford-upon-Avon, Olwen Terris at the BFI, and all the staff at the BFI Library in London. Lyrics from 'Brush Up Your Shakespeare', by Cole Porter, are reprinted by kind permission of Warner Chappell Music and the Cole Porter Musical and Literary Property Trusts.

I'd like to thank Peter Cowie for his initial guidance and my agent, Laura Morris, for all her assistance. Finally, I am very fortunate to have had invaluable advice and support from my parents, Ann Warnford-Davis and Tom Rosenthal, and from Cally Poplak.

Daniel Rosenthal, London, October 2000

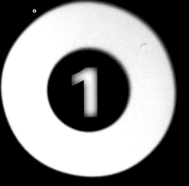

AS YOU LIKE IT

Hath not old custom made this life more sweet than that of painted pomp? Are not these woods more free from peril than the envious court? Duke Senior, *As You Like It*, Act II, Scene i

Left: Vanessa Redgrave, left, as Rosalind with Patrick Allen as Orlando in the BBC's black-and-white *As You Like It* (1963).

If the first quarter of *As You Like It* were typical of the whole play, it would surely have inspired more than two feature-film adaptations. By early in Act II, we've already seen a wrestling bout designed as a murder attempt, and our hero and heroine falling instantly in love. She's been unjustly banished, with her best friend and a comedy sidekick in tow, and he's fled separately to escape his wicked brother's second attempt on his life. That's as much excitement as any cinema audience has a right to expect from the opening 20 minutes of a comedy.

And then? Virtually nothing happens. The plot is put on hold, and the eminently hissable villains, Oliver and Frederick, disappear almost completely. The pleasures of what follows are derived from words, looks and sighs, not incident, as Shakespeare celebrates the madness of romantic love, and the merits of pastoral versus court life.

In the Forest of Arden, everybody is basically decent and, be you a duke's daughter or a shepherd, the greatest danger is falling in love, or coming off second best in a witty exchange with Touchstone or Jacques. There's comparable wit in *Much Ado About Nothing* and *Twelfth Night*, but at least those plays boast plots and sub-plots that keep audiences guessing.

By contrast, *As You Like It*'s forest is a tension-free zone, in which confrontation is averted by the bad guys' 'magical' conversions. That quality, which can work wonders on stage, severely restricts the play's cinematic mileage, as can be seen in both of the films discussed in this chapter: Paul Czinner's ortho-dox 1936 treatment and Christine Edzard's 1992 modernization.

Arguably, *As You Like It*'s most distinguished place in the history of Shakespeare on screen is as the first play to appear on television. On February 5, 1937, the BBC's Friday afternoon schedule included an 11-minute scene featuring West End actors Margaretta Scott as Rosalind and Ion Swinlay as Orlando.

Of the four full-length BBC productions that followed, three had notable lead actors: Laurence Harvey as Orlando in 1953, shortly before he starred in Renato Castellani's *Romeo and Juliet*, and Vanessa Redgrave (1963) and Helen Mirren (1978) as Rosalind, the latter production shot on location at Glamis Castle in Scotland, more famously associated with *Macbeth*.

The next screen adaptation may come from Kenneth Branagh. When this book went to press, his Shakespeare Film Company had announced tentative plans to produce a version of *As You Like It* with the magical wood situated in Kyoto 'at cherry blossom time'. It would be fascinating to see if the combination of Branagh's assured touch with Shakespearean comedy and the talents of his production designer, Tim Harvey, could succeed where Czinner and Edzard failed – by making *As You Like It* cinematic.

Duke Senior, deposed and banished by his brother, Duke Frederick, lives happily in the Forest of Arden with the melancholy Jacques and other lords.

At Frederick's court, Oliver, a malicious nobleman, wants his younger brother, Orlando, dead and asks Charles, a wrestler, to break the former's neck, but Orlando wins their bout. When he is congratulated on his victory by Rosalind, Duke Senior's daughter, they fall in love.

Fearful that the public's affection for Rosalind might cause problems, Duke Frederick banishes her. She disguises herself as a boy, 'Ganymede', and goes to seek her father. Frederick's daughter, Celia, who is disguised as the shepherdess 'Aliena', and Touchstone, a clown, accompany her.

Old Adam, a servant of Oliver's but faithful to Orlando, warns the latter that Oliver is planning to set fire to his lodging and the pair head for the forest where they are made welcome by Senior.

Meanwhile, Rosalind and Celia find shelter with an elderly shepherd, Corin. Touchstone falls in love with a country girl named Audrey. 'Ganymede' persuades Orlando that he can be cured of his love for Rosalind by wooing the boy as if he *were* Rosalind. Ganymede will behave so badly that Orlando will be disgusted and so cured. To confuse matters further, Phebe, a shepherdess who is adored by Corin's fellow shepherd and friend Silvius, falls for 'Ganymede'.

Oliver arrives in the forest to carry out his plot of murdering Orlando and, while sleeping, is saved by the latter from being attacked by a lioness, an act of mercy which instantly converts Oliver to goodness. He takes a message from Orlando to Rosalind and he and Celia instantly fall in love.

Rosalind and Celia reveal their true identities to Orlando, Senior, Oliver, Phebe and Silvius. The goddess Hymen marries the four couples: Rosalind and Orlando, Celia and Oliver, Phebe and Silvius, Touchstone and Audrey. Frederick, who was also coming to the forest to murder his brother, meets an 'old religious man' and miraculously renounces the dukedom, so allowing Senior and his companions to return to court.

Right: Miriam Margolyes as Audrey, left, with Griff Rhys Jones as Touchstone in Christine Edzard's modernized *As You Like It* (1992).

AS YOU LIKE IT (1936)

GB 95 MINS B/W

CAST	LAURENCE OLIVIER (Orlando), ELISABETH BERGNER (Rosalind), SOPHIE STEWART (Celia), JOHN LAURIE (Oliver), MACKENZIE WARD (Touchstone), LEON QUARTERMAINE (Jacques), HENRY AINLEY (Duke Senior), FELIX AYLMER (Duke Frederick), DORICE FORDRED (Audrey), J. FISHER WHITE (Adam)
DIRECTED BY	PAUL CZINNER
PRODUCED BY	PAUL CZINNER
SCREENPLAY	R.J. CULLEN
PHOTOGRAPHY	HAL ROSSON
MUSIC	WILLIAM WALTON

Paul Czinner's **As You Like It** provides sprightly entertainment by presenting Shakespeare's play as two parts fairy-tale to one part pantomime.

Entrusted with $1 million (perhaps $40 million now) to make Britain's first feature-length Shakespeare talkie, Hungarian-born Czinner cast a major star, his wife Elisabeth Bergner (a Polish-born Jew who left Germany with Czinner in 1933 to escape Nazi persecution), as Rosalind. He proved more loyal to her than to Shakespeare: by omitting virtually all of Jacques's melancholy musings and Touchstone's cynical humour, he did the play a disservice, but ensured that no shadows could fall across his wife's carefree performance.

Bergner and Sophie Stewart's radiantly cheerful Celia start off like rivals for the title role in *Sleeping Beauty*. Dressed in matching white satin, they walk dreamily through elaborate sets that make Duke Senior's palace a marvel of high arches and reflective floors. Bergner's Prince Charming arrives in the athletic form of Laurence Olivier's Orlando, who defeats a bare-chested Charles in an excitingly staged wrestling match.

Once our heroine has fallen in love with him, even banishment cannot dent her happy mood. It is a jolly adventure, rather than a test of character, with Touchstone (a loose-limbed Mackenzie Ward, in full jester's outfit) and Celia along for the ride. With Bergner in doublet and hose, the influence of J.M. Barrie – who wrote the treatment on which this adaptation was based – begins to tell: as Ganymede, she's a combination of Peter Pan and Tinkerbell.

Bergner does not give the faintest masculine edge to her voice or gait, which probably explains why Olivier chose to make Orlando appear slightly insane: he'd have to be to believe in Bergner as Ganymede. Where Olivier's delivery is lively and clear, Bergner's incongruous German accent ('a nuisance' to *Variety*'s critic) and bouncy enthusiasm (at one point she even turns a somersault) give Rosalind's poetry an unvarying and eventually tiresome jollity.

Too sanitized

This approach, and the perfunctory attention given to the philosophy of Leon Quartermaine's pompous Jacques, prompted Graham Greene, reviewing for *The Spectator*, to note: 'The streak of poison which runs through the comedy has been squeezed carefully out between hygienic fingertips.' Most of what remained, Greene added, was 'Shakespeare at his worst'.

Greene also had little time for the aspect of Czinner's direction that seems to ask the audience: 'Why listen to the verse when you can admire the animals?' Fawns and rabbits share the studio forest with Corin's flock of some 20 sheep; Audrey milks a cow while surrounded by hens and goats; Rosalind and Celia's thatched cottage has a duck pond. 'How the ubiquitous livestock weary us before the end,' complained Greene.

That ending should provide Shakespeare's peculiar brand of last-scene magic that works so well in *Twelfth Night* and *The Winter's Tale*, as Ganymede's 'transformation' back into woman's form leaves her father and Orlando joyously wondering 'if there be truth in sight'. However, presumably aware that cinema audiences would not buy such a theatrical moment (particularly as Bergner had looked so feminine throughout), Czinner omits this revelation, cutting straight from Rosalind's last speech as Ganymede to the moment when she and Celia reappear in matching wedding dresses.

Czinner replaces Hymen's contribution to the play with a more appropriate, if equally over-the-top, production number: dozens of flute-playing shepherds and skipping milkmaids singing a 'La-la' chorus in celebration of Shakespeare's absurdly happy ending.

The inherent problems with the play as screen fodder were pointed out in *Variety*'s guarded welcome: 'Lovers of Shakespeare will appreciate the fidelity with which the poetry ... has been presented. The vast army of motion picture supporters will wonder why some more dramatic and lively subject was not chosen.'

Apart from the palace sets and the livestock, there is little in Czinner's vision that you could not find in a theatre; and several of its performances (notably those by Quartermaine and Aylmer) belong there, rather than on screen. As *The New York Herald Tribune* said in 1936, this early attempt at filmed Shakespeare 'remains more a photographed version of a stringently cut stage presentation than a comic classic shaped to the cinema'.

Far left: Elisabeth Bergner, left, in Rosalind's disguise of doublet and hose with Mackenzie Ward in sheep's clothing as Touchstone.

Above: Sophie Stewart, radiant and cheerful as Sylvia, relaxes in the Forest of Arden.

Right: Elisabeth Bergner's relentless jollity as Rosalind wears thin long before the end of the film.

AS YOU LIKE IT (1992)
UK 114 MINS COLOUR

CAST	ANDREW TIERNAN (Orlando/Oliver), EMMA CROFT (Rosalind), CELIA BANNERMAN (Celia), GRIFF RHYS JONES (Touchstone), JAMES FOX (Jacques), DON HENDERSON (Duke Senior/Duke Frederick), MIRIAM MARGOLYES (Audrey), CYRIL CUSACK (Adam)
DIRECTED BY	CHRISTINE EDZARD
PRODUCED BY	SANDS FILMS
PHOTOGRAPHY	ROBIN VIDGEON
MUSIC	MICHEL SANVOISIN

This low-budget **As You Like It** leaves the audience bored and baffled. It's hard to believe that Christine Edzard, the director responsible for the moving, Oscar-nominated Dickens adaptation, *Little Dorrit* (UK, 1987), could make such a hopelessly misguided film.

Edzard presents Duke Frederick's court as a 1990s business empire, with Oliver as a smug yuppy with slicked-back hair and Orlando as a surly, shabbily dressed scrounger. The Forest of Arden becomes a concrete jungle of cranes and warehouses, where Duke Senior and his fellow exiles live like down-and-outs in cardboard boxes or polythene tents. Within a few minutes it is clear that this switch from Shakespeare's idealized pastoral setting to a realistic cityscape is going to blend with *As You Like It* like oil with water.

Distracting questions constantly pop into one's head. Would a mogul like Frederick interrupt a party at his businees HQ by holding a wrestling tournament in the lobby? Of course he wouldn't. In any case Edzard does not actually show the Charles v Orlando bout (we only see onlookers' tame reaction shots), and therefore ruins the incident which provides both the play's one burst of exciting action and Rosalind's prime motive for falling in love with Orlando.

The court scenes unfold on a single set ('marble' columns, chess-board floor and multiple, mirrored doors) which serves as the lobby, Oliver's office, old Adam's workshop *and* Rosalind's bedroom. This might be a reasonable, economic approach for theatre, but it is deeply unconvincing on film.

Next come the casting problems. In Shakespeare, Celia and Rosalind are clearly of an age, inseparable since early childhood. So why is Celia played by Celia Bannerman, who looks old enough to be Rosalind's mother? Edzard alone knows, since her choice makes a nonsense of Celia's girlish devotion to her cousin.

Double trouble
Elsewhere, Edzard opts for theatrical doubling: the two dukes are played by husky-voiced Don Henderson and Orlando and Oliver by Andrew Tiernan, who has a slightly creepy screen presence. This sounds like a neat trick: one actor representing both the malevolent and kindly sides of human nature, like Jeremy Irons as the twin gynaecologists in *Dead Ringers*. There is no problem with Henderson's dual role, since his slightly fey

Frederick never appears alongside his phlegmatic Senior. Orlando and Oliver, however, must face each other at key moments in the story, first as deadly enemies then, after the latter's conversion, as bosom buddies. But because Edzard's budget (about $1.5 million) wouldn't stretch to split-screen trickery, she could never show the two Tiernans in the same frame – an absurd visual flaw that scuttles the play's only confrontational relationship.

Nonsensical casting is compounded by lifeless direction, with every scene played at the same, gentle pace. It's doubtful, though, that any director could have made a success of the 'forest' segment, shot in London's docklands. If Edzard had been bold enough to rewrite Shakespeare's poetry to match the setting, the film might have stood a chance; instead, the clashes between his

words and her images come thick and fast: Corin and Silvius tend their sheep (we only see one animal) on fields of concrete; Rosalind refers to her doublet and hose while wearing jeans and a hooded top; and Oliver talks about being menaced by a lioness when we see him threatened by a mugger. The most willing theatre audience in the world would struggle to suspend its disbelief at so much incongruity; cinemagoers can't possibly do so.

City settings like Edzard's have been brilliantly employed by theatre directors to update *The Merchant of Venice* and *Timon of Athens*, but they succeeded because those plays comment forcefully on the corrupting influence of commerce. Not a word of *As You Like It*'s poetic celebration of country life merits transforming the forest into an urban wasteland.

Some of the cast give equally out-of-place performances, notably Griff Rhys Jones as Touchstone, who appears to have wandered in from a 1950s Ealing comedy, gabbling unintelligibly in a strangulated cockney accent. James Fox takes Jacques's melancholy to exhaustingly dull lengths and only Emma Croft, as an attractive, spirited and – when required – convincingly boyish Ganymede, emerges with credit.

The Independent found the film 'perversely endearing', but otherwise the critical response was damning. Described by *The Observer* as 'listless, fuzzy and unfocused' and by *The Guardian* as 'a dead-as-mutton film that is poor Shakespeare and even worse cinema', **As You Like It** took less than $30,000 at the UK box-office and did not get a theatrical release in the US.

Above: Emma Croft, convincingly disguised as 'Ganymede'. The paintwork behind her is evidence of Orlando's love for Rosalind.

HAMLET

So shall you hear of carnal, bloody, and unnatural acts, of accidental judgments, casual slaughters, of deaths put on by cunning and forced cause. Horatio, *Hamlet*, Act V, Scene ii

Elsinore, Denmark. Following the death of old Hamlet, Denmark's king, his brother Claudius now reigns. Hamlet, the dead king's grieving son, is appalled by his mother Gertrude's abrupt marriage to Claudius. Old Hamlet's ghost appears to Hamlet and reveals that he was murdered by Claudius. Hamlet swears revenge.

Concerned by Hamlet's distracted behaviour, Claudius and Gertrude have summoned his boyhood friends, Rosencrantz and Guildenstern, to sound him out. Hamlet sees through their intentions and reveals nothing.

Polonius, Claudius's Lord Chamberlain, suggests that Hamlet's madness is caused by his love for Polonius's own daughter, Ophelia. With Claudius and Polonius looking on, however, Hamlet meets Ophelia and viciously denies that he ever loved her.

A company of travelling players arrives and Hamlet asks them to stage a play mirroring the ghost's description of his murder. During the performance, Claudius, observed by Hamlet's university friend, Horatio, storms out in distress. Hamlet views this as confirmation of his uncle's guilt but stops short of killing him while he's at prayer.

Hamlet confronts Gertrude in her bedroom and when she cries out he stabs Polonius, who's been hiding behind a wall-hanging, thinking that it might be Claudius. Moments later, the ghost appears and urges Hamlet to fulfil his oath of vengeance. Hamlet begs Gertrude not to return to Claudius's bed, then drags out Polonius's corpse.

Claudius, secretly planning to have Hamlet executed by the English king, orders him to sail to England with Rosencrantz and Guildenstern.

Laertes, Polonius' son, returns from France and demands revenge for his father's murder. Ophelia, driven mad by Hamlet's scorn and her father's death, drowns herself.

Hamlet has returned to Denmark on a pirate ship, leaving Rosencrantz and Guildenstern to continue to England with a letter from Claudius that he has forged, ordering their execution. Arriving at Elsinore he encounters Ophelia's funeral procession and has a violent confrontation with Laertes.

Claudius and Laertes have devised a plot to kill Hamlet in a fencing bout. Using a poison-tipped sword, Laertes wounds Hamlet, but in the scuffle they exchange foils and Hamlet wounds Laertes. Gertrude accidentally drinks poisoned wine from the cup that Claudius offers Hamlet and dies. Laertes dies denouncing Claudius. Hamlet kills his uncle, moments before dying himself. Fortinbras, Prince of Norway arrives to lay claim to the Danish throne.

Hamlet is Shakespeare's longest, most celebrated and most filmed play, with more than 50 adaptations made for cinema or television. In some respects, it's obvious why the play has proved so popular on screen. *Hamlet* is a rattling good story, a supernatural revenge thriller whose hero's hesitancy generates unique tension: not a 'whodunit?' but a 'why-doesn't-he-do-it?'

Despite his royal blood and university education, the prince is nonetheless an everyman figure whose reflections on the human condition speak to us regardless of age or nationality. Small wonder, then, that screen Hamlets have emerged from Africa, Asia, South America and the United States, as well as his 'natural' home, Europe.

Yet two of the qualities that make *Hamlet* such a great play for the stage are precisely those that strain directors' ingenuity in transferring it successfully to the screen. Intriguingly, its immense length, dominated by the thoughts of one man – to a much greater degree than *King Lear* or *Othello* – deepens its relentless, cumulative impact.

Before Kenneth Branagh in 1996, every *Hamlet* director discarded hundreds of lines of verse and, often, several minor characters to deliver a running time acceptable to cinema audiences - always less willing than theatregoers to devote four hours to the Bard. But if a director cuts too much from the 'wrong' places he risks reducing Shakespeare's minutely detailed characterizations – not only of the prince, but of Claudius, Polonius and Ophelia – to sketches.

Most importantly, film-makers must try to replicate the intense bond between their lead actor and his audience, established and sustained in live performance by that most theatrical of devices, the soliloquy. Since so much of the drama takes place in the prince's mind, the voice-over has proved a godsend for many *Hamlet* films.

The art of filming *Hamlet* lies in making Shakespeare work with the medium, not against it. This chapter looks at how this challenge has been met by movies staring Laurence Olivier, Innokenti Smoktunovsky, Richard Burton, Nicol Williamson, Mel Gibson, Kenneth Branagh and Ethan Hawke. They have continued the line which began in 1900, with the great French actress Sarah Bernhardt. A three-minute record of the 55-year-old Bernhardt's swordplay in the duel scene from a 1900 stage *Hamlet* in Paris was the second Shakespeare film ever made.

Top left: Arnold Schwarzenegger as cinema's least likely Hamlet in the spoof movie trailer from *Last Action Hero* (1993).

Right: S.A. Cookson as Horatio, left, with 60-year-old Johnston Forbes-Robertson as the prince in a silent *Hamlet* (UK, 1913).

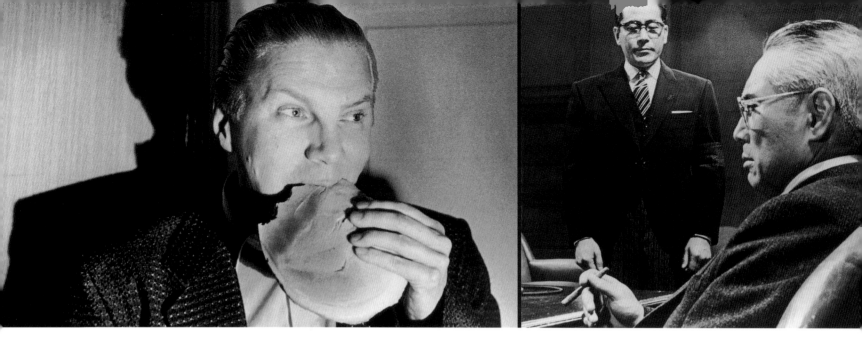

The rest and the silents

At least ten more silents had followed by 1920, in Italy (four), France (two), Britain (two), Denmark and Germany. The British contributions included the 1913 film of a West End production, starring Johnston Forbes-Robertson, then 60 years old. *Hamlet: The Drama of Vengeance* (Germany, 1920) took Bernhardt's cross-dressing to extremes, with the premise that Gertrude gave birth to a daughter who has been raised as a boy. Played by Danish actress Asta Nielsen, a superstar of early European cinema, the adult Hamlet falls in love with Horatio and as she dies Horatio feels her chest to locate the fatal wound and suddenly realizes that the prince is really a princess.

Beyond Europe, *Hamlet* (India, 1955), directed by Kishore Sahu, was accused by *FilmIndia* magazine of slandering the Bard's memory; Ghanaian university students made *Hamile: The Tongo Hamlet* (1964), setting the story among the Fafra tribe in northern Ghana; Brazilian audiences saw a Portuguese-language version, *Hamlet, a Heranca* in 1970

British television Hamlets have included John Byron (1947), John Neville (1959), Christopher Plummer (1964; in a production filmed at Elsinore's Kronborg Castle), Ian McKellen (1972) and Derek Jacobi (1980). America offered small-screen Hamlets starring Maurice Evans (1953) and Richard Chamberlain (1970). Maximillian Schell took the role for West German television in 1960, and Stellan Skarsgård, now familiar from Hollywood movies such as *Good Will Hunting* and *Ronin*, played a long-haired, unkempt prince in a frequently outrageous 1984 Swedish TV production (Claudius vomits over his neighbours during the play scene).

Spanish director Celestino Coronado made the most disturbing and visceral of all screen adaptations with his 65-minute *Hamlet* (UK, 1976), shot on video for less than $5,000. In a mesmerizing representation of the hero's divided nature, Hamlet is played by blue-eyed, lean and frequently naked twins, Anthony and David Meyer. They deliver the soliloquies as duologues, so the prince literally talks to himself; while one Hamlet gently informs Helen Mirren's Ophelia 'I did love you once', the other yells 'I loved you not'. Since Mirren doubles as Gertrude, incest becomes another unsettling theme of this stunning experiment.

Three years after Akira Kurosawa filmed *Macbeth* as *Throne of Blood* (*see* page 76), Hamlet had a significant influence on his gritty tragedy of corporate corruption in contemporary Japan, *The Bad Sleep Well* (Japan, 1960). Its hero, Nishi (a restrained Toshiro Mifune), assisted by a Horatio-like friend, Itakura, seeks vengeance against his boss and the story's Claudius equivalent, Iwabuchi (Takeshi Kato). Iwabuchi, president of the Japan Land Corporation, had elicited a huge bribe from a construction firm in a deal that drove Nishi's father to suicide. Nishi marries Iwabuchi's fragile, Ophelia-like daughter, Keiko, and her brother emulates Laertes by trying to kill Nishi after he mistreats her.

For two gripping hours, Nishi, like Hamlet, wrestles with his conscience finding it impossible to behave as ruthlessly as Iwabuchi. Kurosawa then supplies a less bloody, but more pessimistic climax than Shakespeare: Nishi's hesitation allows Iwabuchi to have him murdered, and the corruption remains unexposed.

Shakespeare's plot also inspired Enzo G. Castellari's mediocre Western, *Johnny Hamlet* (Spain, 1968), and thanks to Disney's *The Lion King* (US, 1994) millions of children will be familiar with Hamlet's predicament when they first encounter the play, although Shakespeare's ending might prove a surprise.

Mocking the prince

Spoof Hamlets include *Oh'phelia*, a British cartoon short from 1919, in which cheeky 'Amlet drives Ophelia crazy by cutting off her hair, asking 'To bob or not to bob?' Marvellous, deadpan mockery was supplied by *Hamlet Goes Business* (Finland, 1987), a typically quirky black-and-white feature from Finnish director

Above left: Pirkka-Pekka Petelius as a gluttonous Hamlet in Finnish director Aki Kaurismäki's deadpan spoof, *Hamlet Goes Business* (1987).

Above: Toshiro Mifune as the Hamlet-like hero, left, in *The Bad Sleep Well* (1960) with Takeshi Kato as the Claudius-like villain.

Right: Innokenti Smoktunovsky as Hamlet, left, with V. Kolpakor as the gravedigger in one of the finest scenes from the Soviet *Hamlet* (1964), directed by Grigori Kozintsev.

Aki Kaurismäki, who needed just 75 minutes to debunk every famous scene and speech from the play.

Following the suspicious death of old Hamlet, boss of a drab industrial complex in present-day Helsinki, his brother Klaus (Claudius) wants the family firm to buy a majority holding in Swedish Rubber Ducks, but is opposed in this project by Hamlet (the lugubrious Pirkka-Pekka Petelius), a smug, gluttonous, horny idiot who reflects on his depression by whining: 'I feel like spewing all the time.'

After Gertrude is accidentally killed by eating the poisoned roast chicken which Claus intended for his nephew, Hamlet kills Lauri (Laertes) - by smashing a large radio over his head – and shoots Klaus. He is then poisoned by his chauffeur, Simo (the

Horatio figure), who turns out to be a trade union spy intent on safeguarding jobs in the Hamlet family sawmill. The more seriously the cast play it, the funnier Kaurismäki's film becomes, though it can't top the one inspired sequence in *Last Action Hero* (US, 1993), the otherwise disastrous Hollywood flop about Danny, a schoolboy obsessed with movie hero Jack Carter (Arnold Schwarzenegger).

Early on, Danny is shown a clip from Olivier's *Hamlet* by his English teacher (Joan Plowright, Olivier's widow) and imagines it as a trailer for a black-and-white epic, with Schwarzenegger as cinema's most unlikely Dane. In close-up, Arnie asks: 'To be, or not to be?' He pauses, lights an enormous cigar, adds: 'Not to be', and Elsinore is blown to smithereens.

HAMLET (1948)
UK 153 MINS B/W

CAST	LAURENCE OLIVIER (Hamlet), EILEEN HERLIE (Gertrude), BASIL SYDNEY (Claudius), JEAN SIMMONS (Ophelia), FELIX AYLMER (Polonius), TERENCE MORGAN (Laertes), NORMAN WOOLAND (Horatio)
DIRECTED BY	LAURENCE OLIVIER
PRODUCED BY	LAURENCE OLIVIER
PHOTOGRAPHY	DESMOND DICKINSON
MUSIC	WILLIAM WALTON

Laurence Olivier's **Hamlet** is a hybrid: part grim fairy-tale, part psychological case study. The colourful pageant of his *Henry V* (*see* page 42) gives way to an equally stylized, monochrome engraving: sombre, disturbing *and* accessible. 'The greatness of the Olivier Hamlet is that he has made it a movie for everybody', declared *The Washington Post*. 'Be you 9 or 90, a PhD or just plain Joe, *Hamlet* is the movie of the year.'

Verdicts like that, following outstanding reviews in Britain, helped **Hamlet** to box-office success on both sides of the Atlantic, and its $3 million US gross was an exceptional figure for a non-Hollywood picture. It became the first film of a Shakespeare play to win the Academy Award for Best Picture – still a unique achievement – and Olivier's virile prince remains the only performance of a Shakespeare role to have won Best Actor.

His approach to the tragedy also brought controversy. With Alan Dent, who repeated his role as text adviser on *Henry V*, Olivier removed several of Shakespeare's characters and 50 per cent of his verse. Out went Reynaldo (Polonius's spy), the second gravedigger, Fortinbras, Rosencrantz and Guildenstern. Out went two of the prince's most famous speeches ('What a piece of work is man' and 'How all occasions do inform against me'). In the interests of accessibility supposedly arcane words were changed (for example, 'maimed rites' became 'meagre rites'). The cuts and, in particular, the rewriting prompted a leading article in *The Times* headlined 'Alas, Poor Hamlet!' and furious letters to the editor from critics who regarded the play as a sacred text.

Olivier had tried to pre-empt such a response in his introduction to *The Film Hamlet: A Record of its Production*, published to coincide with the Royal Première in London in May 1948. Because, he wrote, the screenplay had required 'so much more than mere condensation, I feel the film *Hamlet* should be regarded as an "Essay in *Hamlet*", and not as a film version of a necessarily abridged classic'. That is a fair description of a movie that completely ignores the play's politics in favour of the domestic tragedy and the troubled mother-son relationship that lies at its core.

A tale of indecision

The 'essay' cost £500,000 (about $17 million today), and begins with Olivier's famous declaration, in voice-over: 'This is the tragedy of a man who could not make up his mind'. Mist swirling around Elsinore clears to reveal a glimpse of four soldiers on a circular platform, bearing aloft a man's dead body. His face can't be seen, but to anyone who knows the play this can only be Hamlet. Olivier starts by revealing where indecision will lead his hero, then a dissolve returns to the beginning of the play.

Hamlet's home was designed at Denham Studios by Roger Furse and Carmen Dillon, costume designer and assistant art director on *Henry V*. Fulfilling Olivier's desire for 'a significant austerity in the background', they created a cliff-top Elsinore of cold stone, long, arched passageways and steep, winding staircases, a place which feels not quite real, somehow timeless.

Above: Laurence Olivier as Hamlet contemplating mortality with Yorick's skull.

Above: Jean Simmons as an ethereal Ophelia floating downstream to a watery death.

The actors' aristocratic English voices resound in rooms largely devoid of decoration and furniture, unless chairs or table are actually needed. With William Walton's marvellously varied score largely confined to interludes between spoken passages, there is virtually nothing to distract us from the verse. The intense character study is heightened by Desmond Dickinson's deep-focus photography, which keeps figures sharply defined irrespective of their distance from the camera.

Such an effect would have been impossible with colour film, and Olivier opted for deep-focus black-and-white to achieve 'a morre majestic, more poetic image, in keeping with the stature of the verse'. The result is startling, particularly in a sequence involving Olivier, his hair dyed an arresting blond, and Jean Simmons's captivating Ophelia, which the director nicknamed 'the longest-distance love scene on record'.

Dressed in flowing, virginal white, the 18-year-old Simmons is an ethereal presence who seems to glide across floors, as though Hamlet has gained a second ghost, accompanied by Walton's suitably haunting oboe motif. The 'love scene' occurs after Felix Aylmer's grandiose Polonius has told his daughter to avoid the prince's company. We see Hamlet seated 40 m (120 ft) away from her, as she stands looking at him from the opposite end of an arched corridor; the point of view is then reversed and yet in both shots the features of both actors are in perfect focus. Hamlet and Ophelia are, as the verse makes painfully clear, very close and very far apart.

Dickinson's camerawork speaks just as eloquently in the numerous crane shots: zooms, climbs and descents that could be the Ghost's-eye view of the drama and that give the action a dreamy fluency, pushing the audience towards fairy-tale territory.

②

Left: Laurence Olivier as Hamlet climbing Elsinore's fog-shrouded fortifications to confront the Ghost.

Take, for example, the prelude to the play's most famous speech (interestingly moved from before Hamlet's 'Get thee to a nunnery' tirade against Ophelia to just after). The camera pulls back from Simmons, who's weeping prostrate on a staircase, and then rises up and up until it reaches the battlements, zooms towards the back of Olivier's head and appears to disappear inside it, just as he begins 'To be, or not to be', delivered, like most of the soliloquies, as a voice-over. He makes it the speech of a man on the brink of suicide, staring vertiginously into the waves below, then holding up his dagger, as if to stab himself. As with so much else in **Hamlet**, this is pure cinema from a director still new to the medium.

As an actor, however, Olivier still had one foot on the stage. His portrayal is less obviously theatrical than his Henry V, but his contemplative poses and lyrical verse-speaking are still a world away from the naturalism of Nicol Williamson's Hamlet in 1969 (*see page 29*). In 1948, *Time* suggested that 'in its subtlety, variety, vividness and control, Olivier's performance is one of the most beautiful ever put on film'; today, its style has worn less well than its psychology.

At times, Olivier appears such a courageous figure that the label of 'a man who could not make up his mind' seems utterly inappropriate. Look at how boldly he confronts the Ghost (voiced, through buzzing distortion, by Olivier himself), or the sequence showing him swinging, Errol Flynn-like on to the pirate ship. He is admired by all types of men, from Norman Wooland's upstanding, handsome Horatio to the Chief Player (Harcourt Williams), from soldiers like Barnardo (Esmond Knight, retained, like Williams and Aylmer, from *Henry V*) and Marcellus (Antony Quayle), to the lowly gravedigger (Stanley Holloway). Even Laertes (Terence Morgan, like Quayle making an assured film debut) cannot bring himself to hate the man who killed his father, and the absence of Rosencrantz and Guildenstern spares us awkward questions about Hamlet's ruthlessly condemning them to execution.

In male company, then, Olivier is wholly admirable and decisive, every inch the 'sweet Prince'. With the two women in his life he's a disaster, incapable of responding normally to Ophelia because of his warped relationship with a ravishing Gertrude (Eileen Herlie) who looks young enough to be his wife: at 27, Herlie was 13 years Olivier's junior.

The potent, lovers' chemistry between prince and queen dates back to Olivier's stage *Hamlet* of 1937, when a paper by Dr Ernest Jones, biographer of Sigmund Freud, convinced him that

Hamlet's Oedipus complex (repressed sexual desire for Gertrude, jealousy of Claudius) was responsible 'for a formidable share what is wrong with him'. Throughout the film, Hamlet's desire is clearly reciprocated by Gertrude and reaches its peak in their confrontation after the murder of Polonius: they exchange a brief, passionate kiss that would be shockingly casual even without the grotesque presence of the corpse beside them.

Herlie carries off this scene superbly, and *The Observer* called her portrayal 'the most remarkable thing in the film'. She outshines Basil Sydney, whose Claudius lacks depth and menace, and the Freudian interpretation affords her an unforgettable death scene. During the duel, the audience realizes that Gertrude *knows* that the wine is poisoned, and so swallows it happily, killing herself to save her son. Added to Olivier's suicidal rendition of 'To be, or not to be' and his decision to show a few seconds of Ophelia's drowning, his adaptation is unusually preoccupied with 'self-slaughter'.

The duel in Elsinore's great hall provides a thrilling climax, ending with Hamlet, rapier in hand, leaping on to Claudius from a landing some 5 m (15 ft) above the throne, a daredevil feat that Olivier described in his memoirs as the one 'truly brave' thing he ever did.

After Horatio has spoken the closing lines that rightfully belong to Fortinbras, the camera reverses the journey it made during the opening seconds, a trick copied from *Henry V*, past the prince's empty chair, the chapel where Claudius knelt at prayer, Gertrude's bed and, finally, the four soldiers with the prince's body.

When **Hamlet** won the Best Picture Oscar, it became the first non-American film to take the top prize in the 21-year history of the awards. There were also victories for Furse and Dillon's art direction, Furse's classically simple medieval costumes, and nominations for Olivier as Director, Simmons as Supporting Actress, and Walton for the music. **Hamlet** also won the BAFTA for Best Film and the Golden Lion at the Venice Film Festival.

Since Olivier's movie is, rightly, still regarded as a classic, it's worth recalling one response from 1947 that spoke volumes about movie industry attitudes to the Bard's work, attitudes that still prevail today. Early on in **Hamlet**'s six-month shoot, an anxious J. Arthur Rank, head of the Rank Organization (which funded the film), sent a member of staff to view some early footage and report back. The minion's reassuring verdict? 'Wonderful, Mr Rank. You wouldn't even know it was Shakespeare.'

I feel the film *Hamlet* should be regarded as an 'Essay in *Hamlet*', and not as a film version of a necessarily abridged classic.

Laurence Olivier

Right: Eileen Herlie as Gertrude, left, lies on her bed in terror behind Laurence Olivier as Hamlet. The prince is about to kill Polonius.

Below: Laurence Olivier disrupts Ophelia's funeral and declares: 'This is I, Hamlet the Dane.'

HAMLET (1964)

USSR 140 MINS B/W
RUSSIAN TITLE: GAMLET

CAST	INNOKENTI SMOKTUNOVSKY (Hamlet), ELSA RADZINA (Gertrude), MIKHAIL NAZVANOV (Claudius), ANASTASIA VERTINSKAYA (Ophelia), YURI TOLUBEYEV (Polonius), STEPAN OLEKSENKO (Laertes), VLADIMIR ERENBERG (Horatio)
DIRECTED BY	GRIGORI KOZINTSEV
PRODUCTION COMPANY	LENFILM
SCREENPLAY	GRIGORI KOZINTSEV, BASED ON BORIS PASTERNAK'S TRANSLATION
PHOTOGRAPHY	JONAS GRITSUS
MUSIC	DMITRI SHOSTAKOVICH

Hamlet's belief that 'Denmark's a prison' could serve as a subtitle for this thrilling, moving adaptation. In the opening sequence, Innokenti Smoktunovsky's prince gallops through the main gate of a vast castle, its iron portcullis closing behind him. The portcullis clanks shut again, more ominously still, on his return from Ophelia's funeral while, inside, Mikhail Nazvanov's menacing Claudius presides over a 'big brother' regime.

As the prince walks through the castle's wide stone halls he is deep in solitude, although seldom alone, spied on by Claudius, Polonius, Rosencrantz and Guildenstern and dozens of armoured guards and courtiers in exquisite 16th-century costumes. When he reveals the whereabouts of Polonius's corpse, a scribe notes down his testimony, as though in a show trial. 'Hamlet is tormented by what is happening in the prison state around him', said Kozintsev during production.

He based the film on his 1954 version of *Hamlet*, staged in Leningrad just a year after Josef Stalin's death, and Kozintsev's casting in 1964 of Smoktunovsky would have carried an art-imitating-life edge for many Russian cinemagoers as, it was well

Left: Elsa Radzina as Gertrude, left, with Innokenti Smoktunovsky as Hamlet in the great bedroom confrontation between mother and son.

Right: Innokenti Smoktunovsky as Hamlet before his life-affirming meeting with the gravedigger.

known that after fighting heroically against the Germans during World War II, the actor had been sent to the Gulag Archipelago by Stalin's regime.

The film's ending has been interpreted in allegorical terms: the tyrannical Claudius (Stalin) is replaced by the more tolerant Fortinbras (Khrushchev), who will eradicate some of the corruption in Denmark (Russia). However, as in Kozintsev's *King Lear* (1971, *see* page 64), the political resonance fuelled by Russian history never compromises his compelling and humane treatment of Shakespeare.

Smoktunovsky gives a lucid performance, neatly balanced between internalized and externalized emotions; some soliloquies are delivered quietly as voice-overs, others out loud with unrestrained passion. The prince starts off distracted, moves through dazed disbelief after the ghost's revelations, and on to self-knowledge, accompanied by engaging reminders of his own mislaid mirth.

Smoktunovsky's interpretation is centred around the absence of purpose to Hamlet's life – until, that is, he fully accepts the

role of avenger on his return from his pirate adventure. More than any other film Hamlet, Smoktunovsky appears a completely changed man at this point and his new-found resolve turns his conversation with the plump, bald gravedigger into a remarkably life-affirming moment, with the prince now as certain as the workman that in confronting death 'the readiness is all'.

Motion and music

The rhythms of Hamlet's thoughts are matched by Kozintsev's wonderfully fluid camera movements, particularly in the prince's frequent walks on the castle's spectacular cliff-top fortifications, although the director overdoes expressionistic shots of fluttering banners, scudding clouds and waves crashing against rocks to reflect the mental turmoil already expressed so vividly by the verse (Pasternak's translation is subtitled with Shakespeare's original).

By contrast, Shostakovich's supple score provides perfectly judged accompaniment. The orchestra is at full tilt for Hamlet's encounter with the Ghost. Panting woodwind drives the exhilarating stampede of courtiers following Claudius's exit from the players' night-time performance in the castle forecourt, a sequence that is lit with the same moody precision as the interior scenes.

Shostakovich devises a string lament for the madness of 18-year-old Anastasia Vertinskaya's fragile, blonde Ophelia and composer, director and actress evoke immense sympathy for this trusting young woman who aches with love for Hamlet and is callously manipulated by her self-important father (rotund, bearded Yuri Tolubeyev). Kozintsev turns Ophelia into Elsinore's second prisoner, attended by wizened old women who seem more like gaolers than maids, especially in an unforgettable moment, after Polonius's murder when they lock her into the black iron corset that supports her mourning gown. Minutes later, their harsh ministrations are beautifully contrasted when Kozintsev has a soldier tenderly place a blanket around Ophelia's shoulders as she wanders madly in her nightgown.

The film described by the *Financial Times* as 'arguably the most intelligent and certainly the most *contemporary* interpretation of Shakespeare for the screen' is full of such inspired touches and the last transforms our connection to Radzina's elegant, inscrutable Gertrude. Cuts in the text have left her a peripheral figure until Kozintsev allows her to come tantalizingly close to surviving the climactic massacre. She is enjoying a brisk stroll when the cannon blast signalling the start of the duel between Hamlet and Laertes arouses her curiosity and sends her indoors. It's clear that Claudius, true to his secretive nature, has not even told her of the bout and her accidental death becomes more devastatingly ironic than Shakespeare intended.

Hamlet is tormented by what is happening in the prison state around him. Grigori Kozintsev

HAMLET (1964)

US 199 MINS B/W

CAST	RICHARD BURTON (Hamlet), EILEEN HERLIE (Gertrude), ALFRED DRAKE (Claudius), LINDA MARSH (Ophelia), HUME CRONYN (Polonius), JOHN CULLUM (Laertes), ROBERT MILLI (Horatio), JOHN GIELGUD (Voice of Ghost)
DIRECTED BY	BILL COLLERAN (Film)
	JOHN GIELGUD (Stage)
PRODUCED BY	WILLIAM SARGENT, ALFRED W. CROWN

None of the actors made any concessions to this new process. In other words, we didn't tone it down in order to seem like film actors. Richard Burton

This **Hamlet** is unique amongst Shakespeare films, because of both the way it was made and the fortune Richard Burton made from it.

In 1964, John Gielgud directed Burton as Hamlet in a modern-dress production at the Lunt-Fontanne Theatre on Broadway. Three performances were recorded through the 'revolutionary' Electronovision process, which used small, electronic cameras that could deliver adequate picture quality using only available stage lighting. Five cameras were used and their positions switched nightly so that the edited 'theatrofilm', as **Hamlet** was billed, could combine 15 viewpoints. The result is, as *Variety* noted, 'distressingly dark', and mixes riveting close-ups with flat, long shots. 'None of the actors made any concessions to this new process', said Burton. 'In other words, we didn't tone it down in order to seem like film actors.'

As the brisk production unfolds on bare boards, Burton, dressed in close-fitting black, is physically intimidating yet as light-footed as a dancer, a brooding Hamlet who vacillates between self-love and self-disgust. His booming voice caresses and scours the poetry, creates extraordinary tension from brief, unexpected pauses and then deflates it with startling, mocking chuckles.

It's remarkable how much humour he wrings from the text, with assistance from Hume Cronyn, who displays exquisite timing as an elderly, spry Polonius. The audience's laughter is preferable to their absurd habit of applauding the principal characters' exits, no matter how highly charged the moment.

Beside Burton and Cronyn, the rest of the largely American cast seem terribly wooden. Alfred Drake's Claudius, unwisely kitted out in cosy slacks and cardigan, is more a self-satisfied Manhattan executive than a ruthless killer, Linda Marsh's Ophelia is a nondescript sophomore. As befits Gielgud's spare production, Eileen Herlie is less regal as Gertrude than in Olivier's film – and has a much healthier relationship with her stage son.

Keen to preserve the live audience for any future Shakespeare performances that he might give, Burton insisted that **Hamlet** be shown for just two days. Released in 970 American cinemas in September 1964, it was a huge success, seen by an estimated 5 million people, and netted Burton about $500,000 – perhaps $5 million today.

The 1964 deal also required that all the prints were destroyed and **Hamlet** was thought to have been lost forever until 1991 when Burton's widow, Sally, discovered three rusty film cans at their Swiss home. They contained a complete version, which, carefully restored, has enabled a new generation to discover Burton's **Hamlet** on video.

Above: Alfred Drake as Claudius, bottom, is forced to drink from the poisoned cup of wine by Richard Burton's Hamlet.

HAMLET (1969)
UK 117 MINS COLOUR

CAST	NICOL WILLIAMSON (Hamlet), JUDY PARFITT (Gertrude), ANTHONY HOPKINS (Claudius), MARIANNE FAITHFULL (Ophelia), MARK DIGNAM (Polonius), MICHAEL PENNINGTON (Laertes), GORDON JACKSON (Horatio)
DIRECTED BY	TONY RICHARDSON
PRODUCED BY	NEIL HARTLEY
PHOTOGRAPHY	GERRY FISHER
MUSIC	PATRICK GOWERS

Acclaimed by the *Daily Sketch* as 'a classic for the modern age', this intimate Hamlet belongs to Nicol Williamson: the most neurotic, fastest talking Prince of Denmark in screen history.

Williamson and his co-stars had appeared in the stage production directed earlier in 1969 by Tony Richardson at the Round House, a Victorian locomotive-turning shed-turned drama venue in north London, and the film was shot there over a period of just ten days.

Richardson was equally accomplished in the theatre and the cinema (he won an Oscar for 1963's *Tom Jones*), and utilizes techniques from both forms here. As on stage several actors appear (sometimes distractingly) in two or three minor roles each and the production design is pure theatre with no sets, blacked-out backgrounds and the Ghost represented by a spotlight shone onto Williamson's face. The camerawork, however, creates the unerringly narrow focus that is only possible on screen.

About 90 per cent of the shots are close-ups, generating a claustrophobic mood that is feebly undramatic for the crowded play and duel scenes, but tailor-made to carry the audience into Hamlet's mind. In tune with late 1960s counter-culture, Williamson plays him as a feverishly sardonic, anti-Establishment drop-out, in a hyperactive performance that, said *Time*, 'transcends celluloid and holds the audience in a dramatic vise'. His strangulated vocal ticks and proletarian accent irritated many British reviewers, and he is nobody's idea of a romantic pin-up, yet the poetry has rarely sounded more spontaneous or heartfelt, connecting us with every aspect of Hamlet's fears and frustrations.

Williamson's breathtakingly rapid, though still crystal-clear, delivery, particularly when addressing soliloquies to camera, enables Richardson to retain considerably more of the text than Olivier's film, which is more than half-an-hour longer. The cuts are nonetheless severe on the supporting cast and although Gordon Jackson impresses as a studious, bespectacled Horatio Anthony Hopkins's lusty Claudius barely registers.

Judy Parfitt's prim Gertrude looks younger than her son, but instead of having Williamson hint at oedipal desire for her, Richardson provocatively suggests an incestuous relationship between Michael Pennington's rakish Laertes and Marianne Faithfull's vacant, mannequin-like Ophelia. Faithfull, as you'd expect from a pop star, sings Ophelia's mad lament for Polonius beautifully and in that scene you can glimpse a lady-in-waiting played by a 17-year-old Anjelica Huston, destined for Oscar-winning success in 1985's *Prizzi's Honour*.

Right: Marianne Faithfull as a doll-like Ophelia, left, with Nicol Williamson as cinema's fastest-talking Hamlet.

HAMLET (1990)

US 135 MINS COLOUR

CAST	MEL GIBSON (Hamlet), GLENN CLOSE (Gertrude), ALAN BATES (Claudius), HELENA BONHAM CARTER (Ophelia), IAN HOLM (Polonius), NATHANIEL PARKER (Laertes), STEPHEN DILLANE (Horatio), PAUL SCOFIELD (Ghost)
DIRECTED BY	FRANCO ZEFFIRELLI
PRODUCED BY	DYSON LOVELL
SCREENPLAY	CHRISTOPHER DE VORE, FRANCO ZEFFIRELLI
PHOTOGRAPHY	DAVID WATKIN
MUSIC	ENNIO MORRICONE

When a rumour first began to circulate that Mel Gibson was going to play Hamlet, *The Independent* assumed it was 'no more than a spicy practical joke'. Who would dream of casting Mad Max as the 'Mad' prince? Franco Zeffirelli. He knew that employing such a megastar would give him another great opportunity to bring the Bard to mass cinema audiences. Gibson knew he could earn the critical kudos never accorded to his action roles. Together, they made a $15 million movie that looks great and contains some compelling moments without so much as scratching the surface of Shakespeare's great tragedy.

To achieve a two-and-a-quarter hour running time, more than 60 per cent of the text was ditched ('Frankly, Franco, this ain't cutting; it's axplay,' cried *Vogue*), with the opening scene and the Fortinbras sub-plot among the most notable casualties. The script, structured along similar lines to Olivier's *Hamlet* (which Zeffirelli adored), serves a dual purpose: it ensures that Gibson dominates virtually every scene, and leaves him only a handful of the longer, most demanding speeches.

Since on this occasion he has no cars and gun-wielding criminals to chase, Zeffirelli has him chase words instead. Few soliloquies or conversations pass by without Mel's bearded, nimble Prince running up or down stairs, or along the Elsinore battlements (actually bits of Dunnottar and Blackness castles in Scotland, and Dover Castle, in Kent). Hamlet as a contemplative soul? No. Gibson's still an action man: he almost stabs Rosencrantz (Michael Maloney) with a barbecue skewer, half throttles him with a recorder and demonstrates jokey prowess with three different types of sword in the climactic duel.

Gibson handles the verse competently enough, in a semi-convincing English accent. His dazzling blue eyes dart around expressively and he manages an impressive outpouring of grief and disgust when he confronts Gertrude in her bedroom, throwing in some simulated, incestuous thrusting in homage to Olivier's oedipal interpretation. Otherwise this Hamlet never stands still or speaks long enough for us to judge what's really happening in his head or heart – or care when he dies.

Gibson divided the critics, with responses varying from *The New York Times*'s 'strong, intelligent and safely beyond ridicule', to the *Mail on Sunday*'s: 'He blunders into the poetry as though it were awkwardly placed furniture'.

The authenticity is all

The prince's melancholy is slightly at odds with the warmth of the film's coastal exteriors, all sunshine, seagulls and windswept heather. As one would expect from Zeffirelli after *The Taming of the Shrew* (*see* page 140) and *Romeo and Juliet* (*see* page 128), the production design looks faultlessly authentic and the medieval furnishings and outfits brought Oscar nominations for art direction and costume design.

Yet some of this 'colour' could be sacrificed happily if it meant that Zeffirelli could have given greater depth to the rest of Shakespeare's characters. It's as if he told the other actors 'Your character's only allowed to have one personality trait.' Close's Gertrude, complete with haughty English accent, remains simply a lusty widow unable to keep her hands off Claudius for more than a few seconds. Bates, denied Claudius's great confessional soliloquy, makes him a raucous, Henry VIII-style monarch rarely seen without a tankard in his hand and a hearty laugh on his lips.

Bonham Carter's Ophelia is distracted, fidgety and clearly halfway to insanity from the moment we see her, so there's precious little shock when she really loses her mind, and Ian Holm is obliged to make Polonius an absurdly gnomish chatterbox. Only Paul Scofield's despairing Ghost – the smallest of the five key supporting roles – retains enough of the script to make a telling impact.

The film's box-office performance was respectable, with a $20 million US gross (less than a fifth of the average take for Gibson's 1990s action films). Those who saw it without having seen or read *Hamlet*, would not have realized how much of the original was missing, but might come away wondering what all the fuss was about. Even **Hamlet**'s voice coach, Julia Wilson-Dickson, admitted that 'It is, slightly, the comic-book version'.

Above left: Glenn Close as Gertrude, left, Alan Bates as Claudius, centre, and Ian Holm as Polonius. The performances of all three were hampered by heavy cuts in the text.

Right: Mel Gibson as Hamlet in the arresting pose used for one of the film's posters.

HAMLET (1996)
US/UK 243 MINS COLOUR

CAST	KENNETH BRANAGH (Hamlet), JULIE CHRISTIE (Gertrude), DEREK JACOBI (Claudius), KATE WINSLET (Ophelia), RICHARD BRIERS (Polonius), MICHAEL MALONEY (Laertes), NICHOLAS FARRELL (Horatio), BRIAN BLESSED (Ghost)
DIRECTED BY	KENNETH BRANAGH
PRODUCED BY	DAVID BARRON
SCREENPLAY	KENNETH BRANAGH
PHOTOGRAPHY	ALEX THOMSON
MUSIC	PATRICK DOYLE

After persuading Castle Rock Entertainment to fund a $15 million **Hamlet** that uses every line of the play, Kenneth Branagh made the longest Shakespeare movie in history, and the longest English-language feature since *Cleopatra*.

Grosses of $4.7 million in the US and about $1 million in Britain suggested that the running time was a major deterrent to cinemagoers, and reviewers either found the marathon exhausting (*The New York Post* paraphrased Hamlet: 'To die, to sleep through half the movie'), or admirable, the *Evening Standard* noting that 'Branagh hasn't bought length at the cost of *longueurs*, and that's an achievement'.

The latter was the fairer view, because here, at last, was a film that did justice to the extraordinary depth of Hamlet *and* the supporting characters. The portrayals of Claudius, Ophelia and Polonius alone were enough to vindicate Branagh's faith in the uncut text (he decided to use it after starring in a full-length RSC *Hamlet* in 1992-93, his third stage appearance in the role).

He moves the action to the late 19th century and elegant, Oscar-nominated costumes designed by Alex Byrne evoke Ruritania rather than gloomy Denmark. For the snowy exteriors, Elsinore is represented by Blenheim Palace in Oxfordshire (its owner, the Duke of Marlborough, appears as one of Fortinbras's guards). Inside, at Shepperton Studios, Alex Thomson's shimmering, 70mm photography brings out every detail of Tim Harvey's opulent production design and both men were deservedly Oscar-nominated.

Harvey's centrepiece is a grand hall neatly encapsulating Elsinore's luxury and secrecy, its chessboard floor edged with full-length mirrors that open onto small rooms connected by concealed doors. The hall's long balconies serve Branagh well in the many 'walk and talk' scenes on which he relies heavily to keep things moving, as his restless Hamlet converses with one or more of Horatio, Polonius, Rosencrantz and Guildenstern.

Family tragedies
He makes the prince a remarkably sane, sensible hero, tearfully dedicated to his father's memory but also displaying the requisite mean streak. His verse-speaking is crisp and fluent, although he errs towards theatrical roaring in some of the soliloquies, ludicrously so when he leads into the Intermission (still 80 minutes to go). Against a superimposed backdrop of Fortinbras's army marching across an icy plain, he must virtually scream to make the 'How all occasions do inform against me' speech audible above Patrick Doyle's Elgar-like score (overblown and over-used but Oscar-nominated).

Branagh establishes a strong rapport with Julie Christie's Gertrude, although hers seems an underwritten part compared to Derek Jacobi's Claudius, the greatest beneficiary of the unexpurgated text. Jacobi is chillingly composed, even with Laertes's sword at his throat, and utilizes the speeches cut by other films to fashion a disturbingly complex villain.

The screenplay, which earned Branagh **Hamlet**'s fifth Oscar nomination, skilfully keeps Kate Winslet's Ophelia in view when Shakespeare has forgotten her and a flashback showing her and Hamlet making love introduces shame at her lost virginity as a plausible strand to her suffering. Winslet's decline from rosy-cheeked happiness to haggard lunacy, straitjacketed in a padded cell, is devastating.

As her father, Richard Briers rescues Polonius from harmless, doddery caricature; instead we see an ambitious, unsympathetic figure, with a taste for young whores. Michael Maloney's sensitive Laertes completes the ensemble of fuller characterizations and enables Branagh to succeed where briefer adaptations fail, by stressing that *Hamlet* charts the destruction of two entire families.

If only these engrossing performances did not have to fight against star cameos. 'Oh, look!' you keep thinking, here's Jack Lemmon as Marcellus, the guardsman, and there's Gérard

Above: Derek Jacobi as Claudius, left, Kenneth Branagh as Hamlet, centre, and a veiled Julie Christie as Gertrude in the film's second scene.

Right: Kenneth Branagh delivers the 'To be, or not be be' soliloquy in Elsinore's mirrored hall, the centrepiece of Tim Harvey's Oscar-nominated production design.

Depardieu as Polonius's spy, Reynaldo, and Charlton Heston as the Player King. Billy Crystal turns up as a Brooklyn-accented gravedigger, and Robin Williams as a cartoonish Osric. None is around long enough to make you forget their stardom and accept the character. Silent appearances from John Gielgud and Judi Dench, in a redundant sequence dramatizing Heston's speech about Priam and Hecuba, are equally distracting.

Misguided casting is **Hamlet**'s greatest flaw, closely followed by Branagh's hit-and-miss direction. It would be hard to imagine either a more disturbing 'Get thee to a nunnery' scene, as Claudius and Polonius observe Hamlet and Ophelia through a two-way mirror, or a more riveting play-within-a-play, with the hall converted into a vertiginously raked auditorium.

Yet the audience must also endure a sub-Hammer House of Horror encounter between Hamlet and the Ghost (Brian Blessed, in ghoulish contact lenses), complete with a laughable mini-earthquake, and towards the end Branagh cross-cuts awkwardly between the fencing match and an SAS-style invasion by Fortinbras's army, a ploy that feels like action for action's sake.

Across four hours, **Hamlet** leaves an indelibly frustrating impression, neatly summed up by *The Independent* as 'good and bad ideas scrambled together on a huge scale'.

HAMLET (2000)
US 111 MINS COLOUR

CAST	ETHAN HAWKE (Hamlet), DIANE VENORA (Gertrude), KYLE MACLACHLAN (Claudius), JULIA STILES (Ophelia), BILL MURRAY (Polonius), LIEV SCHREIBER (Laertes), KARL GEARY (Horatio), SAM SHEPARD (Ghost)
DIRECTED BY	MICHAEL ALMEREYDA
PRODUCED BY	ANDREW FIERBERG, AMY HOBBY
SCREENPLAY	MICHAEL ALMEREYDA
PHOTOGRAPHY	JOHN DEBORMAN
MUSIC	CARTER BURWELL

American writer-director Michael Almereyda loves shooting contemporary stories set in New York. His drama, *Another Girl, Another Planet* (US, 1992), and unsettling vampire movie, *Nadja* (US, 1994), were both low-budget black-and-white features set in 1990s Greenwich Village. So it was no surprise that for this fast-moving, inventive **Hamlet** he not only updated the action but also moved it to Manhattan.

The Danish kingdom is now the Denmark Corporation, a vaguely defined multinational conglomerate whose headquarters are the luxury, high-rise Elsinore Hotel in Times Square. Kyle MacLachlan's forceful, elegant Claudius has taken over from his murdered brother as chief executive. He and Gertrude wear dark power suits and use public relations to keep a lid on their corruption. It's rapidly apparent that the ruthless values of big business are what's rotten in this Denmark.

Almereyda has acknowledged that this corporate environment was inspired by Finnish director Aki Kaurismäki's 1987 spoof, *Hamlet Goes Business* (*see* page 21). Where Kaurismäki mocked the play with banal dialogue and grey, unappealing locations, Almereyda retains Shakespeare's verse (heavily and skilfully edited) and finds an equivalent visual poetry in Manhattan's chrome and glass skyscrapers or the sleek interiors of Gideon Ponte's production design, all dominated by shades of blue, red and green.

Prince of New York

The director roams effectively around the city, using such locations as a supermarket, a laundry, JFK airport and the coiled walkways of the New York Guggenheim Museum. By opening the play out he sacrifices the sense of claustrophobia that's so powerful in *Hamlet* films (notably Olivier's and Richardson's (*see* pages 22 and 29) that keep the action within Elsinore, and demonstrates instead how Hamlet might feel equally trapped within a vast metropolis. 'Shakespeare and New York have a strong natural chemistry', Almereyda told an interviewer, adding that living in the city can induce Hamlet-like symptoms: 'It's easy to be lonely and alienated here, but it's also easy to be exhilarated.'

Loneliness and alienation are stock-in-trade qualities for Ethan Hawke, a specialist in 'pale and interesting' roles. At 29,

he is, unlike most screen Hamlets, young enough to convince as a man fresh out of university although, disappointingly for most reviewers, his prince becomes a variation on the self-pitying, 'slacker' he first played in *Reality Bites* (US, 1994).

Hamlet is a poor little rich kid, sporting a five-day goatee and a Peruvian woollen hat, spending his trust fund on making experimental films with a digital camera. In short, said *Variety*, he is 'the very model of a modern moping malcontent', a slightly obnoxious hero with an infuriating habit of mumbling, even during 'To be, or not to be', spoken in an outrageously ironic setting: the 'Action' movie aisle of a Blockbuster video store.

He delivers another speech via pixel-vision on his laptop computer, and Almereyda constantly translates *Hamlet's* fixation with eavesdropping and covert communication into an obsession with modern technology. *Los Angeles Weekly* called Almereyda's vision 'a media-saturated hell' in which 'Hamlet's agony of indecision about whether and how to seek vengeance ... is propelled, as much as anything, by information overload'.

Shakespeare and New York have a strong natural chemistry. It's easy to be lonely and alienated here, but it's also easy to be exhilarated. Michael Almereyda

HAMLET (2000)

There is gadgetry in virtually every scene: fax machines, phones, answerphones and TV screens. The Ghost (sternly played by Sam Shepard) is first glimpsed on a security camera, and Ophelia is made to wear a wire-tap for her 'accidental' meeting with Hamlet. Hamlet discovers the wiretap when she relents and kisses him. After she gathers up her belongings and leaves, Hamlet continues his speech on her answerphone. The film's most stunning coup arrives when Almereyda cuts the play-within-a-play and Hamlet shocks his uncle with an extremely hilarious, short experimental film. This multimedia obsession continues beyond a gripping, roof-top finale that blends Shakespearean swordplay with gunfire: an epilogue is delivered by a TV newsreader (as in Baz Luhrmann's *Romeo + Juliet*) with a background still of Denmark Corporation's new boss, Fortinbras.

There is fine work from Diane Venora (who has played Hamlet on stage) as a sensual, disarmingly contented Gertrude, Liev Schreiber, as an authoritative Laertes, and Bill Murray whose middle-aged Polonius is part buffoon, part concerned father. As a pouting, petulant Ophelia, Julia Stiles is more mannered here than in 1999's *Shrew*-inspired high-school comedy, *10 Things I Hate About You* (*see* page 142). Carter Burwell supplies a moody score that incorporates both electronic and orchestral themes.

The most favourable verdict in a largely positive set of reviews came from *The New York Times*, which said that in this 'voluptuous and rewarding' film, Almereyda 'has created a new standard for adaptations of Shakespeare'. By contrast, *The New York Post* exclaimed: 'This Manhattan-set massacre of the play may well be the dullest and most pointless version ever filmed.'

When this book went to press, the critics' collective influence on **Hamlet**'s box-office performance had yet to be determined, as it had only been on limited release for a week in the US and was awaiting distribution in Britain. Almereyda had, however, already made a lasting impression by providing the most unusual self-assessment yet from a director confronted by *Hamlet*. He was, he said, 'just one more blind man fumbling his way around this particularly spectacular elephant'.

But for sweet Jack Falstaff, kind Jack Falstaff, true Jack Falstaff, valiant Jack Falstaff ..., banish not him thy Harry's company ..., banish plump Jack, and banish all the world.

Falstaff, *Henry IV, Part 1*, Act II, Scene iv

HENRY IV

Right: William Richert as the Falstaff-like Bob, left, with River Phoenix in *My Own Private Idaho* (1991). The film's *Henry IV* scenes, as a comparison with the picture opposite shows, were closely modelled on *Chimes at Midnight*.

Part 1 England, 1403. After ordering the murder of King Richard II, the Earl of Bolingbroke reigns as Henry IV. Noblemen loyal to Richard, led by the impetuous Harry 'Hotspur', set out to depose Henry and divide the kingdom.

Meanwhile, Henry's son and heir, Prince Hal, devotes himself to wine, women and song with his friend, Poins, the fat, cowardly Sir John Falstaff, and other wastrels at Mistress Quickly's tavern, the Boar's Head, in London. Falstaff and company rob some Canterbury-bound pilgrims, but are ambushed by Hal and Poins. Hal then saves Falstaff from arrest for the robbery.

Hal and Falstaff are called to arms as civil war looms. At the Battle of Shrewsbury, Hal saves his father's life and kills Hotspur. Falstaff, who has played dead, claims he killed Hotspur. King Henry's army is victorious.

Part 2 1405. Henry faces another rebellion, led by the Archbishop of York, but war is avoided when another of the king's sons, Prince John, tricks the rebels into dispersing their armies. Hal continues in his 'loose behaviour' until just before the king's death, when he promises his father that he will mend his ways. Falstaff attends Hal's coronation as King Henry V at Westminster Abbey, confident of preferment, but Hal contemptuously rejects him.

FILM BACKGROUND

The *Henry IV* plays can be slotted into a popular screen category: historical drama. As always with Shakespeare, however, a label like that cannot begin to do justice to the plays' multi-layered structure, action and characterization.

Fine movies such as *Cromwell* (UK, 1970), or the Oscar-winning *A Man for All Seasons* (UK, 1966) dramatize events in English history comparable to those in *Henry IV*: civil war and the rise and fall of kings and archbishops. Yet those two scripts made much more straightforward demands of directors than Shakespeare's would, since their focus remains on the high and mighty figures.

By contrast, anyone wishing to film *Henry IV* must switch back and forth between the fate of the kingdom, and the bawdy antics of the Boar's Head gang, between tense verse and jovial prose. They must also shade in the extraordinary relationships between Hal and Henry and Hal and Falstaff, relationships that

Left: Orson Welles as Falstaff, left, with Keith Baxter as Prince Hal at the Boar's Head tavern in *Chimes at Midnight* (1966).

are at the heart of Orson Welles's **Chimes at Midnight** (1966), the only conventional feature adaptation of the plays to date.

It was seeing Welles's film in the 1980s that inspired American director Gus Van Sant to turn the screenplay he was writing about gay hustlers in Portland, Oregon, into a modern-day *Henry IV*. This revised script emerged as *My Own Private Idaho* (US, 1991) and provided perhaps the clumsiest 'modernization' of Shakespeare ever attempted.

It follows the friendship between Van Sant's Prince Hal figure, Scott (Keanu Reeves), and Mike (River Phoenix), a narcoleptic gay hustler (the equivalent of Poins). Scott, son of Portland's ailing, wheelchair-bound mayor, has been 'slumming', but on his 21st birthday — just a week away — will inherit a fortune and, like Hal, reform completely.

This pair are joined by Bob (William Richert), an ageing, obese drop-out (Van Sant has him drink Falstaff Beer) and the characters begin paraphrasing dialogue from *Henry IV, Part 1*, or speaking Shakespeare's lines verbatim. In scenes closely modelled on **Chimes at Midnight**, Bob leads a night-time mugging of a rock band, then Scott and Mike rob him and expose his cowardice at their squat, a derelict hotel 'managed' by Jane Lightwork (the Mistress Quickly figure).

Shakespeare is abandoned as the boys fly to Italy in search of Mike's long-lost mother. She is not to be found, but Scott falls in love with a beautiful Italian girl and brings her back to Portland. After claiming his inheritance, Scott rejects Bob in a swish restaurant (rather than Shakespeare's Westminster Abbey) and Bob dies of a broken heart.

None of this works. Bob is a deeply unappealing substitute for Falstaff, and the Shakespearean language is poorly spoken and wildly incongruous amid so much modern, colloquial dialogue. Van Sant shortened the *Henry IV* segments during editing, because, he said, 'the Shakespeare scenes were becoming like a movie within the movie'. That's precisely the problem: viewers who don't know *Henry IV* wonder what is going on, those familiar with the plays wonder *why* it's happening. Van Sant, noted *The Guardian*, had made 'a monumental Shakespeare gaffe'.

Aside from these two features, both *Henry IV*s have been filmed twice by the BBC. The second production, in 1979, had Anthony Quayle as Falstaff, the first, in 1960, was most notable for its handsome, muscular Hotspur, played by a soon-to-be-world-famous Scotsman — Sean Connery.

CHIMES AT MIDNIGHT (1966)

SPAIN/SWITZERLAND 119 MINS B/W
US TITLE: FALSTAFF

CAST	ORSON WELLES (Sir John Falstaff), KEITH BAXTER (Prince Hal), JOHN GIELGUD (King Henry IV), TONY BECKLEY (Poins), JEANNE MOREAU (Doll Tearsheet), MARGARET RUTHERFORD (Mistress Quickly), NORMAN RODWAY (Hotspur), FERNANDO REY (Mortimer), ALAN WEBB (Justice Shallow)
DIRECTED BY	ORSON WELLES
PRODUCED BY	EMILIANO PIEDRA, ANGEL ESCOLANO
SCREENPLAY	ORSON WELLES
PHOTOGRAPHY	EDMOND RICHARD
MUSIC	FRANCESCO LAVAGNINO

Chimes at Midnight boasts spectacular action and a cast of hundreds, but it's really about three men. Orson Welles' masterful screenplay fillets and re-arranges the *Henry IV* plays to fit his vision of them as the tragi-comic story of a human triangle: 'the prince, his king-father and Falstaff, who's a kind of foster father'.

Welles evokes the worlds occupied by his own vast Falstaff and Gielgud's pale, troubled Henry in richly contrasted tones, casting a spell that is never broken, not even by the atrocious, disjointed soundtrack (virtually all of the dialogue was re-recorded during postproduction) or improbable landscapes (the plains of southern Spain doubling for damp Olde England).

Welles's Falstaff, looking every inch the 'huge hill of flesh' conjured by Shakespeare, with the beard and strawberry nose of a boozy, 15th-century Santa, is at home amid the warm timbers and giggling blonde whores of the Boar's Head. Here he drawls self-mocking jokes, refuses to pay Margaret Rutherford's long-suffering, jittery Mistress Quickly, and is waited on by a cute page (Beatrice Welles, the director's then nine-year-old daughter). Miraculously, he is also adored by Doll Tearsheet, convincingly so thanks to a marvellous cameo from Jeanne Moreau, who instantly makes you believe that she loves this dissolute coward 'with a most constant heart'.

Prince of thieves

Falstaff's wit is still in fine shape, but there is something pathetic about his devotion to Keith Baxter's calculating Hal, so that the great comic set pieces of *Henry IV, Part 1* – the robbery of the pilgrims (wondrously filmed in a wintry, sunlit wood) and the mock trial of Falstaff – are heavy with foreboding.

Baxter, who had also played Hal in 1960 in Welles' staged *Chimes at Midnight* in Belfast, scarcely disguises his character's contempt for Falstaff. Their every moment together and Baxter's conspiratorial, whispered soliloquies pave the way for the betrayal that will come when Hal ascends the English throne, a position that, in the hands of Welles and Gielgud, seems the coldest, loneliest place on earth. Welles contrasts the wide, low angles of the Boar's Head with the forbidding height of Henry's throne room (Spain's Soria Cathedral). Gielgud, his breath condensing in the chilly air, invests the verse with majesty and the simple pain of a father who has lost touch with his wastrel son.

Henry and Falstaff's worlds finally meet in the astonishing scenes of the Battle of Shrewsbury, shot in a Madrid park. For ten minutes, knights and soldiers hack at and batter each other with lances, swords and clubs. Welles intermingles close-ups of dying men writhing on the muddy ground with shots of Falstaff encased in a gigantic suit of armour, frantically waddling to his next hiding place. Somehow, his absurd cowardice renders even more horrifying the battlefield terrors suffered by braver men rather than undermining them.

Then the two great scenes of **Chimes**' second half complete its symmetrical pattern, in which Hal has moved back and forth between 'king-father' and 'foster father'. First comes Hal's reconciliation with the dying Henry (described by *The Guardian* as 'more moving than one would have thought possible') and then his shattering rejection of Falstaff in the coronation ceremony.

Above: Jeanne Moreau as Doll Tearsheet, left, and Margaret Rutherford as Mistress Quickly watch Falstaff's antics inside the Boar's Head.

Shakespeare ends *Henry IV, Part 2* here, but Welles needed to round off the knight's tragedy with his death, and so has Rutherford deliver Quickly's speech from *Henry V*, describing Falstaff's last hours, and **Chimes**' final image is of 'plump Jack' in his coffin, on a cart, pulled away from his beloved Boar's Head by Pistol and Bardolph. It is an indelible conclusion to a movie which earned Welles the Grand Prix at Cannes.

Read *Henry IV* after seeing **Chimes**, and you will appreciate what a brilliant feat of adaptation the film is. Welles lifts marvellous comic scenes featuring Alan Webb's rickety Justice Shallow from *Part 2* and fits them seamlessly into **Chimes** while still depicting events from *Part 1*. He discards most of the rebels from *Part 1*, and ignores *Part 2*'s Archbishop's revolt, so only two of Henry's opponents leave an imprint: Fernando Rey's sinister Mortimer, and Norman Rodway's raucous Hotspur. Historical omissions are glossed over with extracts from Shakespeare's main historical source, Raphael Holinshed's *Chronicles*, read in sonorous voice-over by Ralph Richardson.

Welles's magpie approach means that no responsible teacher would ever recommend **Chimes** to Shakespeare students seeking an accurate screen version of *Henry IV*, but it is hard to imagine any other film-maker capturing the plays' essence with such affecting economy.

Above: Orson Welles as Falstaff encased in armour before the Battle of Shrewsbury, a devastating sequence filmed in a Madrid park.

Right: John Gielgud as King Henry IV, right, confronts Prince Hal, played by Keith Baxter.

We few, we happy few, we band of brothers;
For he to-day that sheds his blood with me
Shall be my brother. Henry, *Henry V*, Act IV, Scene iii

HENRY V

England, 1414–15. King Henry is convinced by the Archbishop of Canterbury that ancient laws allow him to claim the French throne. France's King Charles refuses to yield, so Henry prepares to invade. Before his fleet sails from Southampton, he orders the execution of three noblemen who have conspired to murder him.

Henry's former drinking companions, Bardolph, Pistol and Nym, briefly mourn the death of Falstaff, then join the army. The trio are caught up in the bloody siege of Harfleur, where the brave Welsh captain, Fluellen, condemns their cowardice. Henry urges his men to greater efforts, and Harfleur's governor surrenders.

Charles' daughter, Princess Katharine, anticipating marriage to Henry, learns some basic English from her maid, Alice. Charles, urged on by his son, the Dauphin, sends a vast army to confront Henry's exhausted soldiers as they retreat to Calais.

Henry rejects the French offer to allow his army safe passage back to England in return for a large ransom. Bardolph is executed for robbing a church. That night, Henry wanders, disguised, amongst the common soldiers; their fears make him question his kingly responsibilities. Next day, his rousing speech spurs his army – outnumbered five to one – to an astonishing victory at the battle of Agincourt.

At the French court, Henry woos Katharine, and King Charles consents to their marriage – a perfect seal to the peace between the two countries.

FILM BACKGROUND

Shakespeare's portrait of the English army in *Henry V* is classic war-movie material. In *The Longest Day*, *A Bridge Too Far*, or any number of other World War II adventures, scriptwriters have personalized conflict by showing us three levels of soldier: the generals making big, strategic decisions; the captains and lieutenants commanding smaller units and the 'grunts' in those squads. If they can concoct some jokey regional tension in the ranks, so much the better.

Just over 400 years ago, the Bard placed Henry, Exeter and company in command, with Fluellen, Gower and MacMorris as the junior officers (who also supply the regional jibes). The privates included Pistol, Nym and the soldiers who meet Henry on the eve of Agincourt. All military life was there.

In essence, modern scriptwriters are not doing anything in their war stories that Shakespeare did not do, more powerfully, in the late 16th century. *Henry V* achieves greatness through its detailed, humane portrayal of men at arms, even before one considers Henry himself, and Shakespeare's astute exploration of what it means to be king. Only his jingoistic characterization of the French knights has dated.

Two feature films have attempted to do the play justice, and are the focus of this chapter. The contrasts between Laurence Olivier's **Henry V** (UK, 1944) and Kenneth Branagh's **Henry V**

(UK, 1989) are immense. Olivier's was epic, romantic and rousing, exactly what the wartime mood required. Branagh's was intimate, gritty and moving, a reflection, some critics argued, of Britain's ambivalence to military confrontation seven years after the Falklands War (by the same token, post-World War II patriotism might explain why the BBC produced *Henry V* four times between 1951 and 1960).

Although both directors achieved much, neither could prevent Shakespeare's ending from seeming anti-climactic. At the Globe in 1599, where, it's safe to assume, Agincourt was represented by a few actors fighting carefully for two minutes with blunt swords (as happens in today's stage productions), the shift in temperature from the fire of battle to Henry's tepid wooing scene would not have felt too great. On a big screen, after Branagh and Olivier's prolonged battles, this change is enormous and deflating.

A simple experiment would demonstrate the problem. If the post-Agincourt scenes were cut from both films, so that their last line became Henry's 'to England then; Where ne'er from France arriv'd more happy men', and a few lines added as a Chorus epilogue, explaining that Henry married Katharine, uniting France and England and these modified prints shown to viewers who had never read or seen the play or the movies, no one would feel short-changed.

When Branagh's film was first released, a spontaneous variation on this test occurred. Shakespeare scholar Kenneth Rothwell reports that when the post-Agincourt 'Non Nobis' hymn began at one New York screening, members of the audience started to put on their coats and head for the exits.

HENRY V (1944)
UK 137 MINS COLOUR

CAST	LAURENCE OLIVIER (Henry V), LESLIE BANKS (Chorus), NICHOLAS HANNEN (Exeter), ESMOND KNIGHT (Fluellen), ROY EMERTON (Bardolph), ROBERT NEWTON (Pistol), HARCOURT WILLIAMS (King Charles VI of France), RENÉE ASHERSON (Princess Katharine), IVY ST HELIER (Alice)
DIRECTED BY	LAURENCE OLIVIER
PRODUCED BY	LAURENCE OLIVIER
PHOTOGRAPHY	ROBERT KRASKER
MUSIC	WILLIAM WALTON

Henry V is the perfect marriage of great dramatic poetry with the greatest contemporary medium for expressing it. Time

Laurence Olivier's **Henry V** was not designed primarily to fulfil its director/star's artistic ambitions, win awards or succeed at the box office – although it would eventually do all three.

In 1943, at the height of World War II, the British government approached Olivier because it believed that filming the Bard's account of a great English military triumph would boost morale as British troops fought the Germans. This would be Shakespeare as propaganda.

This was an extension of work that Sub-Lieutenant Olivier was already doing: he was used to being called away from non-operational duties as a Royal Naval Volunteer Reserve, to make stirring speeches throughout Britain, always ending his medley with Henry V's 'Once more unto the breach'.

He was summoned by Jack Beddington, the Ministry of Information civil servant responsible for showbusiness propaganda. Beddington wanted Olivier to play a Russian engineer in *Demi-Paradise*, a contemporary film drama designed to make the British more sympathetic to their Eastern European allies, and then to turn his attention to *Henry V*.

Olivier loved this idea (the brainchild of Dallas Bower, associate producer of the 1936 *As You Like It*) and set to work on the script, aided by *News Chronicle* theatre critic Alan Dent. He reduced the play from 3,000 to 1,500 lines; in his autobiography, he justified the cuts by suggesting: 'The audience must not be allowed to miss the poetry; nor must they be surfeited with it.'

But he was reluctant to star *and* direct and approached three experienced film-makers, William Wyler, Terence Young and Carol Reed. They all declined, so he decided to do it himself.

Even though experienced editor Reginald Beck would be on hand to act as Olivier's assistant, senior film industry figures believed the Rank Organization was mad to entrust an actor directing for the first time with such a vast project. **Henry V** would eventually cost £475,000, 50 per cent more than the original budget, and, up to that point, the largest sum ever spent on a British feature.

Olivier used his budget to fashion a stylized and sanitized Technicolor vision of medieval heroism, which feels like three films rolled into one. An amusing simulation of spare Elizabethan stagecraft gives way to more elaborate, fairy-tale scenery and performances, as Olivier's righteous monarch in shining armour is opposed by sneering, caricatured villains.

Then this story-book treatment is spectacularly interrupted by the epic, open-air realism of the Agincourt battle: galloping French knights brought down by a shower of arrows from English bowmen and messy hand-to-hand combat.

In November 1944, the battle brought a round of applause from critics at a London press screening, and they peppered their reviews with superlatives. 'Easily the most spectacular triumph of the British studio,' roared the *Daily Herald*. The *Sunday Pictorial* acclaimed it as 'easily the most important film ever made'. *The People*, perhaps more realistically, acknowledged the flaws within the triumph, calling **Henry V** 'the most difficult, annoying, beautiful, boring, exciting, wordy, baffling picture yet made'.

Today, the most engaging segment is the first half-hour, which vividly depicts a 1600 performance of *Henry V* at the Globe. It resembles a trial run for the theatre scenes in *Shakespeare in Love*, with raucous groundlings jeering at the players. Backstage, a nervous boy actor dresses up as Princess Katharine, and on stage there are stumbling performances from Felix Aylmer's elderly Archbishop, and Robert Helpmann's bizarre-looking Bishop of Ely (picture a balding Harpo Marx).

As Olivier nonchalantly establishes Henry's magnetic nobility (he memorably tosses the crown over a corner of his throne), the audience might wonder if they are in for two more hours of filmed theatre – until Olivier pulls off a great coup.

'Unto Southampton do we shift our scene', announces Leslie Banks, as Chorus, and a curtain fades away to reveal the prow of Henry's ship, moored at the Southampton quayside. We have moved from the simple staging of the Globe to the grander illusion of Paul Sheriff's sets.

Left: Laurence Olivier as Henry as the English fleet prepares to set sail from Southampton.

Below: Laurence Olivier as Henry, centre, listens as the French herald, second right, concedes defeat after the Battle of Agincourt.

His insubstantial, out-of-scale depictions of French court and castles were built at Denham Studios and inspired by *Les très riches heures du duc de Berri*, a 15th-century book of hours. As the film's cinematographer Robert Krasker said, they look 'terribly phoney', yet they are the perfect backdrops for the one-dimensional performances by the actors playing French characters.

Harcourt Williams is the worst offender, playing the French king as a timid, half-senile fool who swoons when the imposing Exeter (Nicholas Hannen) warns him that Henry's army is approaching. The French knights are even more effete and vain than the text suggests, and, in true propaganda style, such lame villains could never be a match for a hero as formidable as Olivier's Henry.

Despite talk of exhausted English troops and impossible odds, despite Olivier's soaring Saint Crispian speech, the build-up to Agincourt lacks tension. The battle itself is a magnificent spectacle, but less involving than it should have been.

It took eight weeks to film, with the estate of Lord Powerscourt in Enniskerry, Ireland, doubling for France. The Irish extras who made up the two armies were paid £3, 10 shillings a day – and a pound more if they brought their own horses.

More than a kilometre (half a mile) of camera track was needed to follow the line of French knights as they build from a trot to a canter to full gallop, spurred on by William Walton's marvellous orchestral crescendo. Then the English bowmen (whom Shakespeare does not even mention) make their mark, their first volley producing an unforgettable 'whoosh' (created by a technician swishing a willow switch 100 times in front of a microphone).

Back to the 'wooden O'

Once the French have conceded defeat, Olivier reverses the filmic journey. We return to studio sets for our last glimpse of the fearless Fluellen (Esmond Knight, with the broadest of Welsh accents, a fiery temper and beetle-like eyebrows), and then Henry's awkward wooing scene with the demure Katharine (Renée Asherson). As the couple join hands, the scene dissolves back to the Globe, the actors take their bows and the camera pulls back to repeat the bird's-eye view of an elaborate model of Elizabethan London which opened the film.

The propaganda element is most noticeable in what Olivier omits: namely all of the incidents which, in the play, take the gloss off Henry's heroic sheen. We do not hear anything of the traitorous earls, and the governor of Harfleur surrenders without Henry threatening him with the sight of 'your naked infants spitted upon spikes'. Nor, after the French knights murder the baggage boys, does Henry give the order that 'every soldier kill his prisoners'. There is hammy, low-life comedy from Robert Newton (Pistol), and Roy Emerton, as Bardolph, but the latter's execution is not mentioned.

In the circumstances, these omissions are understandable. With British troops dying in France during production, Olivier felt 'shadowed' by his responsibilities to king and country. Even though it meant compromising Shakespeare's play, there could be no hint of treason or disobedience in the English ranks, or Henry's 'war crimes'.

Despite the cuts, certain scenes must have had immense resonance for cinemagoers in 1944-45, all of whom will have had relatives, friends or acquaintances in the armed forces. When Henry celebrates the glory of fighting for one's country, and when he listens to a soldier complaining that 'there are few die well that die in a battle', Shakespeare's words will have meant far more to those wartime viewers than they can to today's audiences. **Henry V**'s opening title card: 'To the commando and airborne troops of Great Britain, the spirit of whose ancestors it has been humbly attempted to recapture in some ensuing scenes, this film is dedicated', will always provide a reminder of those times.

Whether audiences went out of patriotic duty or, more probably, for entertainment, **Henry V** was a major hit, its success boosted by local councils who paid for school parties to see it and thus created the educational sector of the Shakespeare movie market that thrives to this day.

When the film was finally released in the US in April 1946, *Time* considered **Henry V** the 'perfect marriage of great dramatic poetry with the greatest contemporary medium for expressing it', and it grossed over $1 million. None of its four Oscar nominations (Best Picture, Best Actor, Art Decoration and Best Score) brought victory, but Olivier's achievements were honoured with a Special Oscar. He gave the statuette to Filippo del Giudice, the Italian producer who had put together the deal with Rank.

In his memoirs, Olivier wrote of **Henry V**: 'I look back on it always with a happy glow'.

Left: Laurence Olivier as Henry, right, woos Renée Asherson as Princess Katharine at the fairy-tale French court.

Right: English archers prepare to loose the arrows that will devastate the French cavalry charge. Shakespeare does not even mention their contribution to the Agincourt victory.

HENRY V (1989)

UK 137 MINS COLOUR

CAST	KENNETH BRANAGH (Henry V), DEREK JACOBI (Chorus), BRIAN BLESSED (Exeter), IAN HOLM (Fluellen), RICHARD BRIERS (Bardolph), ROBERT STEPHENS (Pistol), PAUL SCOFIELD (King Charles VI of France), EMMA THOMPSON (Princess Katharine), GERALDINE MCEWAN (Alice), MICHAEL MALONEY (Dauphin)
DIRECTED BY	KENNETH BRANAGH
PRODUCER	BRUCE SHARMAN
SCREENPLAY	KENNETH BRANAGH
PHOTOGRAPHY	KENNETH MACMILLAN
MUSIC	PATRICK DOYLE

The scene that best describes the tone of Kenneth Branagh's **Henry V** is not to be found in Shakespeare's play. As the English army retreats to Calais, Bardolph (Richard Briers) stands on a cart in tattered clothes, with blood streaked across his bulbous nose and a noose around his neck; the rope has been thrown over a high tree branch.

A brief flashback, lifted from *Henry IV, Part 1*, shows Henry (Branagh) recalling a raucous night with Bardolph at the Boar's Head. Then, close to tears, the king gives a signal, and Bardolph is kicked off the cart and hauled aloft by soldiers, his body jerking horribly as he dies.

Shakespeare deals with this execution by report only; Olivier's *Henry V* omitted it completely. Branagh's decision to show the hanging and its effect on Henry and his soldiers in harrowing detail typifies his bold, moving treatment of the play, concentrating on the human cost of war, rather than its heroism.

As Henry's ragged soldiers trudge through the rain, looking as 'sick and famished' as Shakespeare pictured them, cinematographer Kenneth MacMillan gives the countryside a murky, medieval feel, while parts of the Harfleur sequence feel like a World War I movie, as MacMorris (John Sessions) and Fluellen (Ian Holm) seek cover from explosions in a narrow trench.

Branagh's Agincourt (filmed on a field behind Shepperton Studios) is much closer to Welles' Shrewsbury sequence in *Chimes at Midnight* than Olivier's battle, as knights and soldiers hack away in agonized slow motion. The sordid Pistol (Robert Stephens) and Nym (Geoffrey Hutchings) loot the fallen men, and Nym is killed as he steals.

For this relief ...

When victory has arrived, the overwhelming relief, exhaustion and grief amongst the English is captured in a magnificent, three-minute tracking shot which follows Branagh as he carries a murdered baggage boy (Christian Bale) across the corpse-strewn field, and the '*Non Nobis*' hymn swells on the soundtrack.

Branagh has led from the front, with a thoughtful, understated performance, based on his Henry for the Royal Shakespeare Company in 1984. Slight, boyish-looking and, when not rousing his troops, quietly-spoken, he is an inexperienced, God-fearing man who attains heroic stature almost in spite of himself. Yet he also demonstrates the ruthless streak that Olivier erased: violently condemning the Southampton conspirators and yelling spittle-flecked threats at the Harfleur governor, after a night-time rendition of 'Once more unto the breach'.

When he woos Katharine (skittishly played by Emma Thompson, who married Branagh soon after filming ended), Henry's awkwardness is affecting and amusing – although still anti-climactic – because we have a vivid sense of what he has endured to reach this point. Olivier's king was essentially the same man in his first and last scenes, Branagh's has undergone a profound transformation.

Below: Emma Thompson as Princess Katharine, left, listens to a marriage proposal from Kenneth Branagh as Henry. In real life, the stars married soon after filming ended.

He has sterling support, notably from Holm's fierce, tearful Fluellen, Brian Blessed, repeating his 1984 RSC performance as a bellicose Exeter, and Paul Scofield as a careworn French king. Early on, Judi Dench delivers a memorable account of Falstaff's death.

Although Tim Harvey's production design is dominated by stark realism (notably in the squalid Boar's Head and spartan French court), Branagh uses Derek Jacobi's excitable Chorus to draw our attention to cinematic illusion, just as Shakespeare and Olivier used this figure to 'excuse' theatrical artifice. In modern dress, Jacobi turns on the lights of a Shepperton soundstage during his opening speech, then reappears several times in the midst of the action, when voice-overs would have made his contributions less intrusive, but also less true to Shakespeare.

From a first-time director aged 28 (the same age as Henry at Agincourt), **Henry V** was a stunning debut, described by the *Sunday Times* as 'compelling entertainment; superbly acted, bristling with energy and power' and by *Rolling Stone* as 'hot-blooded, lively and moving'.

Phyllis Dalton collected an Oscar for her earthy costume design; Branagh was Oscar-nominated as director and actor, and also won the BAFTA for Best Direction and two European Film Awards. In the history of screen Shakespeare, however, **Henry V**'s commercial performance was more important than its critical acclaim. Made for about $9 million, it took that much in the US alone, and, more impressively, roughly the same amount (£5.7 million) in Britain. **Henry V** was a hit – and Shakespeare's cinematic renaissance had begun.

Below: Kenneth Branagh as Henry, centre, rousing his 'band of brothers' before the Battle of Agincourt sequence, which was filmed on a field behind Shepperton Studios.

Laurence Olivier's first attempt at screen stardom was a disaster. In 1930, his good looks and immense talent as a stage actor had earned the 23-year-old a contract with the RKO studio in Hollywood, but his first appearances were in melodramas that flopped at the box office and he left California convinced of the theatre's superiority over the cinema – so much so that he declared Shakespeare's plays could 'never work on film'. RKO formed an equally dismissive opinion of Olivier, with one member of staff confidently predicting that the Englishman would never become a great movie star, 'because he has no screen personality'.

Over the next 20 years, Olivier proved both himself and RKO wrong. As star of *Henry V*, *Hamlet* and *Richard III*, he confirmed his formidable and versatile film presence, and as a director he established beyond doubt that Shakespeare and cinema could form a mutually rewarding partnership – something that Hollywood's initial stumbles with *The Taming of The Shrew* (1929) and *Romeo and Juliet* (1936) had called into question. Without Olivier, the history of Shakespeare on screen would have been very different.

He believed that he was 'born to be an actor', and his lifelong stage and screen commitment to the Bard began when he was just ten. Born in May 1907, the son of an Anglican clergyman, he attended All Saints choir school in London and made his Shakespearean debut there as Brutus in *Julius Caesar*, in 1917; at 15, he played Katharina in *The Taming of the Shrew*.

After training at the Central School of Drama, he served his stage apprenticeship as a junior company member with Birmingham Repertory Theatre during 1927 and 1928. After that, a string of appearances in the West End, including the title role in *Beau Geste*, marked him out as a dashing leading man, and brought him a film debut in an Anglo-German drama, *The Temporary Widow*, in 1929; his £58 fee helped to pay for his wedding to actress Jill Esmond in 1930.

That year he and Jill Esmond caught Hollywood talent scouts' attention in the Broadway première of Noël Coward's sparkling comedy, *Private Lives*. They signed two-year, three-picture contracts with the studio on weekly salaries of $700 (perhaps $28,000 today), but all three films Olivier made for RKO were poor, and he believed that his roles, such as an impetuous lover in *Westward Passage* (1932), were beneath him. With Jill Esmond's prospects at RKO being stifled by the rise of the young Katharine Hepburn, the couple returned to England.

Disenchantment with Hollywood led Olivier to turn down the chance to star in MGM's *Romeo and Juliet* (*see* page 122). One can only imagine how passionate it might have been with Romeo portrayed by 29-year-old Olivier, rather than 43-year-old Leslie Howard. He did agree to play Orlando in the British *As You Like It* (*see* page 14), although his first attempt at screen Shakespeare gave him little satisfaction. In his memoirs, *Confessions of an Actor*, the film doesn't merit so much as a line.

The wide media of films and television do not usually tax one's energies beyond the normal capabilities. But the playing of a great stage role does exactly this.

Laurence Olivier

A theatrical sensation

He now began to dedicate himself to Shakespeare on stage, and rapidly confirmed Coward's 1930 prediction that he would soon be acknowledged as Britain's greatest actor. His alternating performances as Romeo and Mercutio, with John Gielgud, at the Old Vic in 1936 were the first breakthrough, followed by an astonishing string of roles at the same theatre in 1937 and 1938: Hamlet, Henry V, Macbeth and Iago, opposite Ralph Richardson's Othello.

The sheer force of his acting – athletic, virile and quick-witted – was too flashy for some of the critics; others raved; none had seen anything quite like it before. Theatregoers adored him, with *Henry V* breaking box-office records and establishing Olivier as a paragon of national virtues, a quality that would be brilliantly exploited in *Henry V* (*see* page 42). 'Do you know why you're so good in this part? 'Charles Laughton asked Olivier after seeing him as Henry. 'Because you are England!' That ground-breaking Old Vic season also established Olivier's fondness for acting in elaborate make-up, and he would recall that his performance as Sir Toby Belch, in *Twelfth Night*, was 'remarkable only for the weighty encrustation of nose-putty on my face'.

Stage success gave Olivier the confidence to return to Hollywood to tackle a role far superior to anything RKO had offered him: Heathcliff in *Wuthering Heights* (US, 1939), directed by William Wyler. Up until this point, Olivier felt that his screen performances had been 'appallingly rough and ready', from a combination of sheer prejudice against the medium and ignorance of how best to meet the camera's requirements. Some tough talking from Wyler forced him to modify his technique and transformed his screen career: his smouldering Heathcliff earned him his first Best Actor Oscar nomination, not to mention frenzied adoration from female American fans, and he immediately followed up with another Oscar-nominated portrayal, as Maxim de Winter in Hitchcock's *Rebecca* (US, 1940).

That same year, Olivier and Esmond divorced and he was free to marry the woman who had been his lover for several years: Vivien Leigh, then at the height of her fame after *Gone With The Wind*. Heathcliff married to Scarlett O'Hara was a dream come true for the gossip columnists, and the Oliviers became the most celebrated couple in showbusiness.

They acted on stage and screen together numerous times, perhaps most famously as Nelson and his mistress in *Lady Hamilton* (US, 1941), and Leigh was Olivier's first choice to play Princess Katharine in *Henry V*. But *Gone With The Wind* producer David O. Selznick would not release her from her Hollywood contract, and the unknown Renée Asherson stepped in, partly because she fitted the costumes already made for Leigh.

Olivier was equally determined that Leigh should star alongside him in what should have been his fourth Shakespeare outing as a director, a film of *Macbeth*.

Left: Olivier the matinée idol in 1938, a year before his Oscar-nominated Hollywood breakthrough as Heathcliff in *Wuthering Heights*.

Above: Olivier delivers the 'To be, or not to be' soliloquy in *Hamlet* (1948), the film that earned him two Oscars.

Thwarted ambition

In 1955, the couple starred as the Macbeths in Stratford-upon-Avon and, although the critics who celebrated Olivier's performance came down hard on Leigh (always a lesser actor and a more fragile personality than her husband), he was justifiably confident of raising finance for a screen version. After all, in the previous ten years he had won an Oscar for *Henry V*; become the youngest actor ever to receive a knighthood, in 1947; won two more Oscars for *Hamlet* (*see* page 24) and received extraordinary notices for his performance as Shakespeare's hunchbacked king, both on stage and in *Richard III* (*see* page 112) – achievements that he would always cherish.

After *Richard III*'s release, Olivier spent two weeks location-scouting for *Macbeth* in Scotland, wrote a visually ambitious screenplay (including an underwater death scene for Macbeth), and lined up the burly Harry Andrews as his Macduff. The projected budget of £400,000 would surely have come through if Olivier's most loyal patron, the great producer, Sir Alexander Korda, had lived a little longer, but after Korda's death in 1956, Olivier was chastened to discover that no other British or American producer shared Korda's faith in his Shakespearean track record.

After one last, futile effort to raise the money, in 1959, any lingering hopes of Olivier and Leigh as screen Macbeths ended the following year, when they divorced. His regret at failing to film *Macbeth* never faded, and in his memoirs he cursed 'the money men' who had deprived posterity of another version of the Scottish play 'to compare with Orson Welles's or Roman Polanski's'. That lingering frustration may well have contributed to the fact that after *Richard III*, Olivier directed just one more film, a perfunctory version of his stage production of Chekhov's *Three Sisters*, in 1970.

Although he continued to display his chameleon-like range of characters for cinema, including his Oscar-nominated portrayal of Archie Rice, the sour music hall comedian in *The Entertainer* (UK, 1960) and his fanatical Mahdi in *Khartoum* (US, 1965), most of his energies in the 1960s were devoted to the stage. He worked tirelessly to help found Britain's National Theatre and, in 1962, a year after marrying actress Joan Plowright, became the National's first director. He directed numerous productions, appeared in Strindberg, Ibsen and, of course, Shakespeare. His towering *Othello* (filmed in 1965; *see* page 103) ran, on and off, for four years, and he played a harsh Shylock in *The Merchant of Venice* in 1970, soon after becoming the first actor to be made a life peer.

Shylock was to be his last Shakespeare role on stage. During his tenure at the National he had fought funding battles, stage fright and serious illness and, in 1973, exhausted, he announced his retirement from theatre acting and his resignation from the directorship. The largest of the National's three auditoria on London's South Bank is called the Olivier in his honour.

In the final decade of his career, he could still cope with screen work, which he had always found relatively straightforward, because, as he said: 'The wide media of films and television do not usually tax one's energies beyond the normal capabilities. But the playing of a great stage role does exactly this, demanding abundant reserves of vitality and verve.'

Even when vitality and verve were in short supply, Olivier could convince – as a Nazi dentist in *Marathon Man* (US, 1976) or a Nazi-hunter in *The Boys from Brazil* (US, 1978). He happily accepted 'filthy lucre' to support the futures of his children and grandchildren, pocketing $1 million for a Polaroid commercial and fat fees for cameos, such as Zeus in the absurd fantasy adventure, *Clash of the Titans* (UK, 1981).

Six years before his death in July 1989, he had summoned the energy for the last, and most moving of his screen Shakespeare performances, in the television *King Lear* (*see* page 194). To compare Olivier's white-haired, fragile Lear in 1983 with the boundless energy of his Orlando in 1936 was to watch the conclusion of an extraordinary life story, much of it lived through Shakespeare. At Granada Television's Manchester studios, Olivier told an interviewer: 'You know, when you get to my age, you *are* Lear, in every nerve of your body. Here I am, at the very end of myself, in both age and experience.'

Left: Frank Finlay as Iago, left, with Olivier as the Moor in *Othello* (1965), the film version of the National Theatre's acclaimed, sell-out stage production.

Below left: Olivier as Orlando, left, with Elisabeth Bergner as Rosalind in *As You Like It* (1936). The film merits not a single mention in Olivier's memoirs.

Left: Olivier, aged 15, playing Katharina in the All Saints School production of *The Taming of the Shrew* in 1922.

JULIUS CAESAR

As Caesar loved me, I weep for him; as he was fortunate, I rejoice at it; as he was valiant, I honour him; but, as he was ambitious, I slew him. Brutus, *Julius Caesar*, Act III, Scene ii

Rome, 44 BC Julius Caesar has virtually become a dictator. Infuriated by his excessive power, conspirators led by two senators, Cassius and Brutus, plan to destroy him. After an ominously stormy night, the conspirators meet and resolve to kill Caesar in the Senate that day. Portia, Brutus's wife, begs him to reveal what's going on, but he refuses.

Caesar's wife, Calpurnia, has had a dream that he will be murdered and pleads with him to stay at home. Despite having also been warned by a soothsayer to beware this day, the Ides of March, he proceeds to the Senate. The conspirators stab him to death, with Brutus, his close friend, last to strike.

Brutus manages to convince the angry citizens gathered in the forum that this was a just assassination. Then Mark Antony, a staunch ally of Caesar who took no part in his murder, convinces them that Caesar loved ordinary Romans. He turns the mob violently against the conspirators, who flee the city.

Mark Antony joins forces with Octavius, Caesar's nephew and heir, and they pursue the plotters' legions to Philippi, in Macedonia. In the ensuing battle, the armies of Brutus (who has learned of Portia's suicide) and Cassius are routed. Realizing that all is lost, Cassius orders his slave to kill him and Brutus throws himself upon his own sword. Mark Antony eulogizes Brutus as 'the noblest Roman of them all'.

FILM BACKGROUND

Conspiracy, assassination, inspirational speeches, 'heroic' suicides – these are the staple ingredients used by film-makers in the best political thrillers, and *Julius Caesar* has them all.

Although set 2,000 years ago, its account of an overambitious leader brought down by once-loyal deputies has echoes in numerous movies exploring fictional 20th-century American power struggles. *All the King's Men* (US, 1949), which follows politician Willy Stark (Broderick Crawford, in an Oscar-winning performance), from backwoods obscurity to big-time corruption and assassination, is one of Hollywood's finest *Caesar*-like tales. In *City Hall* (US, 1996), the relationship between Al Pacino as the mayor of New York and John Cusack as his aide has a Caesar/Brutus flavour.

The play itself was very popular in the silent era, with no fewer than four versions, two American and two Italian, made in 1908. On television, the BBC filmed *Caesar* seven times between 1938 and 1969, with Peter Cushing taking a break from vampire hunting for Hammer to play Cassius in 1963. The two best-known versions are the focus of this chapter: MGM's black-and-white classic from 1953, with Marlon Brando, and 1970's inferior colour version, starring Charlton Heston.

Heston was still waiting for his Hollywood breakthrough when he made his first two screen appearances in the play, both in 1949. First he was Cinna the poet in a modern-dress TV version for CBS, then he played Mark Antony in one of the most inventive Shakespeare films ever made. *Julius Caesar* (US, 1949) was produced and directed by 28-year-old David Bradley, on a budget of just $10,000. Bradley himself played Brutus, with students from Northwestern University playing centurions whose headgear was made from World War II GI helmets.

Bradley's most inspired decision was to shoot on location at several of Chicago's 'Roman' buildings (Soldier Field football stadium doubled as the Coliseum), giving his 90-minute, black-and-white experiment a more authentic look than achieved in many million-dollar productions.

When it was finally given a limited theatrical release in 1952, the rave reviews were led by the *Los Angeles Daily News*, which hailed it as 'a triumph of ingenuity and imagination over physical odds.' A great future was predicted for Bradley shortly afterwards, when he was given a directing contract by MGM boss Dore Schary, but it never materialized.

Then came *Carry On Cleo* (UK, 1964). Its writer Talbot Rothwell mercilessly parodied *Julius Caesar*, *Antony and Cleopatra* and the Taylor and Burton epic, *Cleopatra* (US, 1963), acknowledging his sources with the immortal credit line: 'Based on an idea by William Shakespeare'. Rothwell responded to the Bard's masterful use of language with a stream of groan-worthy puns, topped by Kenneth Williams's Caesar, wailing as the conspirators close in: 'Infamy. Infamy. They've all got it in for me!'

Left: Charlton Heston as Mark Antony about to ride into the Battle of Philippi in *Julius Caesar* (1970), directed by Stuart Burge.

JULIUS CAESAR (1953)
US 120 MINS B/W

CAST	MARLON BRANDO (Mark Antony), JOHN GIELGUD (Cassius), JAMES MASON (Brutus), DEBORAH KERR (Portia), LOUIS CALHERN (Caesar), GREER GARSON (Calpurnia), EDMOND O'BRIEN (Casca)
DIRECTED BY	JOSEPH L. MANKIEWICZ
PRODUCED BY	JOHN HOUSEMAN
SCREENPLAY	JOSEPH L. MANKIEWICZ
PHOTOGRAPHY	JOSEPH RUTTENBERG
MUSIC	MIKLOS ROZSA

In 1952, MGM announced one of the most surprising and inspired casting decisions in cinema history. A year after he had stunned American audiences as macho, mumbling Stanley Kowalski in *A Streetcar Named Desire*, Marlon Brando would play Shakespeare's 'wise and valiant' Roman, Mark Antony, in **Julius Caesar**. Hollywood columnists expressed astonishment and stand-up comedians treated TV audiences to impressions of Brando reciting Mark Antony's 'Friends, Romans, countrymen' speech as Kowalski.

The star would not be deterred. 'I'm sick to death of being thought of as a blue-jeaned slobbermouth', he declared, having decided that there could be no better way to kill off his *Streetcar* image – and stretch his talents – than by proving he could master Shakespeare.

In the run-up to filming he spent hours studying and imitating recordings by great Shakespearean actors such as Olivier – until **Caesar**'s director, Joseph L. Mankiewicz, told him to 'stop copying the goddamn Limeys' and trust his own acting instincts. For a while, that approach looked as though it would prove disastrous.

At the first cast read-through, producer John Houseman would later recall, Brando 'gave a perfect performance as a stuttering bumpkin only remotely acquainted with the English language'. His inability to handle the verse was shown up by what Houseman called John Gielgud's 'terrifying bravura' as Cassius, a quality that made James Mason (Brutus) and Louis Calhern (Caesar) look almost as inadequate as Brando. On this evidence, MGM's investment of $1.7 million (perhaps $30 million today) in **Caesar**, looked like a tremendous gamble.

Brando sought Gielgud's advice, asked him to record Mark Antony's lines, and went back to his tapes. At some point, he realized that he had to set aside the method acting techniques which made his performance in *Streetcar* so raw. The method is all about playing the subtext, the motivation and emotions *behind* what a character is saying. With Shakespeare, Brando acknowledged, 'the *text* is everything'.

It was this realization, suggested Houseman, that enabled Brando to let the language carry every ounce of Mark Antony's emotion, particularly in the forum scene which would become the high point in one of the most gripping performances in any Shakespeare film.

The first half of the picture, however, belongs not to Brando, but to the conspirators. Gielgud has the right 'lean and hungry look' for Cassius, and condemns Caesar in the opening scenes with enough furious eloquence to corrupt a saint. You can't blame either Mason's aloof, well-intentioned Brutus or Edmond O'Brien's cynical, nervy Casca for succumbing to such vehement persuasion.

As the fatally self-confident dictator, the hulking Louis Calhern gives an ironic edge to the power play: the tallest Roman on view turns out to be the weakest. Deborah Kerr, as Portia, and Greer Garson, as Calpurnia, can do little with one scene each, although the fault lies with Shakespeare's decision to give such scant attention to his politicians' wives.

Superstition and superstar

Mankiewicz, who had won back-to-back Best Director Oscars in 1949 and 1950, spices the urgent, coldly reasoned plotting with just the right measure of supernatural dread, notably when the blind soothsayer rises from within a crowd to tell Caesar to beware the Ides of March, and during the spectacular storm on the eve of the murder.

It's in the assassination scene that Mankiewicz's direction, taut and assured throughout, is shown to greatest effect. As Calhern is stabbed, there are no shouts from the killers, nor screams from the victim. The silence is as shocking as the sight of these civilized men's pristine white togas suddenly stained with blood. It's the perfect prelude to the moment when Brando wrests the plot – and the film – from the conspirators' hands.

Decisively set apart from these older men by his dark robes and tanned, muscular build, Brando first stands beside Calhern's body, steeling himself for revenge. Then, after Mason, a model of rational sincerity, has managed to convince about 250 braying citizens that the dictator deserved to die, they give a collective gasp and we see Brando carrying the corpse down the steps from the Senate.

Mason exits, and for the next ten minutes Brando brings manipulative Shakespearean oratory to life with irresistibly charismatic acting. Reaction shots show the rough-looking plebeians gradually falling under his spell. Cinema audiences followed suit.

At the first cast read-through Brando gave a perfect performance as a stuttering bumpkin only remotely acquainted with the English language. John Houseman

⑤

Biographers have argued that Brando's off-camera turmoil fed his performance (during filming he had several sessions with the Hollywood psychiatrist already treating Mankiewicz), or that the director's instruction to him to 'get mad' during the funeral oration was the key. Never mind the speculation, this is a glorious scene. That the rest of **Julius Caesar** cannot remain at the heights to which Brando lifts it, is to a large extent because the finest moments of the play are concentrated in its first half.

There is, however, much to admire in the second hour. Mankiewicz stages a Western-style Battle of Philippi, as Mark Antony's archers and cavalry take up positions high above a valley floor and swoop down on Brutus and Cassius's infantry like Apaches ambushing the Seventh Cavalry. Gielgud and Mason bring dignity and poignancy to the defeated leaders' suicides.

In the very last shot, Mankiewicz allows himself one theatrical moment. After Brando's final line and exit, the camera zooms in on the lantern beside Mason's head, and its flame is extinguished by a gust of wind – like the blackout at the end of a stage production.

Throughout, as Houseman had hoped before filming began, Mankiewicz refused to 'distort Shakespeare's text with cinematic devices'. He resisted the temptation to show key incidents that are only reported in the text, such as Caesar's fainting fit and the conspirators' flight from Rome, eschewed adventurous camerawork, and used Miklos Rosza's score sparingly, between scenes, so the music never distracts from the speeches.

Great credit must also go to Houseman, who had gained vast Shakespearean experience as producer for Orson Welles's Mercury Theatre company. He had agreed to MGM's demand that **Caesar** save money by re-using scenery and costumes from its last Roman epic, 1951's *Quo Vadis?*, but refused to bow to studio pressure to shoot in colour. Monochrome footage of Roman centurions marching behind eagle-topped standards would, he hoped, remind audiences of still-fresh newsreel images of Fascist and Nazi rallies in Italy and Germany.

Regardless of that historical hook, Houseman's decision was the right one on dramatic grounds. Just as lush colour suits the stirring Roman heroics of later epics such as *Ben Hur* (US, 1959) or *Spartacus* (US, 1960), so stark black-and-white photography was perfect for **Julius Caesar**, echoing they way in which Shakespeare makes it impossible for audiences to identify the 'good guys'.

Hail Caesar

When the film opened in June 1953, some of Brando's detractors still insisted he was miscast and in need of voice training, but *The New York Times* was far from alone in acclaiming him as 'a major talent'; it rated the film as more impressive than Olivier's *Hamlet*. *American Weekly*'s critic declared that Brando could now 'announce that he is going to play King Lear or Peter Pan and nobody will laugh.'

In Britain, the *News Chronicle*'s critic found it 'maddening' to concede that Hollywood had made 'the finest film version of Shakespeare yet'. Five Oscar nominations followed, including Best Picture, and Brando's third citation for Best Actor (he lost out to William Holden in *Stalag 17*). The only win was for Art Direction, thanks to austere but evocative work by a four-man team including Cedric Gibbons and Edwin B. Willis (both previously nominated for MGM's 1936 *Romeo and Juliet*).

Mankiewicz, who rated Brando as 'the single greatest acting talent in the English language', would always dispute Houseman's claim to have come up with the idea of casting the *Streetcar* star. It was his coup, he insisted, devised when Houseman and MGM boss Dore Schary were all set to have Stewart Granger play Mark Antony.

Regardless of who gave him the opportunity, Brando never forgot the experience. In the mid-1980s, when he had virtually disappeared from the world's screens, he would sometimes astonish his friend, Tom Papke, by suddenly launching into scenes from **Julius Caesar**, repeating all the inflections and gestures he had produced more than 30 years earlier.

Left: The mob of Roman citizens listen to Mark Antony praising Caesar on the steps of the Senate.

Top right: Louis Calhern as Caesar, left, is warned to 'Beware the Ides of March' by Richard Hale as the Soothsayer, watched by John Gielgud as Cassius.

Right: John Gielgud as Cassius, left, with James Mason as Brutus, after the bloody assassination of Caesar.

JULIUS CAESAR (1970)

UK 117 MINS COLOUR

CAST	CHARLTON HESTON (Mark Antony), RICHARD JOHNSON (Cassius), JASON ROBARDS (Brutus), DIANA RIGG (Portia), JOHN GIELGUD (Caesar), JILL BENNETT (Calpurnia), ROBERT VAUGHN (Casca)
DIRECTED BY	STUART BURGE
PRODUCED BY	PETER SNELL
SCREENPLAY	ROBERT FURNIVAL
PHOTOGRAPHY	KEN HIGGINS
MUSIC	MICHAEL J. LEWIS

The picture is as flat and juiceless as a dead haddock.

The New York Times

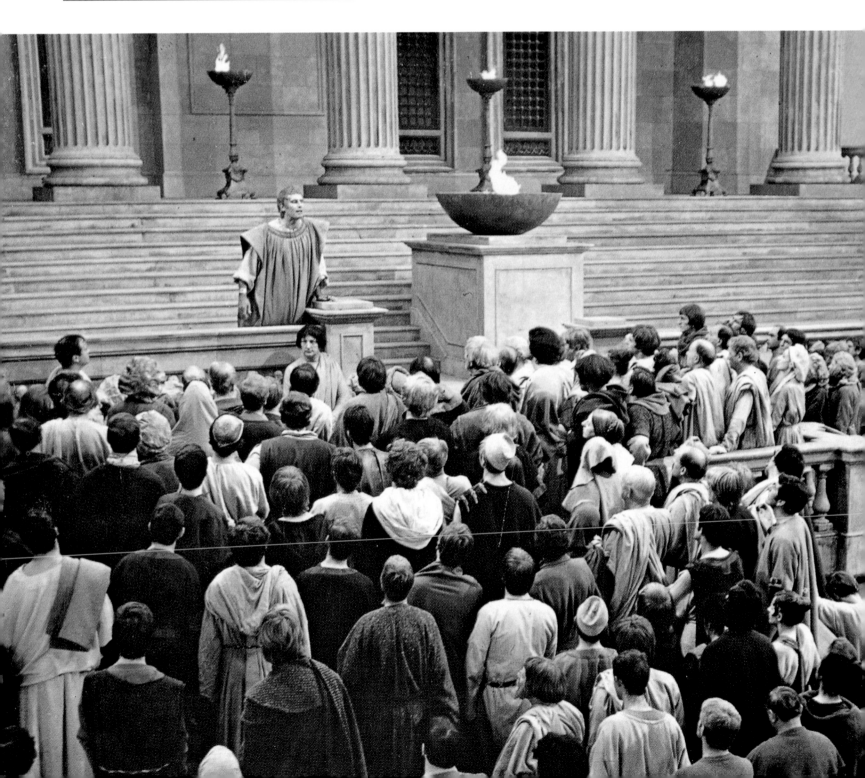

Critics on both sides of the Atlantic could barely muster a kind word for this version of **Julius Caesar**. 'The picture is as flat and juiceless as a dead haddock', said *The New York Times*. *The Daily Telegraph* attacked its 'hotch-potch of styles, both acting and visual'. The studio mock-up of Roman streets and Senate was filled with what *The Sun* described as 'hideous cardboard scenery'.

Stuart Burge's film, his second screen *Caesar* after the 1959 BBC production, has not improved with age. Loud and garish where the 1953 version was thoughtful and restrained, it transforms the play into a weak hybrid that fails as both sophisticated political thriller and straightforward historical epic.

Some of the casting is disastrous. Producer Peter Snell hoped that including Robert Vaughn as Casca and Richard Chamberlain as Octavius would bring in fans of their hit TV shows, *The Man from U.N.C.L.E.* and *Dr Kildare*, but both appear embarrassingly out of their depth; Vaughn's 'English' accent makes him sound like a shifty Cary Grant.

This pair are merely distracting; Jason Robards's Brutus scuppers the entire picture. He turns 'the noblest Roman of them all' into the dullest, delivering Shakespeare's intricate verse as though it were clumsy prose, even managing to ruin Brutus's head-to-head discussions with Cassius – scenes so brilliantly written they should be foolproof. Robards' uninflected, unrhythmical American whine jars against Richard Johnson's measured, RSC-trained English, and while Johnson just about convinces you that the fate of a great empire is at stake, Robards might as well be reading the stock market report.

Some 25 years later, Robards' most famous co-star would be even more damning than the reviewers were in 1970. 'I have never seen a good actor so bad in a good part', Charlton Heston wrote later in his autobiography, *In the Arena*, although his own performance as Mark Antony is not beyond criticism. He reckoned that this was 'the easiest' of the great Shakespearean roles, which may explain why he mistakenly chose to play it in an excessively relaxed, languid style. His oration over Caesar's corpse is simply not in the same league as Brando's (*see* pages 54–57).

He is much happier with the derring-do than the rhetoric, dispatching half-a-dozen centurions from horseback during the Battle of Philippi – an overlong, messy sequence shot in Spain, which used up a large proportion of Burge's $1.4 million budget (approximately $14 million today).

Heston suffers more than anyone from the movie's absurd costume parade, and is obliged to drape his broad-shouldered frame in a virulent green number. Like the pale blue togas and golden cloaks sported by Brutus and Cassius, it would look more at home in *A Funny Thing Happened on the Way to the Forum*.

Over the top

Unfortunately, Burge's direction is as crude as the outfits. His guiding principles are the complete opposite of Mankiewicz's in 1953. First: never allow Shakespeare's words to speak for themselves if you can devise superfluous images or actions to support them. Second: always drench moments of high drama with shamelessly manipulative music.

So, when Jill Bennett's almost hysterical Calpurnia describes her dream, the words merely describe what we've already seen as she writhed in bed: dreadful, superimposed images of mobs running riot and a bust of Caesar weeping blood.

The assassination of John Gielgud's vain, pliant dictator (the least impressive of his screen Shakespeare performances) is a collection of clichés: the camera's vision blurs as the victim loses consciousness, composer Michael J. Lewis supplies an overdose of shrill flutes and frantic xylophone, and there are thumpingly amplified heartbeats on the soundtrack.

Peter Snell told one interviewer that he wanted the scene 'to shake the audience, the women must feel queasy'. Yet the flashing blades and copious blood, like everything else in the film, have a fraction of the impact achieved in 1953. *Julius Caesar* was much better served when Gielgud was one of the murderers, not their target.

Left: Charlton Heston, rear left (on the steps), delivers Mark Antony's 'Friends, Romans, countrymen' speech. *The Sun* attacked the 'hideous cardboard scenery'.

Right: Richard Johnson as Cassius, left, and Jason Robards as Brutus, right, strike at Caesar, played by John Gielgud. Producer Peter Snell wanted the scene to make female cinemagoers 'feel queasy'.

⑤

6 KING LEAR

The oldest hath borne most: we that are young shall never see so much, nor live so long.

Edgar, *King Lear*, Act V, Scene iii

Left: Albert Finney as a cantankerous actor-manager, left, preparing to go on stage as King Lear in *The Dresser* (1983), helped by Tom Courtenay, who plays the title role.

Right: Ermete Novelli as Lear, seated, dividing his kingdom in the opening scene of the silent *King Lear* (Italy, 1910).

Bottom left: Spencer Tracy as a Lear-like cattle baron in the Western, *Broken Lance* (1954).

Britain, 12th century. The ageing King Lear divides his kingdom between his daughters, Goneril, Regan and Cordelia. Enraged by Cordelia's refusal to echo her elder sisters' fawning declarations of love, Lear banishes her and the King of France takes her as his queen.

The Duke of Kent, banished by Lear for criticising his rashness, disguises himself as a servant and rejoins the king and his beloved Fool, who are staying with Goneril and her husband, the Duke of Albany. Goneril asks her father to dismiss most of his 100 knights, he curses her ingratitude and heads for Regan's castle.

Regan and her husband, the Duke of Cornwall, evade Lear by staying with the Duke of Gloucester. They place Kent in the stocks for whipping Goneril's treacherous steward, Oswald. Lear cannot bear this insult, or Regan's ingratitude. Descending into madness, he strides into the countryside, pursued by Kent and the Fool.

Seeking shelter from a storm, they encounter Gloucester's son, Edgar, disguised as 'Poor Tom', a madman, after being falsely accused by his bastard half-brother, Edmund, of plotting to kill Gloucester.

Edmund informs Cornwall that Gloucester is in league with Cordelia, who has landed at Dover with a French army. Cornwall gouges out Gloucester's eyes and is fatally wounded by an outraged servant. Oswald is killed by Edgar, who leads his blinded, dying father to Dover.

Albany and Edmund lead British forces to victory against the French. Goneril, as desperate as Regan to marry Edmund, fatally poisons her sister and then kills herself. Edmund is killed in a duel by Edgar. Lear carries the dead body of Cordelia, hanged on Edmund's orders. Wailing at her loss and the hanging of the Fool, he dies, heartbroken.

FILM BACKGROUND

Some people who adore seeing Shakespeare on stage find *King Lear* unwatchable as they cannot bear to observe so much senseless human suffering depicted with such force. It's a perfectly understandable response to the play, but not one to encourage producers trying to gauge the potential audience for a big-screen adaptation. Put *King Lear* into cinemas today and, in the age of the bite-sized review, a critic might accuse you of making 'the feelbad movie of the decade'.

Although their chances of matching the box-office performance of a *Romeo and Juliet*, say, or a sunny Shakespeare comedy, are remote, the challenge of adapting *Lear* continues to attract film-makers; just as great actors will always relish the challenge of the towering title role. When this book went to press, actor-turned-director Tim Roth, whose debut feature, *The War Zone* (UK, 1999), was a relentlessly bleak tale of a family devastated by incest, was planning a film of *King Lear* from a script that was being written by Harold Pinter.

Roth will be sustaining a tradition that dates back more than 90 years. Four silent *Lears*, two American and two Italian, were made between 1909 and 1910. The second Italian production miraculously crams a slimmed-down plot into 16 minutes, with Lear affectingly played by grey-bearded Ermete Novelli, one of Italian theatre's most celebrated actors.

The sound era's most distinctive feature adaptations, by Peter Brook (**King Lear**, 1971), Grigori Kozintsev (**King Lear**, 1971) and Akira Kurosawa (**Ran**, 1985) are the focus of this chapter, along with Jean Luc-Godard's bizarre hotch-potch, **King Lear** (1987), and **A Thousand Acres** (1997), which attempted to reinvent *Lear* as a contemporary American tragedy.

Notable television adaptations include Brook's 75-minute version for CBS in 1953, with Orson Welles as the king, and a unique double from the BBC, which twice commissioned Jonathan Miller to direct Michael Hordern (better-known for comedy than tragedy) as Lear, first in 1975 and then, more lavishly, in 1982.

Lear inspired the Western, *Broken Lance* (US, 1954), in which Joe (Robert Wagner), youngest son of a tyrannical cattle baron, Matt Deveraux (Spencer Tracy), goes to jail for his father after their raid on a copper mine. On his release, Joe discovers that his father is dead and the family ranch has been divided up and sold by his three older half-brothers, and a violent vendetta ensues.

In Peter Yates's adequate screen version of Ronald Harwood's fine play, *The Dresser* (UK, 1983), Albert Finney, is 'Sir', an elderly, absent-minded actor starring in *Lear* at a provincial English theatre during World War II. His relationship with Norman (Tom Courtenay), his devoted dresser, mirrors the Lear/Fool double-act, and the 'life-imitating-art' storyline ends with 'Sir' dying peacefully in his dressing room, shortly after Lear has died on stage.

KING LEAR (1971)
UK/DENMARK 132 MINS B/W

CAST	PAUL SCOFIELD (King Lear), IRENE WORTH (Goneril), CYRIL CUSACK (Albany), SUSAN ENGEL (Regan), PATRICK MAGEE (Cornwall), ANNE-LISE GABOLD (Cordelia), JACK MACGOWRAN (Fool), TOM FLEMING (Kent), ALAN WEBB (Gloucester), ROBERT LLOYD (Edgar), IAN HOGG (Edmund)
DIRECTED BY	PETER BROOK
PRODUCED BY	MICHAEL BIRKETT
PHOTOGRAPHY	HENNING KRISTIANSEN

Brook will do anything for an effect, however nonsensical, as long as every frame proclaims his supremacy over Shakespeare.

The New York Times

Peter Brook set Shakespeare's bleakest tragedy in one of the coldest, most barren landscapes ever seen on film. Paul Scofield's bear-like Lear divides a dark, windswept kingdom, blanketed with greying snow. Men and women wear thick furs to ward off blizzards and freezing rain. Inside Goneril and Glouces-ter's wooden castles, there are few man-made comforts; even the roaring fires appear to give off little warmth.

More than in any other Shakespeare film, the scenery (Jut-land, in Denmark), weather and production design dictate the story's emotional impact. Against such a harsh background, the inhumanity displayed by Edmund, Goneril, Cornwall and Regan becomes less shocking than it is on stage. It's not surprising to see savagery here – and savage is the only word for Brook's treatment of violence.

All traces of heroism are removed from the 'just' killings com-mitted by Robert Lloyd's Edgar. He murders the squealing Oswald with a pike, like a caveman sticking a wild boar. Brook cuts out Edmund's challenge (which in the play makes his half-brother's appearance a thrilling piece of chivalry) and Edgar becomes a black-helmeted avenging angel, sinking his axe into Edmund's neck with the opening blow of their 'duel'.

All three sisters' deaths (off-stage incidents in Shakespeare) are shown and, instead of theatrically poisoning Regan, Irene Worth's Goneril brains her sister against a boulder, then hurls her own head against a rock face.

An instant later we have a shocking glimpse of Cordelia's neck snapping in the hangman's noose. An entire generation is wiped out in 30 seconds. As Lear dies, farther along the beach where his daughters have fallen, Scofield slips slowly below the bottom of the frame – his, and the film's last moment signified by blank, white sky. After so much suffering, there is literally nothing left to say, or see.

A numbing chill

The problem with Brook's approach, unadorned by so much as a single bar of music, is that it numbs, rather than moves you, extinguishing even the faint glimmers of hope that Shakespeare surely intended to be drawn from the courage and humanity of Edgar, Kent and, belatedly, Albany.

Impressionistic and sometimes symbolic camerawork often make it hard to concentrate on the language, so much so that *The New York Times* accused Brook of doing 'anything for an effect, however nonsensical, as long as every frame proclaims his supremacy over Shakespeare'. Characters appear at weird angles and moments within a given scene. Edgar, in his 'Poor Tom' disguise, is filmed like Jesus on the cross, wearing just a loincloth and a 'crown' of hay, although nothing in his character suggests martyrdom. During the Storm scene, the focus is blurred to suggest, rather obviously, Lear's mental fog. Only once does such trickery enhance, rather than distract from, the horror: as Gloucester's right eye is scooped out by Cornwall with a jagged spoon, the screen goes completely dark, leaving us momentarily 'blind'.

King Lear's dominant sensation is one of cold – physical and emotional – and its dominant sound is Scofield's voice: a parched, echoing growl. As was the case when Brook directed Scofield in the 1962 Royal Shakespeare Company *Lear* on which the film was based, his portrayal of dementia contains no trace of sentimentality. Initially, you even have grudging sympathy for his elder daughters' inhospitable stance: playing host to this irascible, demanding old man and his raucous knights would indeed be a nightmare.

Worth's Goneril, her chilly demeanour thawed by unmistake-able lust for Ian Hogg's brutish Edmund, is an outstanding performance, although Engel's Regan seems too poised and civ-ilized for her primitive environment. Jack MacGowran, as a middle-aged, Irish fool who laughs in order not to cry, and Tom Fleming's gruff Kent are the best of the male supporting actors.

In addition to *The New York Times* attack, Brook's film (made for $1.1 million with a Danish crew) infuriated Britain's *Film Quarterly*, which labelled it 'a travesty', and the headline on a scathing *New Yorker* review compared it to cinema's most famous zombie movie, dubbing it 'Peter Brook's Night of the Liv-ing Dead'. Admirers included *The Boston Globe*, which hailed it as 'a masterpiece', and *Newsweek*, whose critic detected in Brook's vision 'a kind of fractured greatness that makes it a unique addition to screen Shakespeare'. That view is perhaps the fairest; this is a deeply idiosyncratic interpretation of *Lear*, but you have to admire Brook for adhering to it with such discon-certing commitment.

Above: Paul Scofield as a growling, bear-like Lear preparing to divide his kingdom. He had played the role in the 1962 RSC production on which the film was based.

Right: Left to right are Irene Worth, Paul Scofield, Jack MacGowran and Anne-Lise Gabold in the tense opening scene.

KING LEAR (1971)

USSR 137 MINS B/W
RUSSIAN TITLE: KOROL LIR

CAST	YURI YARVET (King Lear), ELSA RADZINA (Goneril), DONATAS BAN (Albany), GALINA VOLCHEK (Regan), VALENTINA SHENDRIKOVA (Cordelia), OLEG DAL (Fool), VLADIMIR YEMELYANOV (Kent), KARL SEBRIS (Gloucester), LEONARD MERZIN (Edgar), REGIMASTAS ADOMAITIS (Edmund)
DIRECTED BY	GRIGORI KOZINTSEV
PRODUCTION COMPANY	LENFILM
SCREENPLAY	GRIGORI KOZINTSEV, BASED ON BORIS PASTERNAK'S TRANSLATION
PHOTOGRAPHY	JONAS GRITSUS
MUSIC	DMITRI SHOSTAKOVICH

No one has illustrated King Lear's dizzying fall from power with greater visual force than Grigori Kozintsev. No one has played the king on screen with more affecting restraint than Kozintsev's Lear, Yuri Yarvet.

Austerely photographed in black and white, the director's epic treatment makes us follow the tale of one man and his daughters in tandem with a more political story, about a king's relationship to the common people. That relationship is the key to Kozintsev's approach and Yarvet's performance: cinematically and emotionally, we see Lear begin as his subjects' god and end as their helpless equal.

In the quasi-biblical opening sequence, hundreds of shuffling, hooded peasants congregate on rocky ground outside Lear's castle (Ivangorod Fortress, on the Russian/Estonian border). After Yarvet's slight, white-haired monarch has divided the kingdom, he appears briefly above the main gate, and the masses kneel and bow their heads as though he were the Messiah.

During the storm, the hovel that Shakespeare leaves empty, save for Edgar as 'Poor Tom', is crammed with shivering vagabonds, and Yarvet's Lear suddenly realizes that he has shamefully neglected his people, these 'poor naked wretches'. This shattering self-knowledge, registered in Yarvet's huge, bright eyes, and quiet, agonized voice, completes the descent into madness initiated by his daughters' ingratitude.

Worse is to come, of course. Lear passes a stream of refugees fleeing homes set alight by Edmund's troops and, after Cordelia's defeat, he and his daughter are cast adrift in a tide of bewildered peasants.

Below: Elsa Radzina, left, Galina Volchek, centre, and Valentina Shendrikova, as Lear's three daughters, entering the throne room for the division of the kingdom.

A Communist king?

This is Kozintsev filtering *Lear* through Russia's obsession with the hungry, oppressed proletariat, and *The Sunday Telegraph* called his film 'a remarkably successful translation of the play into Communist terms'. Yet the director's humanity and some unforgettable performances render Shakespeare's family tragedies as forcefully as the national catastrophe, what Kozintsev called his 'generalized picture of civilization heading towards doom'.

Yarvet, an Estonian who had to learn Russian to play the part, works against the cliché of Lear as bearded lunatic. He starts off with his wits intact and a temper that makes courtiers cower, and seems visibly to age as tragedy takes hold. With his daughters, we sense that for years, the youth and ethereal beauty of Cordelia (Valentina Shendrikova) has been resented by sour-faced Goneril (Elsa Radzina, barely recognizable as the elegant Gertrude from Kozintsev's *Hamlet*), and the fat, frumpish Regan (Galina Volchek); both elder sisters are shockingly callous. Oleg Dal's boyish Fool is a haunting presence, with the shaven head and half-starved body of a prisoner of war. Lear's affection for him is touchingly obvious, and Kozintsev was fonder still: his one liberty with the plot is to spare the Fool's life. At the end, Dal is left to weep, play his recorder and watch soldiers carrying Lear's corpse from the battlefield.

It's difficult to fault Kozintsev's direction. His attention to detail adds new layers of credibility to the play (equipping the King of France with an interpreter in the division scene is one of many plausible additions). His control of large-scale action generates a devastating climax, as the tall, handsome half-brothers (Leonard Merzin's blond, dazed Edgar, and Regimastas Adomaitis's dark, menacing Edmund) fight a thrilling duel, encircled by hundreds of soldiers. The officers dispatched to save Cordelia by Edmund's dying words are stopped in their tracks by Yarvet's Tarzan-like howls, and a shot of Cordelia dangling from the noose. Shostakovich's score adds immeasurably to the mood of despair, with its increasingly ironic trumpet fanfare for Lear, and five-bar 'Call of Death' to greet each character's demise.

Extraordinary effort went into the film, made when Kozintsev was 65. A year of casting, rehearsals and location-scouting was followed by an arduous shoot, in freezing, muddy conditions. 'What hell it all was!', wrote Kozintsev, in his fascinating account of the production, *King Lear: The Space of Tragedy*, published in 1973 – the year in which he died. He left behind one of the greatest books on film-making ever written, and a **King Lear** that *The New Yorker* declared would 'stand as one of the unshakeable edifices of Shakespearean imagination'.

Above: Valentina Shendrikova as Cordelia and Yuri Yarvet as Lear after they have been taken prisoner by Edmund's troops.

RAN (1985)
JAPAN/FRANCE 161 MINS COLOUR

CAST	TATSUYA NAKADAI (Hidetora Ichimonji), AKIRA TERAO (Taro Ichimonji), MIEKO HARADA (Lady Kaede), JINPACHI NEZU (Jiro Ichimonji), YOSHIKO MIYAZAKI (Lady Sue), DAISUKE RYO (Saburo Ichimonji), PETER (Kyoami), MASAYUKI YUI (Tango), TAKESHI NOMURA (Tsurumaru)
DIRECTED BY	AKIRA KUROSAWA
PRODUCED BY	SERGE SILBERMANN
SCREENPLAY	AKIRA KUROSAWA, HIDEO OGUNI, MASATO IDE
PHOTOGRAPHY	TAKAO SAITO
MUSIC	TORU TAKEMITSU

Acclaimed by *The Times* as 'a landmark in cinema history', Akira Kurosawa's vision of *King Lear* overflows with unforgettable images. As this dazzlingly photographed tragedy unfolds on the mountain slopes and broad volcanic plains of Kyūshū, Japan's largest southern island, Kurosawa's mastery of large-scale action, involving hundreds of men and horses, is astonishing. He earned a Best Director Oscar nomination and the BAFTA for Best Foreign Film; costume designer Emi Wada won an Oscar for the multi-coloured armour, banners and kimonos integral to the spectacle. But what makes **Ran** a masterpiece is the skill with which it adapts *Lear* to reflect key aspects of Japanese culture.

Its origins lie in the legend of Motonari Mori, a 16th-century warlord whose three sons were paragons of goodness. Kurosawa wondered how the tale might have changed if Mori's children had been less virtuous, and found his answer in Shakespeare. Lear's daughters become the sons of 70-year-old warlord, Hidetora (the formidable Tatsuya Nakadai). Taro is equivalent to Goneril, but shares Albany's weakness, Jiro is as ruthless as Regan and Cornwall, and Saburo is the devoted Cordelia.

Saburo and Tango (a Kent-like retainer) challenge Hidetora's decision to cede power to Taro and are banished. At the immense First Castle, Taro makes his father sign away all power – a humiliation utterly contrary to *giri*, Japan's system of interpersonal obligations, which places great emphasis on children's respect for elderly parents. In Japanese eyes, Taro's ingratitude is perhaps even more offensive than Goneril's; and it's emulated by Jiro, who treats Hidetora with disdain at Second Castle.

A guilty conscience

As Hidetora storms off into open country, it has become clear that, unlike Lear, Hidetora is not 'more sinned against than sinning' and that his downfall is retribution for having spilled 'an ocean of blood' while suppressing rival families. You feel less pity for Hidetora than for two of his victims: Jiro's deeply religious wife, Sue, who watched Hidetora burn her parents alive, and her beautiful brother, Tsurumaru (an amalgamation of Edgar and Gloucester), whose eyes were gouged out by Hidetora.

Thanks to **Ran**'s most extraordinary creation, Taro's wife, Kaede, whose father and brothers were murdered by Hidetora,

Lear is turned into revenge drama. Played with extraordinary, quiet menace by Mieko Harada, Kaede is like a younger, sexier version of Asaji, the Lady Macbeth figure in Kurosawa's *Throne of Blood*. Hell-bent on vengeance, she manipulates Taro into mistreating Hidetora and, after Taro's death, seduces and marries Jiro so that she can complete her enemy's destruction.

Yet while Hidetora languishes in the countryside, attended by 30 knights, a dozen concubines and his androgynous, graceful fool, Kyoami (Peter, a transvestite singer hugely popular on Japanese television), a happy ending remains possible. All Hidetora need do to find comfort is follow Tango's advice and live with Saburo and his father-in-law, Fujimaki (equivalent to *Lear*'s King of France). But, having misjudged Saburo so badly, Hidetora asks Tango: 'How could I face him?' The Japanese obsession with not losing face prevents Hidetora from rejoining his son, and this remarkable twist on the Lear/Cordelia relationship seals Hidetora's fate.

Taking refuge in the Third Castle, he is attacked by his elder sons' troops, and his knights are wiped out in an astonishing battle. We see, but cannot hear the terrible carnage: men hit by musket rounds and flaming arrows, Hidetora's concubines committing suicide. The strings and muffled timpani of Toru Takemitsu's mournful score are the only sound until Taro is shot in the back by Jiro's wily lieutenant, Kurogane (subtly portrayed by Hisashi Igawa), and the cacophony is suddenly audible.

Jiro lets Hidetora stagger from the burning fortress and in the storm that follows, Nakadai's stylized make-up, based on Noh theatre masks, suddenly changes: he loses the fierce visage of the opening hour, and gains a deeply lined forehead and red-rimmed eyes. The make-up is more expressive of his torment than the script which gives him only the briefest of speeches; when Lear's lines are paraphrased, they are spoken by Kyoami.

After a second remarkable battle, in which Saburo's musketeers slaughter Jiro's cavalry, Hidetora and Saburo are briefly and movingly reunited, before a climax even more apocalyptic than *Lear*'s. Saburo is shot dead, and Hidetora dies of a broken heart. The army of a rival warlord Ayabe (effectively equivalent to *Lear*'s Burgundy) attacks First Castle. Kaede, having engineered the murder of Sue, is beheaded by Kurogane, who goes to join Jiro in suicide. The final shot, of Tsurumaru, helpless on the edge of a precipice, silhouetted against a blood-red sunset, underlines why Kurosawa chose to call the film **Ran**: in Japanese, it means 'chaos' or, more appropriately for *Lear*, 'desolation of the soul'.

Top right: Mieko Harada as the seductive Lady Kaede, desperate to take revenge against Hidetora, the King Lear figure.

Right: Peter as Kyoami, left, with Tatsuya Nakadai as the deranged Hidetora. The actor's face was made up to resemble a Noh theatre mask.

Left: Cavalrymen commanded by Jiro, Hidetora's ruthless middle son, ride into battle. The film's rival factions are dazzlingly colour-coordinated.

KING LEAR (1987)
US/SWITZERLAND 95 MINS COLOUR

CAST	BURGESS MEREDITH (Don Learo), MOLLY RINGWALD (Cordelia), JEAN-LUC GODARD (Professor Pluggy), WOODY ALLEN (Mr Alien), PETER SELLARS (William Shakespeare Junior the Fifth), NORMAN MAILER (The Great Writer)
DIRECTED BY	JEAN-LUC GODARD
PRODUCED BY	MENAHEM GOLAN, YORAM GLOBUS
PHOTOGRAPHY	SOPHIE MAINTIGNEUX

A film of cultural arrogance, and commercial suicide. Daily Mail

Jean-Luc Godard and Israeli producer Menahem Golan famously signed their deal for **King Lear** on a paper napkin over lunch at the 1985 Cannes Film Festival. This unconventional contract generated an almost unwatchable movie, a $1.4 million 'deconstruction' of *King Lear*, rather than an adaptation. It was dismissed by the *Daily Mail* for 'cultural arrogance and commercial suicide'.

Godard, acclaimed in the 1960s as one of the leaders of the French New Wave movement, asks us to believe that the 1986 Chernobyl nuclear accident has wiped out all works of art, including Shakespeare's plays. Geeky William Shakespeare Junior The Fifth (acclaimed American stage director Peter Sellars) is on a mission to reconstruct his famous ancestor's work.

At his lakeside hotel in Switzerland, William encounters short, grizzled Don Learo. This is Burgess Meredith, replacing author Norman Mailer (shown storming off the film in the opening scene) and still sounding like the trainer in the *Rocky* films.

Learo addresses some of Lear's lines to his sullen daughter, Cordelia (Molly Ringwald), although Godard does not want us to establish even a tenuous hold on the characters, since Shakespeare's words are also delivered by unidentified male and female voice-overs.

By eavesdropping on Learo and Cordelia, William recovers some of the lost text, and seeks the remainder from enigmatic Professor Pluggy (Godard). His hair 'dreadlocked' with hi-fi connector leads, Godard chews on a cigar and makes statements about life and art in a semi-intelligible drawl (imagine a Frenchman impersonating Winston Churchill while gargling).

Neither the dialogue nor the random sounds and images (screeching seagulls; models aping William's movements in a forest) have any apparent meaning — unless Godard is trying to suggest the 'impossibility' of filming Shakespeare, in which case why even bother?

After 90 minutes, Pluggy appears to lay down and die, like Lear, while Cordelia and Learo remain alive. Then Woody Allen appears in an editing suite, charged with the task of 'bringing this twisted fairy-tale to the end', which, happily, follows soon afterwards.

After watching this 'massively perverse farrago' (*The Times*), only one thing is certain: like Cordelia in *Lear*'s opening scene, Godard has nothing to say.

Right: Molly Ringwald as Cordelia, bottom, with Burgess Meredith as Don Learo on the shore of a Swiss lake at the end of Godard's massively perverse film.

A THOUSAND ACRES (1997)
US 101 MINS COLOUR

CAST	JASON ROBARDS (Larry Cook), JESSICA LANGE (Ginny Cook Smith), KEITH CARRADINE (Ty Smith), MICHELLE PFEIFFER (Rose Cook Lewis), KEVIN ANDERSON (Peter Lewis), JENNIFER JASON LEIGH (Caroline Cook), PAT HINGLE (Harold Clark), COLIN FIRTH (Jess Clark)
DIRECTED BY	JOCELYN MOORHOUSE
PRODUCED BY	MARC ABRAHAM, STEVE GOLIN, LYNN AROST, KATE GUINZBURG, SIGURJON SIGHVATSSON
SCREENPLAY	LAURA JONES
PHOTOGRAPHY	TAK FUJIMOTO
MUSIC	RICHARD HARTLEY

Jane Smiley transplanted *King Lear* to present-day Iowa in her novel, *A Thousand Acres*, and received the 1991 Pulitzer Prize. By contrast, this screen adaptation received a critical mauling in America and Britain for turning Shakespearean tragedy into soap opera. It leaves an exceptionally strong cast floundering.

Smiley's family of *Lear* counterparts, headed by venerable widower Larry Cook (Robards), live in an outwardly perfect world of whitewashed timber farmhouses and sunny cornfields. When Larry decides to give his three daughters joint ownership of his thousand fertile acres, for tax reasons, the idea is embraced by his elder, married children, who help to run the farm: naive, caring Ginny (Lange), languishing in a childless marriage to Ty (Carradine, a suitably mild-mannered Albany figure), and frustrated Rose (Pfeiffer), married to volatile Peter (Anderson, the story's brooding Cornwall). However, the youngest daughter, Caroline (Leigh), a city lawyer, questions the idea and Larry disowns her.

In *Lear*, and in Smiley's long novel, this father-daughter rift sets the protagonists on clearly defined emotional paths; Laura Jones's overloaded screenplay offers only thinly sketched characters (particularly the men), stilted dialogue and clichéd revelations, all ploddingly orchestrated by Australian director Jocelyn Moorhouse.

Rose and Ginny turn against Larry, who sexually abused them as teenagers, and begin affairs with Jess (Firth, playing a selfish Edmund clone), who's at odds with his farmer father, Harold (a perfunctory Gloucester substitute).

Rose's adultery drives Peter to suicide. Larry and Caroline unsuccessfully sue to reclaim the farm. Ginny leaves Ty, and we leap forward two years to her reunion with Rose, now abandoned by Jess and about to die from breast cancer. Lange's mawkish narration reveals that the farm has been sold and Larry has died of a heart attack.

It feels like six months of daytime soap crammed into 100 minutes, and despite plenty of emoting from Lange and Pfeiffer, the abused sisters fail to evoke the slightest sympathy. As screen Shakespeare, **A Thousand Acres** merits attention mainly as part of an unusual adaptation process, from the Bard to Smiley to Jones: great play, good book, lousy film.

Right: Jessica Lange, left, Michelle Pfeiffer, centre, and Jennifer Jason Leigh as the sisters who come into conflict with their Lear-like father.

MACBETH

7

Not in the legions of horrid hell can come a devil more damn'd in evils to top Macbeth. Macduff, *Macbeth*, Act IV, Scene iii.

Left: Isuzu Yamada as the Lady Macbeth figure in *Throne of Blood* (1957), Akira Kurosawa's magnificent samurai adaptation of *Macbeth*.

Right: Malcolm's army gather in the courtyard of Dunsinane Castle at the climax of Orson Welles's *Macbeth* (1948).

THE PLAY

Scotland, 11th century. Macbeth, thane of Glamis, and his friend, Banquo, encounter three witches, who prophecy that Macbeth will become thane of Cawdor and then King.

Having appointed Macbeth as thane of Cawdor in place of an executed traitor, King Duncan stays at Macbeth's castle, with his sons, Malcolm and Donalbain. Goaded into action by his wife, Macbeth stabs the sleeping Duncan and kills his bodyguards, blaming them for the king's murder. Malcolm and Donalbain flee the country and are suspected of ordering Duncan's death. Macbeth becomes king.

Fearful of losing the crown to Banquo's sons, whom the witches said would become kings, Macbeth has Banquo murdered, but his son, Fleance, escapes. Banquo's ghost torments Macbeth at a banquet. Macbeth revisits the witches, who conjure up apparitions that reassure him that no man born to a woman can harm him and that he will be invincible until Birnam Wood advances on Dunsinane Castle. But he is also shown a vision of seven generations of Banquo's descendants, each as King of Scotland.

Macbeth sends murderers to kill the wife and young children of Macduff, who has joined Malcolm in England, where the latter is rallying an army to claim the crown. Lady Macbeth, already driven to delirious sleepwalking by her guilt over Duncan's murder, dies. Malcolm's soldiers camouflage themselves with tree branches as they approach – and Macbeth sees Birnam Wood marching on Dunsinane. In battle, Macbeth kills Siward, a young nobleman, but is himself beheaded by Macduff, who was 'from his mother's womb untimely ripp'd', thus fulfilling the prophecy. Malcolm is hailed as king.

FILM BACKGROUND

From its supernatural opening to its gruesome climax, *Macbeth* is the Shakespeare play that reads most like a film script. For example, the captain's description in Act I, Scene ii of Macbeth's courageous stand against the Norwegian army might be a shot-by-shot template for a pre-credits battle sequence.

Moments later, the encounter between Macbeth, Banquo and the witches kick-starts a plot that hardly ever lets the audience pause for breath.

Shakespeare, in cinematic terms, cross-cuts at speed between the blasted heath, Forres Castle, a nearby road, the English king's palace, Macduff's castle, Dunsinane Castle and Birnam Wood. Bursts of supernatural or violent action occur at more frequent intervals than shoot-outs in *Die Hard* or *Lethal Weapon*.

The Bard's language creates a uniquely dark and ominous atmosphere, conjuring up a primitive world swarming with serpents, eagles, bats, scorpions and beetles. Moreover, the power struggle in the Macbeths' marriage provides for one of the great actor/actress pairings in screen history and the plot also works as a first-rate psychological thriller, tackling 'big questions' about human destiny and free will.

Macbeth's screen potential was soon tapped in the silent era, beginning with a version produced by William V. Ranous (one of the most prolific early Shakespeare film-makers) in 1908. British, French, German and Italian directors all followed suit.

The five feature versions covered in this chapter range from the 'orthodox' adaptations by Orson Welles (1948) and Roman Polanski (1971), to Akira Kurosawa's extraordinary reinterpretation of the play in 1957's **Throne of Blood**, and two gangster *Macbeths*, **Joe Macbeth** and **Men of Respect**.

Scotland produced its first film of the Scottish play in 1997. A low-budget ($500,000), conventional adaptation, starring Jason Connery, it had a limited theatrical release in Britain, and in the US was distributed only on video. On television, the BBC produced four versions between 1949 and 1983, none as impressive as the 1979 production for commercial television (*see* page 192).

Charlton Heston took the lead for a CBS *Macbeth* in 1949, and NBC filmed their 1960 colour adaptation on location in Scotland. As this book went to press a modern-day, corporate setting of *Macbeth* was on the production slate of Kenneth Branagh's Shakespeare Film Company. If he, or any other director, wanted a tip on the best way to pace future productions, they need look no further than one of Macbeth's most famous lines: 'If it were done when 'tis done, then 'twere well it were done quickly.'

MACBETH (1948)
US 107 MINS B/W

CAST	ORSON WELLES (Macbeth), JEANETTE NOLAN (Lady Macbeth), EDGAR BARRIER (Banquo), DAN O'HERLIHY (Macduff), ERSKINE SANFORD (Duncan), RODDY MCDOWALL (Malcolm), ALAN NAPIER (Holy Father)
DIRECTED BY	ORSON WELLES
PRODUCED BY	ORSON WELLES
SCREENPLAY	ORSON WELLES
PHOTOGRAPHY	JOHN L. RUSSELL
MUSIC	JACQUES IBERT

Made in just 23 days, **Macbeth** is an extraordinary experiment in Shakespeare. Welles combines cinematic techniques with theatrical staging and a radio director's emphasis on the verse; he mixes reverence for the Bard with idiosyncratic revisions.

At times, **Macbeth**'s visual language rivals the eloquence of Shakespeare's poetry. This happens in the banquet scene, when the camera closes in on the feverish brow and haunted eyes of Welles' Macbeth, as he sees a crowded dining table suddenly empty, save for Banquo's ghost. It does so again when a tense, ten-minute take leads through the build-up to and immediate aftermath of Duncan's murder; long takes were possible because the cast had prerecorded their dialogue, in a wide variety of Scots accents, and lip-synched to a playback, allowing Welles to keep rolling without worrying about off-camera interruptions.

In other respects, however, notably some stagey, 'stand-and-deliver' performances (such as Dan O'Herlihy's robust Macduff), it's sometimes painfully obvious that the film's roots lie in the theatre, specifically in Welles' production of *Macbeth* at the Utah Centennial Festival in May 1947 — effectively a dress rehearsal for the movie, which began shooting a month later.

In terms of production design, the $700,000 budget from Hollywood B-movie studio, Republic, did not go far and Welles could only afford abstract sets giving Macbeth a castle unlike anything ever seen in Scotland: its jagged walls are apparently built from quick-dried volcanic lava; its courtyard has the unmistakable smoothness of a studio floor. Copious thunder, lightning and howling wind effects only enhance the artifice.

The bewildering mix of costumes ranges from traditional Scottish (tartan capes for Macduff and Roddy McDowall's thin-voiced, boyish Malcolm) to sci-fi (Macbeth's silver-sleeved jerkin recalls a 1930s *Flash Gordon*), and Welles would later concede that he should never have worn such bizarre crowns, one of which made him look like the Statue of Liberty.

As in his *Othello* (*see* page 98), he towers above his co-stars in a series of low-angled close-ups, and plays Macbeth as a man only half in control of his personality. He murders Duncan in a virtual trance, then, as king, deadens reality by remaining perpetually drunk; sobriety returns only when he faces death. The impression that Macbeth is enduring a nightmarish, out-of-body experience is strongest when Welles, in a fine Scots burr, delivers the most important soliloquies as voice-overs. At such moments, as in Welles's radio Shakespeares, the thoughts belong as much to the audience as to the speaker.

Lust for power
His Macbeth and Jeanette Nolan's Lady Macbeth make a perversely sexy couple, the wife lusting after the husband and power with equal passion. An accomplished radio performer whose inexperience in front of the camera explains her stiff, though still compelling, performance, Nolan has a touch of the dominatrix about her, with a Bride of Frankenstein hairdo and shrill voice.

Nolan benefits from Welles' decision to have Lady Macbeth appear at several points where Shakespeare keeps her off stage. For example, she is given some of Lady Macduff's lines, and talks to Macduff's son (a disturbing part for Welles to give his then eight year-old daughter, Christopher) just before he is killed. This expanded presence deepens the audience's sense of the couple's complicity and her gradual descent into madness.

Welles's other major interpretative stroke — this one more contrived — was to set Macbeth's rise in the context of a religious conflict. The preposterous, white-haired witches are portrayed as the last representatives of paganism, standing opposed to early Christianity, in the form of the blond, pigtailed Holy Father (the imposing Alan Napier), a character invented by Welles and given most of Ross's lines.

Early on, the father leads a service in which Duncan, Malcolm and, ironically, the Macbeths, swear to renounce Satan. He is in the vanguard of Malcolm's invasion force (driven forward by Jacques Ibert's martial score) of soldiers of the cross, carrying long staffs topped with Celtic crosses. Welles allows the forces of darkness a partial victory by having Macbeth kill the father with a well-aimed spear.

It is a rather half-baked addition, its meaning presumably lost on the Republic executives who hated Welles's original cut of **Macbeth** so much that they obliged his assistant, Richard Wilson, to hack it down to 86 minutes, with the dialogue redubbed with American accents. Released in the US in September 1950, this version made Republic a small profit. In Britain, the negative verdicts included *The Observer*'s: 'uncouth, unscholarly, unmusical, and almost without exception abominably acted'. Only in 1980, when Wilson restored the excised footage and Scots dialogue, were audiences able to judge **Macbeth** as Welles said he intended it, as 'a violently sketched charcoal drawing of a great play'.

… uncouth, unscholarly, unmusical, and almost without exception abominably acted.

The Observer

Below: Orson Welles as Macbeth, seated, stares at Banquo's ghost, watched by Jeanette Nolan as Lady Macbeth, third from right.

Right: Erskine Sanford as Duncan, left, with Roddy McDowall as a boyish-looking Malcolm.

JOE MACBETH (1955)

UK 90 MINS B/W

CAST	PAUL DOUGLAS (Joe Macbeth), RUTH ROMAN (Lily), SID JAMES (Banky), BONAR COLLEANO (Lennie), NICHOLAS STUART (Duffy), GRÉGOIRE ASLAN (Duca)
DIRECTED BY	KEN HUGHES
PRODUCED BY	M.J. FRANKOVICH
PHOTOGRAPHY	BASIL EMMOTT
MUSIC	TREVOR DUNCAN

Below: Paul Douglas as Joe Macbeth, left, Sid James as Banky, centre, and Grégoire Aslan as Duca, their boss, who is handing over a diamond ring for Joe to give his new bride.

Macbeth's plot and protagonists were skilfully reinvented by screenwriter Philip Yordan in **Joe Macbeth**, an entertaining, blackly comic gangster thriller, made in Britain with mostly American stars.

Yordan carefully harvested only those aspects of the play that could plausibly be squeezed into Hollywood's tried-and-tested mould: trench-coated, chain-smoking hoodlums plotting in dimly lit offices, dining with glamorous molls and gunning each other down. The middle-aged 'hero', Joe (burly Paul Douglas), is not too smart but has brawn to spare, which makes him an effective, obedient 'number one boy' for Duca (suave, balding Grégoire Aslan), cigar-chewing Italian kingpin of New York gangland.

Joe has a rival mobster rubbed out in the film's opening scene, and Duca rewards him with a diamond ring to give to his gorgeous, domineering new bride Lily (Ruth Roman, a specialist in tough-gal roles). The couple's celebration dinner is interrupted by Rosie (diminutive Minerva Pious), an actress-turned-flower seller who, in Yordan's most blatant nod to his source, once played a witch in a Broadway *Macbeth*. She gives Joe a Tarot reading that says he will become 'Lord of the Castle' and then 'King of the City'. Seconds later, Duca walks in proffering the keys to that 'castle': a gothic, lakeside mansion. Cue ominous brass on the soundtrack, and the start of the Macbeths' rise to power.

Death of a glutton

Sid James, as Joe's pal, Banky, adopts a fine, 'Noo Yoik' accent and, compared to his *Carry On...* roles, plays it shockingly straight. Banky's son, Lennie (pale and fidgety Bonar Colleano) is an amalgamation of Fleance and Macduff. Then Yordan breaks away from the *Macbeth* template. Joe, Banky and Lennie are ordered to take care of another of Duca's enemies, a bloated grotesque named Dutch (Harry Green). They shoot up his nightclub but botch their hasty attempt to kill him, forcing Joe to use shiftier tactics.

Dutch employs a stuttering food taster to make sure that his gargantuan meals are safe, although this doesn't prevent Joe from engineering one of the great movie murders. Dutch is so eager to guzzle a plate of crèpes Suzette that he doesn't let his taster sample them first. Joe's had the pancakes poisoned, with predictable results.

This episode is used by Lily to convince Joe that Duca's only ever going to treat him as dispensable muscle (by making the couple newlyweds, Yordan puts a neat spin on the wife's manipulation of the husband). The couple will remain 'stooges playing big shots unless Joe kills the boss and, after another *Macbeth*-style prophecy from Rosie ('So long as you have no fear, nothing shall stop you'), Joe agrees to murder Duca.

After enjoying himself at a house party thrown by the Macbeths, Duca, who clearly has designs on Lily, invites her for a dawn dip in the lake. He swims out to a diving raft, followed by Joe, who hauls him underwater and stabs him – and the bloody deed sends a flock of birds screeching into the air, an image straight out of the play. Joe becomes kingpin and the violence returns to the Shakespearean model.

Two killers hired by Joe shoot Banky, although Lennie escapes. Banky's ashen-faced ghost appears at Joe's dinner table, prompting some distinctly B-Movie 'mad' acting from Douglas. Knowing that Lennie will be out for revenge, Joe dispatches his hired guns to pressure Ruth, Lennie's wife, into making him leave town. They end up killing her and her baby, and a glimpse of this carnage drives Lily insane (though Roman is, sadly, denied a sleepwalking scene).

That night at the mansion, Joe, thinking she's Lennie, accidentally shoots Lily. Moments later, Lennie kills Joe and is then cut down, off screen, by the police. The only person left standing is Angus, the mansion's sardonic butler (memorably played by Walter Crisham as a mixture of Jeeves and *Macbeth*'s Porter).

British director Ken Hughes, perhaps best known for *Chitty, Chitty, Bang Bang*, switches proficiently between the violent action, comedy and gothic elements – it's just a pity that his lead actors were not stronger. If it had been made ten years earlier, with James Cagney as Joe, Barbara Stanwyck as Lily and Edward G. Robinson as Duca, **Joe Macbeth** might have been a Shakespearean classic. Instead, it's a cherishable oddity.

Below: This poster shows Ruth Roman in *femme fatale* pose and Paul Douglas demonstrating his B-movie 'mad' stare'.

THRONE OF BLOOD (1957)

JAPAN 110 MINS B/W
JAPANESE TITLE: KUMUNOSU-JO

CAST	TOSHIRO MIFUNE (Washizu), ISUZU YAMADA (Asaji), MINORU CHIAKI (Miki), AKIRA KUBO (Yoshiteru), TAKASHI SHIMURA (Noriyasu), TAKAMARU SASAKI (Tsuzuki), YOICHI TACHIKAWA (Kunimaru), CHIEKO NANIWA (Evil Spirit)
DIRECTED BY	AKIRA KUROSAWA
PRODUCED BY	SHOJIRO MOTOKI, AKIRA KUROSAWA
SCREENPLAY	SHINOBU HASHIMOTO, RYUZO KIKUSHIMA, HIDEO OGUNI, AKIRA KUROSAWA
PHOTOGRAPHY	ASAKAZU NAKAI
MUSIC	MASARU SATO

Washizu, the Macbeth figure in **Throne of Blood** has all of his Shakespearean counterpart's courage, but none of his eloquence. This wild-eyed samurai (Toshiro Mifune at his fiercest) rarely says more than a dozen words at a time, and his language is as plain as the floorboards of his castle. There is no poetry in **Throne of Blood**'s sparse dialogue, and little subtlety in its characterization, but its pace, atmosphere and imagery have a power that is absolutely Shakespearean.

The Bard's evocation of 11th-century Scotland and Kurosawa's depiction of late 15th-century Japan are both marked by bestial omens and foul weather. In **Throne of Blood** a horse's wild behaviour presages its master's murder; galloping warriors are buffeted by howling wind and driving rain, or shrouded in fog or mist. The music of Shakespeare's verse is replaced by the woodwind and percussion of Masaru Sato's distinctively Japanese score.

Washizu's story is told in flashback, beginning with a shot of the monument that marks the site of Cobweb Castle, as a male chorus sings of its destruction. Next, we see the impregnable castle in its former glory, as Tsuzuki (the Duncan figure) learns of heroic exploits by Washizu and his best friend, Miki (Minoru Chiaki as a jovial, trusting Banquo), against Inui (the King of Norway) and the treacherous Fujimaki (the thane of Cawdor).

Meanwhile, in a marvellously dynamic and eerie sequence, Washizu and Miki become lost in the maze-like Cobweb Forest, and meet an aged 'evil spirit' (Chieko Naniwa). Her white make-up resembles the ghost-masks of Noh theatre (the ancient Japanese form that Kurosawa adored), and she prophecies in the husky, expressionless tones of Noh actors: Washizu, commander of Fort One, will rule North Mansion and then Cobweb Castle. Miki will take over Fort One, and his son will eventually rule the castle.

Tsuzuki installs Washizu and his wife, Asaji, in North Mansion, and Kurosawa immediately uses Noh to associate Asaji (the mesmerizing Isuzu Yamada) so closely with the forest spirit that the suspicion arises they are in league together. Yamada's long, oval face is like a Noh mask, she walks heel to toe, like Noh actors, and adopts an expressionless voice to suit Asaji's pitiless ambition. She convinces the unambitious Washizu that Tsuzuki and Miki are plotting his death and that he must strike while Tsuzuki is their guest.

Here, Kurosawa devises a night-time sequence of such stealth that it perfectly distils the dreadful tension of Duncan's murder in *Macbeth*. For seven minutes, in the build-up to and bloody aftermath of the crime, no words are spoken – nor are they necessary: the horror of the deed is writ large on Mifune and Yamada's faces.

The 'guilty' flight of Kunimaru, Tsuzuki's son, and Noriyasu (Macduff) makes Washizu lord of the castle, and from now on the script begins to work devastating variations on *Macbeth*. With no children of his own, Washizu has agreed to let Miki's son, Yoshiteru, inherit the castle, but then Asaji suddenly announces that she is pregnant: Washizu *will* have an heir, so Miki and Yoshiteru must die.

Kurosawa now pulls off a unique feat: improving on Shakespeare by *not* showing a murder that is invariably depicted on stage. Miki's horse refuses to be saddled, but he ignores this omen and sets off for Washizu's feast. The horse gallops, riderless, back into Fort One, showing that Miki is dead; his dazed ghost's appearance during the feast provides confirmation.

A final reckoning

Months pass, Asaji has a stillborn child, and the realization that Yoshiteru (who escaped his father's assassin) will still inherit prompts a self-mocking shout from Washizu: 'Fool! Fool!' – the closest Mifune gets to a soliloquy.

With Asaji madly washing Tsusuki's invisible blood from her hands, and his enemies preparing to attack, Washizu rides back to the spirit, who guarantees him invincibility 'until Cobweb Forest comes to Cobweb Castle'.

He reassures his soldiers with this promise, but when they see an army of pines approaching through the mist, we get the last, greatest twist on *Macbeth*: Washizu is killed by his own men. Dozens of arrows whistle into his armour, until one last arrow transfixes his neck and he collapses. Beyond the gates, Noriyasu's men prepare to raze the castle and the screen fades back to its opening image of the monument.

Astonishingly, on its first release, Kurosawa's film was dismissed by *The New York Times* for an 'odd amalgamation of cultural contrasts [that] hits the occidental funnybone'. However, by 1965, Britain's *Sight and Sound* magazine was making a bold and not unreasonable claim for **Throne of Blood**, as the only work that 'completely succeeded in transforming a play of Shakespeare's into a film'.

Left: Toshiro Mifune as the dying Macbeth figure, Washizu, transformed into a human pin-cushion by the arrows of his own soldiers.

Right: Toshiro Mifune as Washizu, lost in the middle of Cobweb Forest during a thunderstorm and about to meet the Evil Spirit.

MACBETH (1971)
UK 140 MINS COLOUR

CAST	JON FINCH (Macbeth), FRANCESCA ANNIS (Lady Macbeth), MARTIN SHAW (Banquo), TERENCE BAYLER (Macduff), NICHOLAS SELBY (Duncan), STEPHAN CHASE (Malcolm), JOHN STRIDE (Ross)
DIRECTED BY	ROMAN POLANSKI
PRODUCED BY	ANDREW BRAUNSBERG
SCREENPLAY	ROMAN POLANSKI, KENNETH TYNAN
PHOTOGRAPHY	GILBERT TAYLOR
MUSIC	THE THIRD EAR BAND

Roman Polanski's **Macbeth** was notorious even before filming began. The announcement that the executive producer who had put up 60 per cent of the $2.5 million budget (about $22 million today) was none other than *Playboy* founder Hugh Hefner made the project appear to be an unholy alliance of Shakespeare and soft porn.

If that was comical, Polanski's choice of play carried horrific echoes of events that had devastated him in August, 1969 when his young, heavily pregnant wife Sharon Tate was murdered at their Los Angeles home, picked on at random by three stoned members of Charles Manson's 'Family' cult. Eight months later, Polanski was in London with theatre critic Kenneth Tynan, scripting the scene that shows Macduff's 'wife and babes savagely slaughtered'.

Only Polanski knows if he chose to make **Macbeth** as a peculiar form of therapy to help him come to terms with Tate's death, but the personal tragedy can only have increased his determination, revealed in an interview, 'to show the [play's] violence the way it is. If you don't show it realistically then that's immoral and harmful.'

True to Polanski's word, **Macbeth** depicts all the deaths that occur off-stage, and more besides: we see Macbeth stabbing Duncan in the chest and neck; the slit throat of Banquo's ghost weeps blood; Macbeth thuds an axe into an enemy soldier's groin and is himself spectacularly beheaded by Macduff. 'All that is good here seems but a pretext for close-ups of knives drawing geysers of blood,' complained *Newsweek*. Yet the gore is justified by Shakespeare's blood-drenched poetry and, by allowing breathing space for the Macbeths' more reflective moments, Polanski does not allow the carnage to swamp the intellectual thrust of the play.

Although he does not always push the drama forward with the requisite speed (the film feels perhaps 20 minutes too long), Polanski has opened out *Macbeth* impressively, shooting on hills and mountains (Welsh rather than Scottish) and in real fortresses (Lindisfarne Castle and Bamburgh Castle in Northumberland). Devised sequences, such as Macbeth's coronation, strengthen our understanding of this 'primitive' Scottish culture, and the spacious, impressively detailed castle interiors (built at Shepperton Studios) bristle with crude life.

Right: Jon Finch as Macbeth, right, and Francesca Annis as Lady Macbeth after the couple have become King and Queen. Annis believed that she was too young for her role.

The young warrior

Distorted bagpipes and bass guitars, courtesy of the Third Ear Band, fuel the supernatural mood and Polanski conjures a wildly over-the-top sequence for Macbeth's second encounter with the witches. The three hags are joined by a dozen more, all grotesquely naked, and a swig of their foul brew sets Jon Finch off on a bad trip: special effects-laden hallucinations, including a baby being 'untimely ripped' from a womb.

Finch, then a relative unknown aged 28, suits Polanski's conception of Macbeth as 'a young, open-faced warrior', starting out neurotic and short of confidence, but imbued with utter conviction once the crown is on his head.

He is spurred into action by tearful, almost girlish reproaches from Annis (who at 25 thought herself too young for the role).

Her flawless porcelain beauty, concealing the inner malice, seems to embody the witches' 'Fair is foul, and foul is fair' and she sleepwalks in the nude.

Although the script leaves the soliloquies largely intact, Annis and Finch are prevented from making the most of them by a distractingly inconsistent technique: the bulk of the lines is delivered in voice-overs, with a few spoken out loud at seemingly random points.

Martin Shaw's intelligent, sober Banquo, and Terence Bayler's stoical Macduff head a solid supporting cast (all of whom, like Finch and Annis, have English, rather than Scots accents), but the most intriguing characterization is the smiling menace of John Stride's Ross. Undoubtedly one of the good guys in Shakespeare, Polanski and Tynan make him a merciless

opportunist (following a radical interpretation put forward in an obscure Victorian essay). Ross is shown trying to kill Fleance (substituting for Shakespeare's Third Murderer), and leaving the gates of Macduff's castle open to his family's killers. Only when it's clear that Macbeth won't reward his vicious loyalty does he join Duncan in England.

At the end, we realize that if Duncan has men like Rosse at his side, he cannot feel secure – a point reinforced by the comparable reinvention of Donalbain (Paul Shelley). An innocent prince in the play, he is more like a junior Richard III here, seething with resentment at Duncan's elevation. A silent epilogue shows him riding to the witches' lair to hear his fortune. Polanski leaves us in no doubt: Macbeth is dead, but the cycle of violence is about to recommence.

7

MEN OF RESPECT (1991)
US 107 MINS COLOUR

CAST	JOHN TURTURRO (Mike Battaglia), KATHERINE BOROWITZ (Ruthie Battaglia), DENNIS FARINA (Bankie Como), PETER BOYLE (Duffy), ROD STEIGER (Charlie d'Amico), STANLEY TUCCI (Mal)
DIRECTED BY	WILLIAM REILLY
PRODUCED BY	EFRAIM HOROWITZ, GARY MEHLMAN
SCREENPLAY	WILLIAM REILLY
PHOTOGRAPHY	BOBBY BUKOWSKI
MUSIC	MISHA SEGAL

Men of Respect is hard to beat when it comes to eccentricity, weird inventiveness and sheer verve. The New York Times

Men of Respect's writer-director, William Reilly, starts off with the same smart idea – 'Let's do *Macbeth* as a gangster thriller' - that worked so well in *Joe Macbeth*. Then, by slavishly updating virtually every detail from Shakespeare, he digs himself and his formidable cast into a very deep hole. A movie that wants to be taken seriously ends up providing the most risible chunks of modernized Shakespeare in screen history.

This is a shame, because Reilly succeeds in revealing some interesting common ground between *Macbeth*'s thanes and 1990s Mafiosi: swearing absolute loyalty to king/Godfather; summary execution of traitors; killing anybody who stands in your path.

His Macbeth, low-ranking wise guy Mike Battaglia (John Turturro), makes an instant impact, walking into a crowded restaurant and fearlessly blowing away the Greek gangster who's been threatening the New York empire of his boss, Godfather Charlie d'Amico. Mike and his best friend, loan shark Bankie Como (the ever-reliable Dennis Farina) then stumble across the three 'witches': an elderly gypsy fortune teller, her husband and their weird male companion. The woman tells Mike that he's going to get promoted and then become Godfather, as will Bankie's son, Phillie. d'Amico (played with merciful restraint by Rod Steiger) promptly elevates Mike to 'man of respect' status.

After d'Amico has dined at the Battaglias' Greenwich Village restaurant, Mike, goaded by his ambitious wife, Ruthie, stabs him as he sleeps in their guesthouse, and the murder sets off a spiral of violence faithfully copied from *Macbeth*, although disappointingly directed in routine, low-budget style. Mike's henchmen gun down Bankie, but Phillie (ludicrously portrayed as a bespectacled MBA graduate) gets away. The wife and young son of Mike's enemy, Duffy (a bored-looking Peter Boyle), are blown up by a car bomb.

Duffy joins d'Amico's sons, Mal and Don, and, on the night that the guilt-ridden Ruthie slits her throat, leads their revenge attack on Mike's restaurant. 'Not of woman born' because he was delivered after his mother died in childbirth, Duffy kills the seemingly invincible Mike, and Mal takes over as Godfather.

Clichés but no poetry
While Turturro's edgy, haunted persona suits Macbeth's psychological peaks and troughs, and Katherine Borowitz's glacial good looks are just right for a role that makes her the only screen Mafia wife who wants her husband to be *more* violent, both are poorly served by Reilly's script. Quentin Tarantino (rumoured to have been preparing a film version of *Macbeth* in 1995) might have created a stylized, poetic form of mob slang to match the Bard's language, but Reilly deals mostly in expletive-heavy clichés. His attempt to tap *Macbeth*'s key philosophical question (does fate or free will drive the action?) goes no deeper than Mike's last words: 'Shit happens.'

When the film had a limited theatrical release in America (grossing just $140,000), *The New York Times* admired Reilly's 'eccentricity, weird inventiveness and sheer nerve', although the supernatural elements that give the standard mob setting a spooky twist (imagine one of the Corleones' victims reappearing in *The Godfather*, as Bankie's ghost does here) become unintentionally hilarious because of Reilly's sombre determination not to ditch Shakespeare's most outlandish images.

How does he find a modern equivalent for the witches' brew made from 'eye of newt' and 'lizard's leg'? He shows the gypsies watching a TV chef outlining, in gruesome close-up, her recipe for lamb's head stew ('Bake for two hours, or until the eyeball becomes opaque'). To approximate Lady Macbeth's attempt to wash away that 'damned spot' of Duncan's blood he gives Borowitz a can of bleach and has her frantically scrub the bath in which she washed Mike's clothes after the d'Amico murder.

Since Greenwich Village cannot offer a version of Birnam Wood, the gypsy has prophesied that Mike will be safe until 'the stars fall from the heavens'. As the assault on the restaurant begins, fireworks start exploding in the sky a block away, for no reason other than shameless plot contrivance, and one of Mike's henchmen says: 'You'd think the stars were dropping.' At which point, neither the gunshots, nor Misha Segal's embarrassingly crude score can drown out the noise of *Macbeth* fans laughing in disbelief.

Top right: John Turturro as Mike Battaglia, left, with Dennis Farina as Bankie, equivalents to Shakespeare's Macbeth and Banquo.

Right: John Turturro as Mike Battaglia is goaded into murdering his Mafia boss by Katherine Borowitz as his wife, Ruthie.

AKIRA KUROSAWA PROFILE

Steven Spielberg once described Akira Kurosawa as 'the pictorial Shakespeare of our time'. *Throne of Blood*, Kurosawa's *Macbeth*, and *Ran*, his transformation of *King Lear*, show precisely what Spielberg meant. From the simple, silent close-up of an actor's face, to an epic battle sequence, Kurosawa controlled moving images with the grace and power of a great poet.

Although the characters in *Throne of Blood* (*see* page 76) and *Ran* (*see* page 66) use much plainer language and speak more sparingly than their Shakespearean models, Kurosawa could distil soliloquies into a single image: the bloody hands of Washizu, his Macbeth figure, clenched around a spear after the murder that makes him lord of Cobweb Castle, or Lord Hidetora, Kurosawa's Lear, staggering down the steps of a burning fortress, like a soul descending into hell. At such moments Kurosawa silently matches Shakespeare in expressing the terrible consequences of ambition and brutality.

All his movies, historical and contemporary, adaptations and original screenplays, were characterized by the profound, frequently hard-edged humanity encountered in Shakespeare. They were always designed, he once said, to confront audiences with the same fundamental theme: 'Why – I ask – is it that human beings ... can't live with each other with more good will?' The fact that he could ask that question by reworking 400-year-old English plays into films as utterly Japanese as *Throne of Blood* demonstrates how Shakespeare crosses all national and cultural boundaries.

This East-West traffic moved in both directions throughout his career. Just as he transformed Shakespeare, so his original, Japanese stories were westernized. *Rashomon* (1950), an extraordinary account of a rape in 12th-century Japan, told from four contrasting viewpoints, was remade as *The Outrage* (US, 1964), starring Paul Newman, with the story moved to 1870s

Above: Kurosawa in his trademark cap, on location during the making of the historical epic, *Kagemusha* (1980).

America. The warriors defending peasant farmers in *Seven Samurai* (1954) became the heroes of John Sturges's Western, *The Magnificent Seven* (US, 1960). The samurai protagonist of *Yojimbo* (1961), who kills for both sides in a violent feud, became the hired guns played by Clint Eastwood in *A Fistful of Dollars* (Italy, 1964) and by Bruce Willis in *Last Man Standing* (US, 1997).

Those pictures entertained millions who had never seen a Kurosawa movie. None of them demonstrated the same thrilling and often affecting artistry of the originals, directed by a man who never liked talking about his work: 'Everything I want to say is in the film itself; for me to say anything more is, as the proverb goes, like drawing legs on the picture of a snake.'

The Tokyo apprentice

Kurosawa was born in Tokyo in March 1910, the youngest of seven children; his father was a disciplinarian army officer turned athletics-instructor. After high school Kurosawa trained at the Doshusha School of Western Painting but, although his gifts as a painter are obvious in the magnificent water-colour storyboards he made for *Ran*, in his early twenties he had struggled to make a living as a commercial artist.

That was why, in 1936, he responded to a newspaper advertisement from Tokyo's P.C.L. Studios inviting applications from would-be assistant directors, even though he had 'no desire at all to make my name in the movies'. From amongst 500 hopefuls, he was one of a handful to secure a job, and started at P.C.L. as assistant to the director Kajiro Yamamoto, who was eight years his senior. 'Yamamoto was a real teacher,' Kurosawa recalled in the 1960s, 'and it was due to him that I settled down and made movies my life's work.'

His apprenticeship covered every aspect of movie-making and, in the years to come, Kurosawa would direct, produce,

Above: Kurosawa, left, jokes with his leading man Tatsuya Nakadai far right, on location for *Ran* (1985), which earned Kurosawa a Best Direction Oscar nomination.

co-write and, with extraordinary skill, edit his own films. His screenplays frequently drew on his own wide knowledge of European fiction and Shakespeare's plays, and he firmly believed that scriptwriters 'must study the great novels and dramas of the world' and try to emulate their 'passion'.

He began directing soon after Japan entered World War II, and his first projects had to tell stories deemed appropriate by state regulation, such as his second feature *The Most Beautiful* (1943), about women working as wartime volunteers at a sewing-machine factory. It starred Yoko Yaguchi, who married Kurosawa in 1945; they stayed together until her death in 1985.

After the war, Kurosawa could choose his projects and began to demonstrate his versatility. When *Rashomon* won the Grand Prize at the Venice Film Festival and then the Oscar for Best Foreign Language Film in 1951 it was both a personal breakthrough and an introduction for western critics and cinemagoers to the richness of Japanese cinema, paving the way for the discovery of other masters such as Yasujiro Ozu and Kenzo Mizoguchi, who made their most celebrated films in 1950s.

Before shooting *Rashomon*, Kurosawa had begun making plans to film his favourite Shakespeare play, *Macbeth*, but postponed them when he heard that Orson Welles was about to do the same, and it would be another seven years before audiences had a chance to see Kurosawa's vision of the parallels between the warlords of medieval Japan and the thanes of Dark-Age Scotland.

When *Throne of Blood* was finally completed and Kurosawa went to London for the British première, it was his first trip outside Japan. He told *The Times* that travel didn't suit him, because he was 'a shy sort of man', yet on location or in the studio, where he saw himself as 'commander of the front line', this tall, imposing figure could be fiercely intimidating, earning himself the nickname of *tenno*, 'emperor', in the Japanese press.

His dictatorial tendencies were the product not of rampant ego but of his perfectionism and the need, on films such as *Seven Samurai* and *Ran*, to shoot immensely challenging sequences out of doors, where the elements rob directors of the control that they enjoy in a studio. 'He can be a real demon,' said Shiro Miroya, an assistant director who worked with Kurosawa several times. 'He'll scream out that "The rain isn't falling like I want it to", or "That damn wind isn't blowing the dust right".'

Conviction and compassion

Had Kurosawa not been inspirational as well as demanding, writers and actors would not have kept working with him as often as they did. Hideo Oguni co-wrote a dozen Kurosawa films; Toshiro Mifune appeared in 15 and developed with Kurosawa one of cinema's greatest actor-director partnerships, to rank alongside that of John Wayne and John Ford, the legendary Western director whom Kurosawa admired and imitated. Mifune, so fearsome as Washizu in *Throne of Blood*, so reserved as the Hamlet-like hero of *The Bad Sleep Well*, described Kurosawa as a man 'both more self-willed and more compassionate than most men are'.

That self-will sustained Kurosawa's absolute commitment to authenticity. He believed that 'the real life of any film lies just in its being as true as possible to appearances', and this meant that

Everything I want to say is in the film itself, for me to say anything more is like drawing legs on the picture of a snake. Akira Kurosawa

his historical pictures required long schedules, expensive sets – and large budgets. Three times Kurosawa set a record for the most expensive Japanese movie ever made: *Seven Samurai* established the first benchmark, the $6.5 million historical epic, *Kagemusha*, set a new high in 1980, and in 1985 *Ran*, with battles involving 1,200 extras and 200 horses, cost $12 million – not much in Hollywood, but a fortune by Japanese standards.

Fed up with his refusal to make inexpensive, populist films, Kurosawa's regular backers, the Toho studio, severed their relationship with him in 1965 and the next five years were filled with abortive projects including, in 1967, being hired as co-director of *Tora! Tora! Tora!*, the Hollywood epic about the Japanese attack on Pearl Harbor, and then fired after just ten days' shooting, largely because of his perfectionism.

He finally raised independent finance for a fable about poverty, *Dodes' Kaden* (1970), but its box-office failure and his frustration at rejection by the domestic studios pushed Kurosawa to his lowest point. In December 1971, he attempted suicide by slashing his wrists.

His comeback over the next 15 years was astonishing, although it was achieved only with financial backing from outside Japan. Russia's Mosfilm studio was the main producer of *Dersu Uzala*, a remarkable tale of survival and friendship made in freezing conditions in Eastern Siberia, which won the 1975 Oscar for Best Foreign Language film. The budget for *Kagemusha*, awarded the Palme d'Or at Cannes, was raised only with the support of Francis Ford Coppola, Steven Spielberg and George Lucas (who owed Kurosawa a great debt: the two comic Japanese peasants in 1958's *The Hidden Fortress* had inspired R2-D2 and C-3PO in *Star Wars*).

Even after those twin successes, Japanese studios still spurned Kurosawa, and it took French producer Serge Silbermann nearly two years to raise the budget for *Ran*, half of it in France and the rest from a Japanese newspaper firm. By 1985, like *Ran*'s Lord Hidetora, Kurosawa was 75 years old and beginning, at last, to slow down, and he would not make another film on such a grand scale. He received an Honorary Oscar in 1989 and directed two final projects, both intimate and reflective: *Dreams* (1990), a series of eight short episodes, and *Rhapsody in August*, (1991).

When he died, in September 1998, tributes were paid by filmmakers all over the world, yet arguably the most fitting epitaph had been written almost 30 years earlier, by another great director of Shakespeare, Grigori Kozintsev. Watching *Throne of Blood*, Kozintsev found Kurosawa working an extraordinary double magic: 'One caught one's breath at the greatness of Shakespeare and at the same time the greatness of cinema.'

Right: Kurosawa at work in the early 1950s, around the time of his Oscar-winning breakthrough with *Rashomon*.

Below: This cavalry charge from *Ran* (1985) demonstrates Kurosawa's consummate control of battle sequences.

A MIDSUMMER NIGHT'S DREAM

Are you sure that we are awake? It seems to me that yet we sleep, we dream. Demetrius, *A Midsummer Night's Dream*, Act IV, Scene i

Left: Kevin Kline as Bottom, left, bewitches Michelle Pfeiffer's Titania in Michael Hoffman's *Dream* (1999).

Right: William V. Ranous as Bottom, left, had to pull on a chord to operate the mouth of his model ass's head in this scene from the silent *Midsummer Night's Dream* (1909).

Ancient Athens. Theseus, Duke of Athens is about to marry Hippolyta, Queen of the Amazons. In the first scene Theseus is accosted by the young lovers, Lysander and Hermia, and her father, Egeus, who has ordered her to marry Demetrius. The lovers flee into the woods, chased by Demetrius, who is himself pursued by the adoring Helena. Meanwhile, Bottom the weaver and his fellow craftsmen are preparing a play in the woods for the duke's wedding celebrations.

In the woods, the fairy king, Oberon, has quarrelled with his queen, Titania, and orders his mischievous sprite, Puck, to gather a potion that will make Titania fall in love with the next creature she sees. This is Bottom, who, transformed by Puck, now has the head of an ass.

Using the same potion, Puck mistakenly makes Lysander fall in love with Helena. After a night of chaos, Titania and Oberon are reconciled and the Athenians, thanks to further use of another of Puck's potions, are correctly paired off: Hermia with Lysander, Helena with Demetrius. They are married in Athens alongside Theseus and Hippolyta. Bottom, in human shape, and his fellows farcically perform their 'Pyramus and Thisbe' play. The newly-weds retire to bed.

FILM BACKGROUND

A Midsummer Night's Dream is a play of three parts: beginning, muddle and end. The beginning introduces the Athenian characters with minimal fuss, and the end requires deft handling on screen if it is not to seem a stagey anticlimax. It is the muddle that offers film-makers the richest material: magical transforma-tion and painful romantic confusions involving desperate lovers, fairies and 'rude mechancials'.

The fairy world gives production designers licence to create as much fantastical imagery as their director and budget allow. Combine this with the emotional highs and lows expressed in the language of three very different types of character – fairy royalty, Athenian nobility and uneducated craftsmen – and the story should provide a feast for eyes, ears and hearts.

The three feature versions directed by Max Reinhardt (1935), Peter Hall (1969) and Michael Hoffman (1999) and assessed in detail in this chapter are the most widely known amongst a host of screen adaptations dating back to the silent era, when versions were filmed in America, France, Germany and Italy.

Vitagraph's 12-minute US production from 1909 is a midsummer day's dream – shot in a real wood in bright sunshine. Oberon is mysteriously absent, replaced by a dark-haired fairy called Penelope. The magical effects vary from the excellent (the boy playing Puck 'flies'), to the laughable: when Bottom has been transformed, the actor pulls on a chord to open and close the mouth of his model ass's head.

The BBC has made four versions, the first in 1946, with Desmond Llewelyn ('Q' in the James Bond films) as Theseus, the most recent, in 1981, with Helen Mirren as Titania. These had none of the irreverence shown by Spanish director Celestino Coronado, who used opera and ballet alongside Shakespeare's text for his outlandish 1984 film, *Sueno de Noche de Veran*. This gave the enchantments a homosexual twist: Hermia briefly falls in love with Helena and Lysander with Demetrius.

Adrian Noble's $4 million version, released in 1996, serves as an adequate small-screen record of his acclaimed 1994 stage production for the Royal Shakespeare Company but should never have been released in cinemas. A stylized production design, filled with light bulbs and umbrellas, and the doubled roles (Alex Jennings as Theseus and Oberon, for example) were the too-theatrical heart of a film which, lamented *The Times*, was 'so lacking in screen presence that it puts the Bard's cause back 100 years'. It was a box-office disaster.

Two dramas have employed extracts from the play to moving effect. In *A Matter of Life and Death* (1946, US title *Stairway to Heaven*) a glimpse of an amateur rehearsal of the 'Pyramus and Thisbe' play shows two lovers trying to communicate through a wall – mirroring dead RAF pilot David Niven's attempt to return from celestial limbo to his girlfriend back on earth. In *Dead Poets Society* (1989), a teenage pupil, Neil (Robert Sean Leonard), is shown playing Puck in a school production as a prelude to his shocking suicide, prompted by his stern father refusing to let him pursue a stage career.

As this book went to press, production was well underway on what may be the most unusual screen *Midsummer Night's Dream* of them all. Christine Edzard, director of the 1992 *As You Like It*, was shooting Shakespeare's text with every character, from Puck to Egeus, played by children aged between 7 and 12.

CAST	IAN HUNTER (Theseus), VERREE TEASDALE (Hippolyta), OLIVIA DE HAVILLAND (Hermia), DICK POWELL (Lysander), JEAN MUIR (Helena), ROSS ALEXANDER (Demetrius), JAMES CAGNEY (Bottom), ANITA LOUISE (Titania), VICTOR JORY (Oberon), MICKEY ROONEY (Puck)
DIRECTED BY	MAX REINHARDT, WILLIAM DIETERLE
PRODUCED BY	MAX REINHARDT
SCREENPLAY	CHARLES KENYON, MARY MCCALL JNR
PHOTOGRAPHY	HAL MOHR
MUSIC	FELIX MENDELSSOHN, ARRANGED BY ERICH WOLFGANG KORNGOLD

For the first time I have realized my own dream of doing this play with no restriction on my imagination. Max Reinhardt

In 1934, Max Reinhardt fled the Nazi persecution of Jews in Germany and sought refuge in Hollywood. The hugely influential Austrian-born director had already staged *A Midsummer Night's Dream* ten times in Europe, and his first assignment in America was yet another production: an open-air extravaganza at the Hollywood Bowl, watched by 15,000 spectators every night and adored by the critics.

Bottom: Mickey Rooney as an 'invisible' Puck, left, torments Olivia de Havilland as Hermia. Both had played the same parts in Max Reinhardt's 1934 stage production of the *Dream* in Hollywood.

Right: Joe E. Brown as Flute, extreme left, and James Cagney as Bottom, second left, lead a chorus of rude mechanicals in the opening sequence.

Soon afterwards, Warner Brothers hired Reinhardt to direct a film version. This would be a classy affair, something that could show cinema-knocking snobs that Warners were capable of making more than just Westerns and gangster movies.

Reinhardt was entrusted with a budget of about $1.5 million (around $60 million today), but studio anxiety over his early footage prompted Warners to install a new cinematographer and to add the more experienced William Dieterle, a former Reinhardt collaborator, as co-director. Together they delivered Shakespeare on the grandest scale; from the opening scene, showing Egeus leading his golden army in a triumphant homecoming parade, it is obvious that drama will take a back seat to spectacle.

The directors' vision of the enchanted wood begins with a seven-minute ballet, accompanied by Mendelssohn's *Midsummer Night's Dream* overture. Blonde 'fairy' ballerinas, in ethereal lace costumes, emerge from the mist and gambol around a giant oak that appears rooted in the sky. Filters make the air sparkle around the black-clad figure of Oberon (a grandiose Victor Jory). Another, shorter piece of ballet closes the fairy segment with genuine menace, as Oberon's bald-headed minions use their sinewy wings to round up Titania's terrified fairies.

'Unquestionably the loveliest fantastic imagery the screen has yet produced', was *Variety*'s verdict, and 65 years later it is still easy to understand why critics were bowled over by the production design. Cinematographer Hal Mohr and film editor Ralph Dawson earned Oscars for their contributions to what *The Daily Telegraph* called 'a gorgeous pageant'.

The boy wonder

At the heart of the pageant is 13-year-old Mickey Rooney's Puck, a hyperactive blonde cherub in a grass skirt. He covers up a loose grasp of the language by punctuating his mischief with whooping laughter, and enjoys the best of the special effects: appearing to fly above the trees and to belch fog.

Reinhardt used him to give 'family' appeal to a play dominated by adult characters and concerns, and does the same with the 'changeling boy' whom Titania (an angelically serene Anita Louise) has refused to hand over to Oberon, causing their rift. Not shown on stage, this turbaned chap is seen riding a unicorn, and weeping when Titania abandons him. Finally 'kidnapped' by Oberon, he becomes the key to the couple's relationship.

Such fanciful additions are irrelevant to the core of the play, unlike the plight of the Athenian lovers which here becomes a tiresome, broadly acted series of shouting matches. *The Observer*'s critic put it well, describing the quartet as 'co-eds who have lost their campus'. Years later, Dick Powell admitted that he had never really understood Lysander's lines. It shows.

Shakespeare is slightly better served by the 'rude mechanicals'. As Bottom, James Cagney distanced himself from his habitual tough-guy roles with a slow-witted turn, enhanced by a magnificent ass's head. He enjoys a necessarily chaste night with Titania (in 1935, any suggestion of sex between 'donkey' and fairy queen would have been unthinkable), then, in the chaotic 'Pyramus and Thisbe' performance, teams up with a dim, seed-munching Flute (Joe E. Brown, fondly remembered as the millionaire who woos Jack Lemmon in *Some Like It Hot*).

Not even this double-act convinced reviewers of the film's comedy value, and perhaps the worst of many British reviews, in *The Sunday Times*, concluded 'Poor old Shakespeare!'

Reinhardt probably didn't care. His one and only Hollywood film earned him an Oscar nomination for Best Picture. More importantly, he had finally achieved a lifelong ambition. 'For the first time', he said, 'I have realized my own dream of doing this play with no restriction on my imagination'.

Unquestionably the loveliest fantastic imagery the screen has yet produced. *Variety*

A MIDSUMMER NIGHT'S DREAM (1969)
UK 124 MINS COLOUR

CAST	DEREK GODFREY (Theseus), BARBARA JEFFORD (Hippolyta), HELEN MIRREN (Hermia), DAVID WARNER (Lysander), DIANA RIGG (Helena), MICHAEL JAYSTON (Demetrius), PAUL ROGERS (Bottom), JUDI DENCH (Titania), IAN RICHARDSON (Oberon), IAN HOLM (Puck)
DIRECTED BY	PETER HALL
PRODUCED BY	MICHAEL BIRKETT
PHOTOGRAPHY	PETER SUSCHITZKY
MUSIC	GUY WOOLFENDEN

I believe that Shakespeare's text only has film value in close-up.

Peter Hall

One Sunday night in February 1969, Shakespeare knocked *Mission: Impossible* and the *Smothers Brothers Comedy Hour* off US prime-time schedules. Some 25 million viewers tuned in to CBS television to watch the Royal Shakespeare Company's (RSC) film of **A Midsummer Night's Dream**, an audience that would fill even the RSC's largest auditorium every night for 30 years.

Positive critical reaction (*Time* praised it as 'richly textured' entertainment) was in stark contrast to the panning that had been handed out by British critics a week earlier, on the film's cinema release. 'Frankly terrible on almost every conceivable level', said *The Times*. 'Drab, mundane and shockingly inept', fumed *The Observer*. More than 30 years later, such verdicts seem both justified and excessive.

In pre-release interviews, director Peter Hall took a dig at Max Reinhardt's 1935 version, dismissing its 'fairies in little white tutus, skipping through gossamer forests'. Hall believed that dance sequences betrayed the Bard, and promised to deliver screen Shakespeare in which there would be 'no shots without dialogue'.

In search of realism, he filmed in autumn daylight, in the grounds of Compton Verney (a manor house near Stratford-upon-Avon). When Puck (a boyishly eager Ian Holm) refers to the wood's 'dank and dirty ground', that is precisely what we see,

Frankly terrible on almost every conceivable level. The Times

and as the four Athenian lovers struggle through tangled undergrowth, their faces and dainty, 1960s outfits become streaked with mud. These vain, Carnaby Street youths really are cold, wet and bewildered. Tracked by a hand-held camera, their ordeal is closer to *The Blair Witch Project* than Reinhardt's film.

Hall's distinctive quartet live up to Shakespeare's description of them as 'quick bright things': Diana Rigg as Helena is a neurotic, willowy brunette who towers over the blonde, girlish Hermia of Helen Mirren, while David Warner's Lysander has a physical and intellectual edge over dark-haired, haughty Michael Jayston's Demetrius. Hall's edgy treatment of the lovers' shifting romantic allegiances, suggested several critics, was in tune with the prevailing ethos of sexual promiscuity in the late 1960s.

Royal Shakespeare Company
in Peter Hall's film of

A Midsummer
night's
dream U

EASTMAN
COLOUR

EAGLE FILMS LTD

Left: Judi Dench, left, and Ian Richardson as Titania and Oberon, fairy queen and king.

Far left: Left to right are David Warner, Helen Mirren, Diana Rigg and Michael Jayston as the Athenian lovers.

No-budget fantasy

Hall's treatment of the fairy world bore the brunt of British reviewers' wrath. Titania, Oberon and Puck are covered from head to toe in sickly, silvery green make-up but wear little else (Dench goes topless, her modesty protected by a few leaves).

Woeful lighting continuity means these characters change colour alarmingly from one shot to the next, as do their equally green fairy minions – urchin-like children with messy hair and little talent. 'Special effects' here means fairies appearing and vanishing in primitive jump-cuts or rushing out of shot in speeded-up footage, accompanied by cartoonish whizzing noises.

Such clumsy techniques suck all visual magic from the film – a pity, since Dench, suitably spellbound for her one-night stand with Bottom (a tiresomely loud Paul Rogers), Richardson's world-weary king and Holm give eloquent voice to the verse's magic.

Derek Godfrey, a kindly, man-of-the-world Theseus, and Barbara Jefford's sultry Hippolyta (dressed in leather mini-dress and knee-length boots) enliven the opening and closing scenes inside the manor house.

They, like all the other actors, are shown in close-up in eight out of ten shots – a monotonous technique adopted to place the greatest possible emphasis on Shakespeare's language. 'I believe that Shakespeare's text only has film value in close-up', explained Hall in an article for *The Sunday Times*. 'In the theatre we make our own close-ups, as eyes switch from actor to actor. Film can do this for us with even greater concentration.'

His wish to stress words over images also prompted a more successful decision: having the actors re-record every line 'in the peace and concentration of a studio' during postproduction. Initially distracting, this dubbing is soon forgotten, and you relish the attentive delivery of the entire cast (several of whom, including Dench and Richardson, were retained from the Hall/RSC *Dream* staged in 1962). As in only the best theatre productions – and Hall has directed dozens – Shakespeare's every word is given precise meaning.

Does such fine acting cancel out the visual flaws? Sadly not. Hall delivered perhaps the only Shakespeare movie that would be more enjoyable if you watched it with your eyes shut.

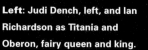

8

WILLIAM SHAKESPEARE'S A MIDSUMMER NIGHT'S DREAM (1999)

US/GERMANY 116 MINS COLOUR

CAST	DAVID STRATHAIRN (Theseus), SOPHIE MARCEAU (Hippolyta), ANNA FRIEL (Hermia), DOMINIC WEST (Lysander), CALISTA FLOCKHART (Helena), CHRISTIAN BALE (Demetrius), KEVIN KLINE (Bottom), MICHELLE PFEIFFER (Titania), RUPERT EVERETT (Oberon), STANLEY TUCCI (Puck)
DIRECTED BY	MICHAEL HOFFMAN
PRODUCED BY	MICHAEL HOFFMAN, LESLEY URDANG
PHOTOGRAPHY	OLIVER STAPLETON
SCREENPLAY	MICHAEL HOFFMAN
MUSIC	SIMON BOSWELL

Bringing together Michelle Pfeiffer, Kevin Kline and Rupert Everett for a heavily promoted Hollywood production of a beloved Shakespeare comedy should have guaranteed solid box-office appeal for 1999's **A Midsummer Night's Dream**. As *Variety* noted, Michael Hoffman's film 'brims with ideas and promises', yet it never quite takes flight. Consistently mixed reviews and grosses of $16 million in America and $2 million in Britain were a disappointing result for such a star-studded team.

Hoffman, who had directed the play twice on stage, moves the story from ancient Athens to the fictional Monte Athena, Tuscany, in the 1890s. The marriage of Sophie Marceau's dreamy Hippolyta and David Strathairn's strait-laced Theseus is a sensible match between aristocrats at his grand villa. This is a reasonable attempt to make the *Dream* more 'accessible' to 1990s audiences – provided that you can overlook the clash of English and American accents amongst the 'Italian' characters, and understand Marceau's Frenchified verse (she makes 'admirable' sound like 'hot mirror ball').

The updated setting allows Hoffman to dress the young lovers in the buttoned-up fashions and romantic conventions familiar from Merchant/Ivory's *A Room With A View*. Before they can begin to lose their inhibitions in the fairy wood, Hoffman introduces his big idea: giving Bottom (Kevin Kline) a background not even hinted at by Shakespeare.

In Monte Athena's bustling market square, we see Kline acting the gentleman in straw boater and cream suit and avoiding his furious wife, who yells in subtitled Italian: 'Where's my husband? Where's that worthless dreamer?' It is a shame Hoffman didn't have the courage to make this character speak English like everybody else, but the two scenes showing Bottom yearning for escape from an unhappy marriage do lift Shakespeare's weaver beyond his stereotypical portrayal as a vain imbecile. Regrettably, Kline sours this refreshing twist by overacting.

Too clean by half

After the action shifts from bright Tuscan locations to a disappointingly cramped and sanitized studio woodland, Kline, transformed into a hairy, though far from grotesque ass, strains too hard to make us sigh at the contrast between his night of bliss with Michelle Pfeiffer's glitter-speckled Titania and his home life with Signora Bottom.

Pfeiffer seems neither turned on by Bottom, nor much moved by Rupert Everett's languid, bare-chested Oberon. This fairy king and queen are impossibly beautiful, which suits Shakespeare's language, and about as engaging as the models in a perfume commercial, which leaves the verse as mere decoration. It is left to Stanley Tucci's Puck to score points for the supernaturals. Bald, Spock-eared and sardonic, he would clearly much rather be boozing, or seducing one of Titania's many gorgeous attendants than chasing after the Athenians.

Perky Anna Friel and her cocky admirers, Dominic West and Christian Bale, are adequately ardent, although you can't believe that these civilized Brits are from the same century, let alone community, as Helena – played by Calista Flockhart as a more neurotic and exasperating version of her TV role as Ally McBeal. Hoffman deserves a special booby prize for making Flockhart and Friel wrestle in a pool of absurdly chocolaty mud.

As the quartet cycle and stumble across unconvincing sets, which give the impression of a wood barely larger than a football field, Hoffman's uncertain direction fails to generate sufficient confusion or enchantment. The special effects, with fairies flying, or fading into invisibility, hardly improve on those in the 1935 film version, despite the use of computer technology that Max Reinhardt could only dream of.

Tucci excepted, none of the performances has the zest found in the music, which includes bustling original themes by Simon Boswell, and the Brindisi, or drinking song from Verdi's *La Traviata*, used as the signature tune for the mechanicals.

When Kline and the other craftsmen launch into their shambolic performance in Theseus's private theatre, Hoffmann doesn't trust us to laugh for ourselves, so each amateurish slip-up prompts canned laughter from a largely unseen audience. It is a grating finale to a production that, suggested *Time*, 'manages to seem both leaden and hasty'.

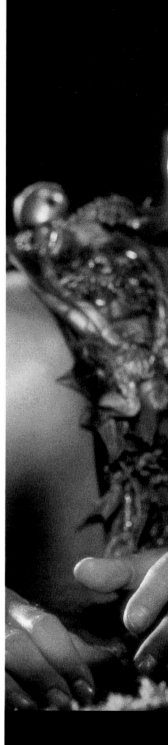

Far left: Dominic West as Lysander, left, with Calista Flockhart as Helena. Flockhart's performance had more than a touch of her TV role as Boston lawyer Ally McBeal.

Above: Stanley Tucci as Puck, left, and Rupert Everett as Oberon with the magical 'love in idleness' flower.

Michael Hoffman's film brims with ideas and promises but suffers from a lack of coherent vision and an incongruous tone.

Variety

O, beware, my lord, of jealousy! It is the green-eyed monster, which doth mock the meat it feeds on. Iago, *Othello*, Act III, Scene iii

FILM BACKGROUND

Othello seems a less obvious candidate for screen adaptation than Shakespeare's other most celebrated tragedies: *Macbeth* and *Romeo and Juliet* have more action-packed plots, and *Hamlet* has more scenes that lend themselves to set piece, cinematic treatment. To put it bluntly, from the Cassio/Roderigo fight, early in Act II, until the night-time ambush which opens Act V, *Othello* is all talk.

Yet the shortage of incident and movement does not matter. Iago's manipulation of the complicated network of racist prejudice and sexual jealousy involving Othello, Desdemona, Cassio, Roderigo and Emilia, gives *Othello* a slow-burning intensity which is unrivalled in Shakespeare – and readily translated to the screen.

Some critics argue that the jealousies have been more authentically depicted on stage and screen than the inter-racial love story, because for generations the Moor was played by white actors in blackface make-up.

That was the case in numerous silent versions produced in Germany, Italy and America, in the BBC's 1981 production, with Anthony Hopkins starring opposite Bob Hoskins' Iago (although the BBC had cast television's first black Othello, Gordon Heat, in 1955) and Franco Zeffirelli's fine film of Verdi's opera, *Otello* (1986).

Of the four 'straight' versions of **Othello** assessed in this chapter – directed by Orson Welles (1952), Sergei Yutkevich (1955), Stuart Burge (1965) and Oliver Parker (1995) – only Parker's has a black Moor: Laurence Fishburne. The white Othellos have still brought out the play's racism, but in the age of political correctness it is unlikely that an actor will ever again black up for the part on screen.

The other movie discussed in this chapter, **A Double Life** (US, 1947), is one of several whose heroes are white actors who become murderously jealous while playing Othello. This formula, which often manufactures a happy ending, was first used in the silent *Carnival* (UK, 1921; remade as a talkie a decade later) and repeated in *Men Are Not Gods* (UK, 1936), in which the Othello actor's affair with a theatre critic's secretary almost leads him to murder his wife, who's playing Desdemona.

Shakespeare's plot was transplanted to the London jazz scene for *All Night Long* (UK, 1961): black musician Aurelius Rex almost strangles his white wife after the Iago figure, drummer Johnny Cousin (Patrick McGoohan) has convinced him that she is having an affair with Cass, Rex's manager.

McGoohan also directed *Catch My Soul* (US, 1974), a tense rock opera (adapted from a London stage hit) with black soul singer Richie Havens as Othello, a preacher who comes to a western desert town run by Iago and marries Desdemona, a young white convert, with familiarly tragic consequences.

Othello has inspired a bleak Western, Delmer Daves's *Jubal* (US, 1956). Rod Steiger's Iago surrogate, Pinky, persuades simple-minded rancher, Shep (Ernest Borgnine), that his wife Mae (Valerie French) is lusting after their tenant, Jubal (Glenn Ford). Jubal kills Shep in self defence. Pinky rapes Mae, whose dying words save Jubal from a lynch mob and enable him to take revenge on Pinky.

In 2000, Miramax Films' *The One* (US) has turned Othello into Odin (Mekhi Phifer, from Spike Lee's *Clockers*), a black, high-school basketball player with a white girlfriend, Desi. The film was scheduled for release in America as this book went to press, so it remained to be seen whether *Othello* can withstand Holly-wood teen treatment.

Venice, 1500s. Desdemona, daughter of Venetian senator Brabantio, has secretly married Othello the Moor, a heroic general. Brabantio accuses Othello of bewitching her, but relents when she confirms that she loves him. The Doge sends Othello to defend Cyprus against the Turkish fleet.

Iago, Othello's 'honest' aide, promises to help Roderigo, a gullible nobleman who is hopelessly in love with Desdemona. Iago's real plan is to destroy Othello, who promoted Cassio to be his lieutenant ahead of him. His other motive for revenge is that he also suspects that Othello has slept with his wife, Emilia, Desdemona's maid.

Othello arrives, victorious, on Cyprus. Iago engineers a fight between a drunken Cassio and a disguised Roderigo, prompting Othello to dismiss Cassio and promote Iago as lieutenant in his place.

Iago tells the Moor that Desdemona and Cassio are lovers. Othello refuses to believe it, but when Desdemona appeals for Cassio's reinstatement becomes insanely jealous. After Othello sees Cassio with a handkerchief that he, himself, had given Desdemona (placed in Cassio's bedroom by Iago), he vows to kill her. Iago promises to kill Cassio.

Roderigo ambushes Cassio, wounding him, then Iago kills Roderigo. Othello wakes Desdemona, condemns her for adultery and suffocates her. Emilia discovers Desdemona's body, realizes that Iago has caused the tragedy and denounces him. Iago kills her and flees but is captured. Realizing his terrible mistake, Othello wounds Iago, then kills himself.

OTHELLO

A DOUBLE LIFE (1947)
US 105 MINS B/W

CAST	RONALD COLMAN (Tony John/Othello), SIGNE HASSO (Brita Kaurin/Desdemona), EDMOND O'BRIEN (Bill Friend), SHELLEY WINTERS (Pat Kroll), PHILIP LOEB (Max Lasker)
DIRECTED BY	GEORGE CUKOR
PRODUCED BY	MICHAEL KANIN
SCREENPLAY	RUTH GORDON, GARSON KANIN
PHOTOGRAPHY	MILTON KRASNER
MUSIC	MIKLOS ROZSA

The magic of the word 'Shakespeare' must simply have made the [Oscar] judges swoon away. The Guardian

Has anyone ever won an Oscar for a less convincing performance than Ronald Colman gives in **A Double Life**? This handsome, smooth-talking Englishman's gifts in light comedies, or adventures such as *The Prisoner of Zenda*, were considerable. In this ridiculous psychological drama, mastering Shakespeare proved way beyond his reach.

We are in post-war New York, and Colman plays Tony John, a leading man famed for immersing himself in his roles. He is persuaded by Broadway producer Max Lasker to star as Othello, with his ex-wife and regular co-star, Brita (Swedish-born Signe Hasso), as Desdemona.

Within minutes, we know that there is big trouble ahead. During a one-night stand with Pat, a lonely blonde waitress (Shelley Winters, giving a sexy, career-boosting performance), Tony starts 'becoming' Othello. He imagines himself wearing blackface make-up, and a voice in his head denounces Desdemona as a 'strumpet'.

Next, a montage sequence charts the *Othello* rehearsals, with Colman's breathless voice-over insisting that the actors go through hell before confronting that 'terrifying monster with a thousand heads' (better known as a theatre audience).

During *Othello*'s opening night we watch the first of the movie's three enactments of Desdemona's murder, with stiff, melodramatic performances from Colman and Hasso – although director Cukor wants us to believe this is great acting, so cuts away to misty-eyed women in the stalls.

Tony becomes convinced that Brita is having an affair with the story's answer to Cassio, unscrupulous Broadway publicist Bill Friend (Edmond O'Brien, who later played Casca in the 1953 *Julius Caesar*). The voice in Tony's head continues quoting juicy *Othello* references to jealousy and at the play's three hundredth performance, he almost strangles Brita for real in the murder scene. Hasso improbably shrugs this off as 'overdoing it'.

Pushed over the brink
The production is two years old before Tony, certain that Brita is going to marry Friend, finally snaps. Incapable of venting his rage on Brita, he returns to the waitress's shabby apartment and suffocates her. Although the police arrest one of Pat's

neighbours for the murder, Friend suspects Tony and convinces a police captain to investigate further.

Incredibly, the script now rips off the famous 'play' scene from Act IV of *Hamlet*. Friend, behaving like a cross between a private eye and the Prince of Denmark, hires an actress who vaguely resembles Pat, dresses her in a blonde wig and gives her the dead woman's earrings. He brings Tony (now more like Claudius in *Hamlet* than Othello) to a bar where the hired 'waitress' serves them and the police captain (now acting as Horatio) watches Tony's horrified reaction as he sees his victim apparently resurrected.

Before Tony can be arrested, however, we must again endure the *Othello* murder scene, and this time Tony really stabs himself. As he lies dying in Brita's arms, Othello's magnificent last speech 'Speak of me as I am ... one that loved not wisely, but too well' becomes Colman's 'Don't let them say I was a bad actor'. Shakespeare it is not.

His death ends a film in which husband-and-wife writers Garson Kanin and Ruth Gordon copy Shakespeare's plot while diluting its shocking impact. Othello rages against 'betrayal' by the woman who defied great prejudice to marry him; Tony and Brita are no longer even married. Without an Iago, we see Tony as his own worst enemy, but Colman's Jekyll-and-Hyde histrionics are a woeful substitute for the Iago-Othello relationship.

Somehow, positive critical reaction in America enabled Colman to win the Oscar for Best Actor (a 'flawless' performance, said *Variety*). The jarring score by Miklos Rozsa, relentlessly employed to amplify Tony's madness, also won an Oscar, and Cukor was nominated for Best Director.

British critics were divided. Several thought Colman's award 'richly deserved'; others labelled him the worst Othello they'd ever seen. *The Guardian* suggested that 'The magic of the word "Shakespeare" must simply have made the [Oscar] judges swoon away'. Years later, even Cukor admitted that Colman's many attributes did not include 'the danger and madness' needed for Othello. We are left with a film worth watching as the perfect demonstration of how tinkering with Shakespearean brilliance can lead to cinematic folly.

Below: Ronald Colman as disturbed actor Tony John, left, and Philip Loeb as theatrical agent Max Lasker discuss staging *Othello*.

Right: Signe Hasso, left, with Ronald Colman, playing Desdemona and the Moor in the film's Broadway production of *Othello*.

A DOUBLE LIFE (1947)

⑨

OTHELLO (1952)
MOROCCO 91 MINS B/W

CAST	ORSON WELLES (Othello), MICHEÁL MACLIAMMÓIR (Iago), SUZANNE CLOUTIER (Desdemona), FAY COMPTON (Emilia), ROBERT COOTE (Roderigo), MICHAEL LAWRENCE (Cassio), HILTON EDWARDS (Brabantio)
DIRECTED BY	ORSON WELLES
PRODUCED BY	ORSON WELLES
SCREENPLAY	ORSON WELLES
PHOTOGRAPHY	ANCHISE BRIZZI, G.R. ALDO, GEORGE FANTO
MUSIC	FRANCESCO LAVAGNINO, ALBERTO BARBERIS

One of the most intellectually stimulating, visually beautiful and emotionally exciting 90 minutes ever to come out of the cinema.

The Times

The making of Orson Welles's **Othello** stretched across three troubled years. Cast and crew shuttled back and forth between locations in Italy and Morocco, never quite sure how long they would be needed. Shooting had to be suspended three times when Welles ran out of money. Somehow the film was completed – and the result is a masterpiece.

Welles begins after the end of the play. His unforgettable pre-credits sequence shows cowled figures silhouetted against a cloudless sky, leading twin funeral processions along the battlements of a fortress. A soundtrack of heavy, repetitive piano chords, timpani and a wailing chorus add to the atmosphere of doom. The corpses are a black man and a white woman: Othello and Desdemona. A chained figure is thrown into a cage by soldiers and winched aloft: Iago. Not a word is spoken.

Then a fade-out carries us back to Venice and, once a mock-Shakespearean Prologue (delivered by Welles in a voice-over) has filled in the background to Othello and Desdemona's secret wedding, *Othello*'s plot starts to unfold in familiar sequence. It does so with speed unimaginable in screen versions that do not slash the text as Welles does. His film lasts 90 minutes; Trevor Nunn's magnificent television production from 1990 (*see* page 195) lasts well over twice as long.

Within this shortened span, some sequences in **Othello** would work just as effectively as silent film, such is Welles's genius for evoking moods through the stark contrasts of black-and-white photography.

Early on, he places the characters in bright, windswept exteriors, but once Iago's plot begins to take hold, darkness spreads into almost every frame. Othello's black features are invariably concealed by shadows; figures hurry down flooded passageways, or eavesdrop from behind pillars. Sometimes the camera looks down on characters from a great height, then suddenly someone towers above us. It make for disorienting viewing – as though Welles wants our perspective to become as warped as Othello's view of Desdemona.

Brief and bloody

The camerawork is perfectly in tune with Welles's concentration on short-lived rage and dread. He was not interested in the long conversations and the 'Will he? Won't he?' tension that Shakespeare wanted to grip theatre audiences once the Moor has sworn to kill Desdemona. Instead, in fewer than 20 bloody minutes, Cassio is wounded, Roderigo, Desdemona and Emilia are murdered and Othello stabs himself.

Towards the end of Othello's final speech, Welles's body disappears, so all we see is a black face surrounded by darkness. The image fades back into the double funeral – allowing Welles to end where he began.

At the heart of this extraordinary film are the performances of Welles and his Iago, Micheál MacLiammóir (co-founder of Dublin's Gate Theatre with his partner, Hilton Edwards, **Othello**'s blustering Brabantio). Amid the film's many contrasts, the differences between their physiques, complexions and voices are the most pronounced.

Far left: Orson Welles, right, lines up a shot of Suzanne Cloutier as Desdemona on location in Morocco. Cloutier was Welles's third choice for the role.

Left: Welles as Othello, left, with Micheál MacLiammóir as Iago. MacLiammóir decided that his character suffered from impotence.

Welles cuts an exceptionally tall, imposing figure, gives full vent to his magnificent bass voice and still manages to reveal the fatally trusting side to a man who, suggested the director, 'is destroyed easily because of his simplicity, not his weakness'.

He looms over MacLiammóir's Iago, a hunched weasel of a man with drooping shoulders and lank hair, who dispenses malicious advice in a blank, Irish-accented whine. He and Welles had devised an unusual key with which the actor might unlock Iago's character: they decided he was impotent. 'That's why he hates life so much', said MacLiammóir, although Welles himself believed there was no need to seek concrete motivation for Othello's destroyer: 'I've known a lot of Iagos in my life, [people] who perpetuate villainy without any motive other than ... the enjoyment of the power to destroy'.

It's clear the Othello-Iago relationship is the only one that really fascinated Welles. Alongside this formidable duo, the Desdemona of Suzanne Cloutier (Welles's third choice for the part) comes across as little more than a saintly, sacrificial victim, a woman of great beauty and scant personality. Desdemona's murder, though, produces an image of horror to rank with any in cinema: as Welles suffocates her with a sheet, Cloutier's features strain against the material like a tormented ghost.

Desdemona is not the only part ill-served by Welles's customized script. Emilia becomes just a middle-aged ballbreaker, Cassio a brainless hunk. Robert Coote's aristocratic Roderigo is a caricature, his simpering, upper-class voice dubbed in by Welles himself. Coote appears pathetically devoted to a white poodle because such pets are carried by gentlemen in portraits by Renaissance Venetian artist Vittore Carpaccio, whose art was the basis for **Othello**'s costumes.

Roderigo is murdered by Iago shrouded in the steam of a Turkish bath, repeatedly stabbed between floorboards as he cowers beneath them, in a shot that could have been a trial run for the *Psycho* shower scene. It seems an inspired choice of location, but it arose because of one of **Othello**'s production hitches.

The cast and crew were in Morocco when their Italian backer went bankrupt. The costumes had yet to be made. They were stranded. How to film without costumes? 'Let's shoot in a bathhouse', said Welles, 'because people won't be wearing clothes'. Roderigo's sweaty fate was sealed.

There was no studio finance behind **Othello** when filming first began in Mogador, Morocco, in June 1949 – the movie would be funded out of Welles's pocket. A haphazard pattern emerged over the next 18 months: Welles would start filming at various Moroccan and Italian locations; after four or five weeks

I've known a lot of Iagos in my life, [people] who perpetuate villainy without any motive other than ... the enjoyment of the power to destroy. Orson Welles

Right: Welles as Othello, about to 'put out the light' by smothering Suzanne Cloutier's Desdemona.

he would run out of money, suspend production and disappear for a month or so to make fast bucks acting in another movie, such as the Tyrone Power vehicle, *Prince of Foxes*. He would then use his fee to resume filming **Othello**. And so it continued.

Rough magic

When a scene in **Othello** does not look or feel as smooth as it should (and most do not), that is probably because one actor's contribution was shot in Italy in 1949, the second actor filmed in Morocco in 1950 and the footage spliced together in an editing room in 1951. An equally erratic dubbing schedule means that voices seldom emerge from mouths in anything close to perfect sync. The miracle is that **Othello** grips *despite* all the inconsistencies.

Every chaotic development in what Welles would later call this 'maddening' process, is catalogued in MacLiammóir's 'The Making of *Othello*' diary, entitled *Put Money in Thy Purse* (after Iago's advice to Roderigo in Act I), and described by *The Sunday Times* as 'one of the funniest books of the 1950s'.

MacLiammóir's account appeared in 1952, around the time that Welles, hugely in debt, had finally completed **Othello** for its premiere at the Cannes Film Festival. It won the Palme D'Or (shared with *Two Cents of Hope* by Renato Castellani, whose next film was *Romeo and Juliet*), although this recognition failed to set **Othello** up for critical and commercial triumph.

It languished unreleased until September 1955, when American critics savaged it. *The New Yorker* felt that Welles had 'destroyed' Shakespeare's 'glorious tale' by 'concentrating on half a hundred cinematic tricks'. It lasted one week in New York cinemas before disappearing.

When it opened in Britain in February 1956, the same reviewers who had recently showered superlatives on Olivier's *Richard III*, now launched venomous attacks. The headlines on three of the reviews said it all: 'Mr Welles murders Shakespeare in the dark'; 'The Boor of Venice'; 'The Crime of Orson Welles'. Welles was labelled a 'big, prankish schoolboy' in *The Guardian*, while the *Daily Mail* said that he had reduced a great tragedy to 'a murky, gloomy charade'.

Two voices took the opposite view. 'One of the most intellectually stimulating, visually beautiful and emotionally exciting 90 minutes ever to come out of the cinema', said *The Times*, and *The Sunday Times* saw in **Othello** 'a kind of genius'. Their praise did not save the film from financial failure.

Yet in 1992, seven years after Welles's death, a restored print was reissued in Britain and America and **Othello** was suddenly a rediscovered classic. The *Independent on Sunday* called it 'the most intense, invigorating, mobile and heart-stabbing Shakespeare film of all time'.

Welles himself remained very proud of **Othello** – which is not to say that he thought it was perfect. Back in 1951, six months before the film's Cannes première, he directed himself as the Moor on stage in London – and judged his performance 'much better' than the one he gave on screen. In *Filming Othello*, a television documentary shown in 1978, he sits watching his film and mutters about all the improvements he would make – if only he could shoot it again.

OTHELLO (1955)
USSR 106 MINS COLOUR

CAST	SERGEI BONDARCHUK (Othello), ANDREI POPOV (Iago), IRINA SKOBTSEVA (Desdemona), A. MAXIMOVA (Emilia), E. VESNIK (Roderigo), VLADIMIR SOSHALSKY (Cassio), E. TETERIN (Brabantio)
DIRECTED BY	SERGEI YUTKEVICH
PRODUCTION COMPANY	MOSFILM
SCREENPLAY	SERGEI YUTKEVICH
PHOTOGRAPHY	EVGENY ANDRIKANIS
MUSIC	ARAM KHACHATURIAN

Below: Andrei Popov as Iago, left, appears to be spying on Irina Skobtseva as Desdemona and Sergei Bondarchuk as Othello in this unusual publicity shot.

Othello has never received more spectacular screen treatment than in this epic Russian adaptation. Before a word is uttered, Sergei Bondarchuk's majestic Othello has fought a naval battle, been whipped and chained as a galley slave, and miraculously escaped drowning – all in a brief, thrilling montage dramatizing the tales with which the Moor has won Desdemona's heart.

That opening sequence is typical of Sergei Yutkevich's achievement in cutting away *Othello*'s theatrical roots, even more decisively than Orson Welles had done three years earlier. Action, spectacle and music (Aram Khachaturian's plaintive strings and emphatic organ blasts) take precedence over language, and the cast speak a heavily edited version of Pasternak's Russian translation of *Othello* (the subtitles use Shakespeare).

Yutkevich's open-air shooting places the intimate Othello/Iago and Othello/Desdemona scenes on Cyprus against breathtakingly photographed locations: vineyards, mountains, golden beaches, azure sea and sky and a vast medieval fortress. This colourful, holiday brochure beauty contrasts superbly with the darkness of the plot. The operatic performances are less effective.

Bondarchuk's bombastic technique sets Othello up as a hero of mythic proportions, full of godlike love and hate, but he gives no hint of the man's inner life. Andrei Popov provides a handsome Iago who seems oddly roguish, rather than evil, and the Desdemona of Irina Skobtseva (plucked straight from drama school in Moscow) is a one-dimensional victim.

When a crazed Othello bears down on her like Frankenstein's monster, bathed in demonic red light, Yutkevich replaces tragedy with melodramatic horror. It is an over-the-top moment, yet not entirely out of place in an adaptation which consistently opts for broad effects. Without ever moving you as the play should, this **Othello** is constantly impressive, and Yutkevich's reward for giving Shakespeare such distinctive, cinematic treatment was the Best Director award at the 1956 Cannes Film Festival.

OTHELLO (1965)

UK 166 MINS COLOUR

CAST	LAURENCE OLIVIER (Othello), FRANK FINLAY (Iago), MAGGIE SMITH (Desdemona), JOYCE REDMAN (Emilia), ROBERT LANG (Roderigo), DEREK JACOBI (Cassio), ANTHONY NICHOLLS (Brabantio)
DIRECTED BY	STUART BURGE
PRODUCED BY	ANTHONY HAVELOCK-ALLAN, JOHN BRABOURNE
PHOTOGRAPHY	GEOFFREY UNSWORTH
MUSIC	RICHARD HAMPTON

Olivier's is a stage performance – outsize, elaborate, overwhelming.

The Spectator

Below: Laurence Olivier as Othello, left, yells in jealous rage at Maggie Smith, his bewildered Desdemona.

Laurence Olivier said that *Othello* demanded 'enormously big' acting. That is what theatregoers queued for hours to see when he played the Moor at London's Old Vic in 1964, and cinema-goers witnessed more of the same when this acclaimed National Theatre production was filmed the following year.

Olivier is astonishing. His gym-enhanced physique coated in thick black make-up, he strides around barefoot, cradling a scim-itar. His voice, deepened a full octave by six months of exercises, sometimes gives the poetry a haunting, West Indian lilt. When jealousy takes hold he roars and howls like a wild animal. It is a uniquely uninhibited portrayal of male hysteria.

Alongside him, Frank Finlay's Iago is excessively restrained, an unassuming chap whose matter-of-fact tone suggests that destroying Othello is a bit of a chore. Maggie Smith brings great spontaneity to Desdemona, perfectly capturing the innocent wife's bewilderment, and Joyce Redman's Emilia is affectingly desperate to win back her husband's affections.

As *The Spectator* magazine pointed out, Olivier had done nothing to tone down his 'outsize, elaborate, overwhelming' per-formance from the stage production directed by John Dexter. His Othello would be horribly out of place in a screen adaptation that attempted to be cinematic, but not in this one, which must be judged as filmed theatre.

It was made in a studio in just three weeks, with Venice and Cyprus represented by simple façades, and the sky by a painted backdrop. The static camerawork obliged the cast to move into view as they would on stage. In short, there is nothing to distract us from the fine acting (all four principals were nominated for Oscars) and the poetry.

This potent combination helped **Othello** to take a remarkable $1.2 million in its first weekend on release in the US, and prompted the great *Sunday Times* film critic Dilys Powell to sug-gest that 'it is difficult not to feel that Shakespeare diminishes everything else on screen'.

OTHELLO (1995)
US/UK 124 MINS COLOUR

CAST	LAURENCE FISHBURNE (Othello), KENNETH BRANAGH (Iago), IRÈNE JACOB (Desdemona), ANNA PATRICK (Emilia), MICHAEL MALONEY (Roderigo), NATHANIEL PARKER (Cassio), PIERRE VANECK (Brabantio)
DIRECTED BY	OLIVER PARKER
PRODUCED BY	LUC ROEG, DAVID BARRON
SCREENPLAY	OLIVER PARKER
PHOTOGRAPHY	DAVID JOHNSON
MUSIC	CHARLIE MOLE

Branagh steals the show … Who steals this picture steals trash.

The New Yorker

In promotional interviews for **Othello**, first-time director Oliver Parker called the play 'an erotic thriller', and insisted that the previous screen adaptations had lacked passion. Did this mean he offered cinemas a steamy tale: the Bard meets *Basic Instinct*? Not quite.

True, Parker goes further than previous versions to underline an intense physical bond between Laurence Fishburne's Othello and Irène Jacob's Desdemona. He shows them making love after the Moor's arrival in Cyprus and, later, twice shows Othello's jealousy-crazed hallucinations, as he imagines Desdemona and Cassio having sex.

All three sequences are brief, discreetly shot and at least partially justified by Shakespeare's verse, which, particularly when Kenneth Branagh's Iago is talking, dwells explicitly on physical betrayal. Still, sex scenes included, there is not really anything in this adaptation to offend those who prefer their screen Shakespeare served straight up, without a twist.

Othello looks good for its $11 million budget, with locations in Venice and the Cyprus citadel (in fact Bracciano Castle, north of Rome) decked out in fine, 1570s style by Tim Harvey (production designer for all Branagh's films) and lushly photographed by David Johnson. When the dialogue is at its most intense, however, there are too many close-ups of talking heads, raising the spectre of staid, television Shakespeare.

A mixed blessing
Parker, who had played Iago in rep six years earlier, skilfully trims about half of the text, delivering an audience-friendly two-hour running time without compromising the clear, briskly paced plotting that drives *Othello* on stage. The script severely restricts the dialogue entrusted to Desdemona, which is a blessing, since Swiss-born Jacob struggles with complex, archaic verse in what is for her a foreign language. At the same time, Parker's cuts leave her virtually no chance to build a Desdemona whose guiltless plight can really move us, which is a pity.

Language also handicaps Fishburne. Physically, he is very impressive, exuding hearty sexual swagger, but Shakespeare's pentameters are alien to an actor who is more at home in the expletive-ridden worlds of 1990s thrillers like *King of New York*. Speaking in a bass, almost Caribbean accent, he sometimes rushes over his lines as though he is trying to spit out something extremely indigestible. *The Sunday Telegraph* felt that he was 'hopelessly at sea'.

Crucially, Fishburne misses Othello's despairing grief in the final scenes, and you end up wondering what Morgan Freeman, slipping back into his Moor's costume from 1991's *Robin Hood: Prince of Thieves*, might have made of the part. A Freeman Othello would have been more of a match for Branagh's sturdy, leather-jacketed Iago. Relishing his first shot at screen villainy, Branagh delivers most of his soliloquies directly to camera, and his brazen running commentary serves as a model lesson in manipulative evil.

He features in **Othello**'s most lingering moments. The best comes when he and Fishburne swear their blood oath to vengeance on the sunlit roof of a turret. The worst has Branagh ending a soliloquy by grasping a smouldering log from a nearby fire, wincing only slightly at the pain, like some slasher movie psycho. Dreadful.

The New Yorker said 'Branagh steals the show', before adding: 'Who steals this picture steals trash.' That's an unkind verdict on a film that is bolstered by intelligent performances from Nathaniel Parker (the director's brother) as Cassio, and Michael Maloney, who makes Roderigo a more plausible victim than is usually the case. This was 'a fair stab at turning the Bard into a decent night at the multiplex', *The Times* suggested.

In the end, neither Parker's 'erotic thriller' hype nor an attempt to generate a topical spin by linking the 'black husband murders white wife' storyline to that year's OJ Simpson trial could turn **Othello** into a hit. It grossed only $2.8 million in America and about $900,000 in the UK.

Above: Laurence Fishburne as Othello, left, listens to poisonous lies from Kenneth Branagh as Iago.

Right: Irène Jacob as Desdemona, left, in bed with Laurence Fishburne as Othello. Director Oliver Parker described his film as an 'erotic thriller' and wrote in three sex scenes.

Right up until his death, Orson Welles was still striving to transfer his vision of Shakespeare to the screen. Aged 80, and in poor health, he continued to develop his script for a film of *King Lear*. He sent producers a six-minute videotape in which he explained how *Lear*, 'Shakespeare's masterpiece [is] as strong now and as simple and as timeless as any story ever told.'

A magician named Abb Dickson would play the Fool, and Welles would play the king, for the third time, following his appearances in a CBS television *Lear* in 1953, and a Broadway run in 1956, when a broken ankle had forced him to perform in a wheelchair. This new, intimate black-and-white version, Welles promised, would be 'epic in its stark simplicity and almost ferociously down-to-earth. In a word, not only a new kind of Shakespeare, but a new kind of film.'

It sounds magnificent. But this was 1985: Welles had not directed a feature for ten years and, in any case, Shakespeare movies were totally out of fashion. No one in America would

back the project and Welles himself withdrew from a possible *Lear* collaboration with French television.

When he died of a heart attack at his Hollywood home, on October 10, 1985, the *Lear* movie became one of the final 'What if ...' footnotes to a career that had earned Welles the Directors' Guild of America's highest accolade, the D.W. Griffith Award, but that also, famously, contained almost as many aborted movie projects as completed productions. If he had been less demanding, less of a perfectionist, or if circumstances had been kinder, his list of credits as director might contain a dozen more titles.

In 1952, for example, he was trying to put together a modern-dress, documentary-style *Julius Caesar*, to be financed by King Farouk of Egypt, when he heard that John Houseman had begun producing the Mankiewicz/Brando version for MGM. Having tried and failed to pay MGM to abandon their film, Welles returned to *Caesar* in 1960, inviting Charlton Heston to play Mark Antony opposite Richard Burton's Brutus. It was just talk then,

Above: Welles in London in his mid-50s, a period when he was much in demand as a narrator for television documentaries.

He was fascinated by the darker side of human nature, and so was Shakespeare, the playwright whom Welles believed 'would have made a great movie writer'.

Orson Welles

and just talk in 1967, when he hoped to play Caesar to Christopher Plummer's Mark Antony and Paul Scofield's Brutus.

Yet by the late 1960s Welles had already done great service to Shakespeare on film, television, stage, radio and record. His admirers' sense of regret at never seeing a Welles *Lear* or *Caesar* is offset by the enduring power of his *Macbeth*, *Othello* and *Chimes at Midnight* – three distinctive achievements that, thematically and cinematically, sit neatly alongside Welles's non-Shakespearean projects.

Whether the setting was 11th-century Scotland or 1940s America, Welles was always drawn to stories of corrupted men of power: from Macbeth to the haunted media tycoon, Charles Foster Kane, in his masterpiece, *Citizen Kane* (US, 1941); from Othello to Gregory Arkadin, the shadowy arch-capitalist in *Mr Arkadin* (France/Spain, 1955, UK title *Confidential Report*); from Prince Hal to Hank Quinlan, the deranged, obese cop in *A Touch of Evil* (US, 1958).

He was fascinated by the darker side of human nature, and so was Shakespeare, the playwright whom Welles believed 'would have made a great movie writer'. Welles had begun reading Shakespeare at an age when most children are still devouring picturebooks. Born in Kenosha, Wisconsin, in May 1915, the son of Richard Welles, a wealthy inventor, and a beautiful concert pianist and suffragette, Beatrice, who died when he was nine, Welles was a child prodigy in art, music and drama. At Todd School for Boys, in Woodstock, Illinois, aged 14, he staged and adapted *Julius Caesar*, playing Mark Antony *and* Cassius.

Orphaned by the death of his father in 1930, Welles headed for Dublin, where he convinced Hilton Edwards and Micheál MacLiammóir, managers of the Gate Theatre (and eventually co-stars in Welles's *Othello*), that he was a star of New York theatre. They gave him several roles, but he left the company in 1932, largely because they would not let him play Othello. He was 17.

After a six-month trip around Morocco, which would influence his choice of locations for *Othello*, Welles returned to America and co-edited *Everybody's Shakespeare*, a textbook that encouraged pupils not to study the Bard's plays, but to 'Read them. Enjoy them. Act them.'

He joined a touring theatre company, playing Tybalt in *Romeo and Juliet*, and married one of his co-stars, Virginia Nicholson. John Houseman saw him as Tybalt, and was astonished by what was perhaps Welles's greatest gift as an actor: 'a voice of such clarity and power that it tore like the wind through the genteel, modulated voices of the well-trained professionals around him.'

Houseman and Welles were soon a producer-director team, collaborating in 1936 on the sensational 'voodoo *Macbeth*', at the Lafayette Theatre in Harlem, with an all-black cast and Haitian magic replacing Highland witchcraft. The following year the pair launched the Mercury Theatre, producing Shakespeare on record and stage (a modern-dress *Julius Caesar*), and the notorious radio broadcast of *War of the Worlds*, for Halloween 1938, when Welles's vivid description of aliens invading New Jersey panicked thousands of listeners.

By 1939, when he played Falstaff in *Five Kings*, a five-hour forerunner of *Chimes at Midnight*, Welles's 'boy wonder' reputation had spread to Hollywood. Executives at the struggling RKO studio hired him to film Joseph Conrad's *Heart of Darkness*, although his plans would, not for the first time, prove too costly to be realized. He wrote two unfilmed screenplays – and then came *Citizen Kane*.

William Randolph Hearst, the model for Kane, tried to have the film destroyed, but RKO held firm, and Welles's devastatingly innovative manipulation of structure, sound, low-angled compositions and deep-focus cinematography in *Kane* would influence a whole generation of film-makers. It continues to top 'Greatest Films of All-Time' polls.

In some respects, Welles's first feature also marked the high point of his career. After *Kane* underperformed at the box office, the RKO executives who had allowed him complete artistic freedom on his debut reimposed the usual studio controls. Welles would never again enjoy the same combination of Hollywood resources and creative licence. His struggles began immediately, on his graceful family drama, *The Magnificent Ambersons* (US, 1942), which RKO hacked from 148-minutes to just 88, giving Welles a foretaste of what Republic would do to his *Macbeth* six years later (*see* page 72).

Professional setbacks went hand in hand with personal failures. After he and Nicholson divorced in 1939, Welles married Hollywood superstar Rita Hayworth in 1943, then saw their relationship collapse immediately after he directed her in the bizarre thriller, *The Lady from Shanghai* (US, 1948); in 1955, he married Paola Mori, who had played the female lead in *Mr Arkadin*.

After Hayworth divorced him and Republic ruined *Macbeth*, Welles left for Europe, beginning a self-imposed 'exile'. Apart from the occasional, brief return to America, this phase would last almost 30 years, during which his abilities as an actor, confirmed by a towering Rochester in *Jane Eyre* (US, 1944), meant that he was constantly in demand for other directors' films. His Harry Lime in *The Third Man* (UK, 1949) was unforgettable, his Cesare Borgia in *Prince of Foxes* (US, 1949) largely forgotten, but in the history of screen Shakespeare both parts were hugely important, because they helped to pay for *Othello* (*see* page 98).

That great film's protracted production history proves that, in spite of all those unfinished projects, Welles could be astonishingly persistent, while the making of *Chimes at Midnight* (*see* page 38), in the winter of 1964–65, highlights the desperate lengths that he would go to in order to retain his collaborators' support.

Producer Emiliano Piedra, not the first man to be mesmerized by the force of Welles's personality, only agreed to invest his share of the $1 million budget (a tiny sum, given the scale of the finished film) because Welles had convinced him they would be shooting a version of *Treasure Island* immediately after the Shakespeare. The set Welles had designed for the Boar's Head would double as the Admiral Benbow Inn for Robert Louis Stevenson's adventure; Welles would play Falstaff *and* Long

John Silver. Simple, really – except that Welles had never intended to make the pirate film.

In order to ensure that his next picture would get made – or at least started, Welles's integrity would evaporate. A pay cheque was a pay cheque, no matter how good or bad the production to which he lent his name; so, in 1966, he could be seen as Cardinal Wolsey in the classy *A Man For All Seasons*, and then as co-host of *Revenge of TV Bloopers*.

The road to appearances on that kind of worthless TV special began with Hollywood's rejection of Welles in the 1940s, and many writers have viewed his preoccupation with Hal's rejection of Falstaff in that context. Keith Baxter, who played Hal in *Chimes*, noted how Welles and Shakespeare's plump knight had much in common: 'always short of money, having to lie, perhaps, and to cheat' to get by. Yet when he dies, Falstaff leaves nothing behind; Welles left us some of the finest movies ever made.

Far left: Welles applies his make-up before going on stage as the Moor in his 1951 production of *Othello* at the Saint James Theatre, London.

Right: Welles, extreme right, with crew members during the making of *Macbeth* (1948) in Hollywood.

10 RICHARD III

Thus I clothe my naked villainy ... and seem a saint, when most I play the devil. Richard, *Richard III*, Act I, Scene iii

'See the greatest film villain of all time!' That is how British cinemas advertised Laurence Olivier's **Richard III** in 1955. Today some people would make different choices: Hannibal Lecter, perhaps, or Darth Vader. But they don't enjoy Richard's greatest asset, the opportunity to stare at his audience and outline his every move. 'I am subtle, false and treacherous', explains Olivier in his opening soliloquy. 'I can smile, and murder while I smile'. There is no conscience, just a relentless quest for power.

Thanks to Richard and the loathing he inspires, the words 'murder', 'hate', 'Hell', 'blood' and 'kill' appear more often in *Richard III* than in any other Shakespeare play, and innocent victims – men, women and children – pile up at an alarming rate. How should film and television directors handle this formidable body count, given that Clarence's and Richard's are the only deaths depicted on stage? Most adaptations have shown some or all of the many reported killings, and the play's copious gore has even inspired two horror movies.

In Rowland Lee's *Tower of London* (US, 1939), Shakespeare's storyline became a bloody vehicle for Boris Karloff, as the king's bald, club-footed executioner, Mord, and Basil Rathbone (Tybalt in MGM's *Romeo and Juliet*) as Richard. 'Crookback and Dragfoot', says Richard to Mord. 'Well, what we lack in physical perfection we make up in brains'. Vincent Price (Clarence in the 1939 film) played Richard in master of schlock Roger Corman's remake, also called *Tower of London* (US, 1962).

Richard III has two other distinguishing features that make it problematic as screen Shakespeare: its great length (only *Hamlet* is longer) and its dependence on a vast array of important – and memorable – subsidiary characters (Lady Anne, Clarence, Hastings, etc.). Shakespeare's text must be heavily and judiciously cut if an adaptation is to run at a tolerable length, function as a wonderful star vehicle *and* allow a heavyweight supporting cast to shine. Separated by 40 years, the Olivier and Ian McKellen films achieved all three targets magnificently. So, by very different methods, did Al Pacino's **Looking for Richard** (1996), and all three versions of the play are described here.

Television's treatment of the play is dominated by three BBC productions, made in 1960, 1964 (both as part of major adaptations of Shakespeare's history plays) and in 1983. Back in the silent era, hugely condensed versions of the play were produced by directors in America, Germany and Britain, where a 20-minute film provided a marvellous record of director/star Frank Benson's stage production at Stratford-upon-Avon in 1911.

Benson is a remarkably able-bodied Richard, laughing with delight at every piece of villainy. After stabbing one victim, he casually wipes his bloody dagger on the dead man's cloak, and seems to cast a magic spell over the grieving Lady Anne (played by Benson's wife, Constance).

Impressive use of dissolve techniques allows the ghosts of Richard's victims to melt in and out of view in the nightmare scene, and a furious swordfight between Richard and Richmond ends a film which serves as a vivid record of early 20th-century stage and screen techniques.

As with so much of Shakespeare, *Richard III* has been the target of occasional spoofs alongside more serious screen versions, none more outrageous than the film of Neil Simon's *The Goodbye Girl* (US, 1977). Aspiring actor Elliot Garfield (Richard Dreyfuss) is cast as Richard in an off-Broadway production, and plays him as cinema's first homosexual hunchback.

Left: Ian McKellen in 1930s costume, in the title role of the BAFTA-winning *Richard III* (1995), directed by Richard Loncraine.

Bottom left: Richard Dreyfuss as actor Elliot Garfield, who plays a homosexual Richard III in *The Goodbye Girl* (1977).

England, 1471. Richard, hunchbacked Duke of Gloucester, sets out to seize the throne occupied by his ailing older brother, King Edward IV. He engineers the murder of his other brother, Clarence, and marries Lady Anne, widow of the Prince of Wales, one of his earlier victims.

After Edward IV's death, Richard quickly has his opponents, Lords Grey, Dorset, Rivers and Hastings executed. Aided by the Duke of Buckingham and Sir William Catesby, he has Edward's two young sons, the rightful heirs to the throne, wrongfully declared bastards and imprisoned. Richard is crowned King and immediately has the two princes murdered.

Queen Anne dies and Buckingham, who has joined the rebel forces led by Henry, Earl of Richmond, is captured and executed. On the night before the climactic Battle of Bosworth Field, Richard is tormented by the ghosts of his victims. Richmond leads the rebels to victory in battle, kills Richard and is crowned King Henry VII.

Above: Frank Benson as Richard, right, preparing for the Battle of Bosworth Field in the British silent *Richard III* (1911).

RICHARD III (1955)
UK 157 MINS COLOUR

CAST	LAURENCE OLIVIER (Richard), CLAIRE BLOOM (Lady Anne), RALPH RICHARDSON (Buckingham), JOHN GIELGUD (Clarence), NORMAN WOOLAND (Catesby), MARY KERRIDGE (Queen Elizabeth), ALEC CLUNES (Hastings), STANLEY BAKER (Richmond)
DIRECTED BY	LAURENCE OLIVIER
PRODUCED BY	LAURENCE OLIVIER
PHOTOGRAPHY	OTTO HELLER
MUSIC	WILLIAM WALTON

Olivier puts a bloodstain on your memory that you can't rub out.

Daily Express

When he watched Laurence Olivier on stage as Richard III in 1944, Noël Coward called it 'the greatest male performance' he had ever witnessed. Ten years after that wildly acclaimed Old Vic production, Olivier transferred his portrayal of the hunchback king to film – with such devastating results that *Variety* greeted 'one of the major classics of the screen'.

For two hours, the action stays firmly within Roger Furse's spacious sets. Dressed in the dark colours of Carmen Dillon's velvet-rich costumes, Richard, his allies and his victims plot and plead in palace corridors, courtyards and throne room, or at the Tower of London. Olivier shuns elaborate camerawork, allowing static scenes to run for as much as ten minutes, fuelled by the brilliance of script and cast. There is not a dull moment.

Stressing the darkness in Richard's soul, Olivier is repeatedly shown as a humped shadow, limping across the floor. His wig of straight, shiny black hair and false, witch's nose are mesmerizingly ugly – based, he said, on the looks of 'the most loathsome man' he'd ever met, American theatre director Jed Harris.

And that voice! Even while outlining his machinations to the audience in a conspiratorial soliloquy, Olivier can retreat into the background, safe in the knowledge that his extraordinary vocal delivery would still cast a spell. He overemphasizes odd syllables, often at close to shrieking pitch. He suddenly accelerates through the last few words of a sentence – a tactic he strengthens by following moments of stillness with abrupt surges of movement.

'Olivier puts a bloodstain on your memory', was The *Daily Express*'s reaction, and Olivier's bravura techniques would make this one of cinema's most parodied performances, with Peter Sellers memorably impersonating Richard singing The Beatles'

'A Hard Day's Night' on British television in 1965. Olivier was easily imitated, yes, but never surpassed.

Villains and victims

Olivier does not, however, steal every scene. As his partners in crime, Norman Wooland makes a suavely menacing Catesby and Ralph Richardson's apparent benevolence makes Buckingham's power-hungry malice singularly unnerving. John Gielgud gives great dignity to the imprisoned Clarence, and his murder – skull bashed in before he is drowned in a barrel of wine – is horrific.

Claire Bloom, tearful and saintly as Lady Anne, provides a stunning climax to the wooing scene when she kisses Richard with unmistakeable passion. Our shock at her capitulation is matched by the fleeting glimpse of the bloody axe which beheads Hastings – skilfully played by Alec Clunes, who combines a politician's fatal vanity with patriotic woe at his country's fate.

Pamela Brown's is the most interesting performance. She hovers in several scenes as Jane Shore, mistress to Hastings and King Edward, and, without delivering a single word, makes this woman's sexual and emotional hold over both men a major thread in the story. It is the most telling screen appearance by a Shakespearean character never seen on stage.

Only in the film's set-piece finale does Olivier's directing disappoint. Although no amount of cinematic flair could have made the Battle of Bosworth Field equal the victory-against-impossible-odds impact of *Henry V* 's Agincourt sequence, Olivier delivers a disappointingly muddled affray. There are deflating cuts between long- and medium-shots filmed on the bleached Spanish earth of a bull farm outside Madrid, and close-ups of the

Above: Laurence Olivier as Richard, left, with Ralph Richardson as Buckingham. The king dismisses his accomplice's request for an earldom by declaring 'I am not in the giving vein today'.

Right: Laurence Olivier as Richard before the climactic Battle of Bosworth Field, filmed on a bull farm outside Madrid.

mounted duel between Richard and Richmond, obviously shot on the fake grass of a Shepperton soundstage.

The anticlimax is offset by another rousing William Walton score, and by Richard's demise. Twenty soldiers swoop down to stab and batter him, then retreat to watch his agonized death, as Olivier's body writhes and twitches in time to the music. It is an astonishing end for a character that earned Olivier another Oscar nomination for Best Actor (he lost out to *The King and I*'s Yul Brynner).

He won the BAFTA for Best British Film, and **Richard III** did excellent business in UK cinemas. It fared less well at the American box office because of an unprecedented deal with NBC, worth $500,000 (about $7 million today). On the same day as its US theatrical release, in March 1956, **Richard III** was transmitted on television in 45 states. Some 25 million people watched it in black and white – almost certainly a larger audience than had watched *Richard III* in 350 years of stage productions.

Right: Claire Bloom as the sleepless Lady Anne, centre, with Laurence Olivier as Richard.

RICHARD III (1995)

UK 104 MINS COLOUR

CAST	IAN MCKELLEN (Richard), KRISTIN SCOTT THOMAS (Anne), JIM BROADBENT (Buckingham), NIGEL HAWTHORNE (Clarence), TIM MCINNERNY (Catesby), ANNETTE BENING (Queen Elizabeth), ROBERT DOWNEY JNR (Rivers), JIM CARTER (Hastings), BILL PATTERSON (Ratcliffe), EDWARD HARDWICKE (Stanley), DOMINIC WEST (Richmond)
DIRECTED BY	RICHARD LONCRAINE
PRODUCEED BY	LISA KATSELAS PARÉ, STEPHEN BAYLY
SCREENPLAY	RICHARD LONCRAINE, IAN MCKELLEN
PHOTOGRAPHY	PETER BIZIOU
MUSIC	TREVOR JONES

A powerful contender for the title of most entertaining Shakespeare film ever made. Independent on Sunday

A tank smashes through the wall of an army base. A soldier wearing a gas mask climbs from the turret and shoots dead a handsome young officer and his elderly father. The killer peels off his mask and reveals the sneering features of Ian McKellen, as gunshots on the soundtrack blast letters onto the screen: RICHARD III.

Director Richard Loncraine said that this stunning opening was designed to grab the attention of sceptical cinemagoers: 'people going "Oh, yeah, bloody Shakespeare, what time's it finish?"'. It set the tone for an intelligent and dizzyingly paced adaptation, driven forward by Loncraine with all the economy that you would expect from a man who had directed 400 commercials.

The $10 million film was developed from 1990's justifiably acclaimed National Theatre production, starring McKellen and directed by Richard Eyre, which had relocated the action from the 1480s to the 1930s and linked Richard's reign of terror to those of Mussolini and Hitler. Retaining this modern setting, McKellen and Loncraine's BAFTA-nominated screenplay tinkers with the status of Shakespeare's characters and brings crystal clarity to the original plot's fiendishly complex York v Lancaster rivalries.

Out go all those earls, dukes and knights to be replaced by a more familiar, modern style of military dictatorship (Richard, Buckingham, Catesby, Tyrrel, Ratcliffe), opposed by the Prime Minister (Hastings), air force chief (Stanley) and naval commander (Richmond).

The screen is filled with fascist imagery, thanks to Shuna Harwood's costumes and Tony Burrough's evocative production design, which makes brilliant use of some skilfully chosen locations (London's then disused Bankside Power Station – now the Tate Modern art gallery – became the Tower). Harwood and Burrough, who both won BAFTA awards and Oscar nominations, turn Richard's coronation rally into a mini-Nuremberg, but McKellen does not play him as a ranting Führer.

His BAFTA-nominated portrayal has authority, mischief and malice to spare. Pale and sickly (prosthetics made the left side of his face appear to sag), with a pencil moustache above chain-smoking lips, his deformity is more discreet than Olivier's Richard – and so is his acting technique. Like his famous predecessor, he delights in speaking directly to camera (even concluding his opening solioquy while taking a pee), but he does so in softer, less mannered tones, and creates a more human anti-hero than Olivier's.

Around him, Annette Bening hits the right, despairing notes as Queen Elizabeth (her casting was a historical nod to Edward VIII's scandalous 1937 marriage to American divorcee Wallis Simpson) and Kristin Scott Thomas's Lady Anne chillingly consumes assorted narcotics to blot out the horror of sharing Richard's bed.

Jim Broadbent is ambitiously oily as Buckingham and Adrian Dunbar plays Richard's hitman, Tyrrel (a role greatly expanded from the play), with sneering menace. Robert Downey Jnr, as Elizabeth's brash brother, Rivers, is the only actor unable to make the verse seem as if it is his character's natural way of speaking.

Violent ends

Rivers is stabbed while in bed with an air hostess – the most specatcular death in a movie overflowing with horrors that Shakespeare kept off stage. In addition to the opening carnage (showing the murders of the Prince of Wales and King from *Henry VI, Part 3*), Richard's victims are hanged, strangled and suffocated. Nigel Hawthorne's pitiful Clarence has his throat slit.

Richard even blows away one of his own men in the explosive Bosworth sequence, which is marred slightly by the film's overblown final shot: Richard's slow-motion tumble from a high girder into a hellish inferno, as Al Jolson croons 'I'm Sitting on Top of the World'.

Moments like that irritated some American reviewers, with *The Village Voice* dismissing the film as 'flashy and lurid ... a wild bore'. *Variety* praised the 'machine-gun pacing', and a set of overwhelmingly positive British reviews included that in the *Independent on Sunday*, which called **Richard III** 'a powerful contender' for the title of most entertaining Shakespeare film ever made.

Grosses of just $2.7 million in the US and about $1.5 million in the UK were lower than the film deserved, perhaps bearing out the prediction made by Hollywood producer Sam Goldwyn, who warned McKellen that the play was 'too dark' for a public that 'only wants Pollyanna Shakespeare'. Dark it most certainly is, yet this realization of **Richard III** also vindicates McKellen's firm belief that 'you don't have to treat Shakespeare reverently to revere him'.

Below: Kristin Scott Thomas as Lady Anne, visiting a hospital mortuary to view the corpse of her murdered husband.

Right: Ian McKellen as the hunchback king, firing at enemy aircraft in the explosive finale.

RICHARD III

LOOKING FOR RICHARD (1996)

US 112 MINS COLOUR

CAST	AL PACINO (Narrator/Richard III), WINONA RYDER (Lady Anne), KEVIN SPACEY (Buckingham), ALEC BALDWIN (Clarence), AIDAN QUINN (Richmond)
DIRECTED BY	AL PACINO
PRODUCED BY	MICHAEL HADGE, AL PACINO
PHOTOGRAPHY	ROBERT LEACOCK
MUSIC	HOWARD SHORE

Left: Al Pacino as Richard, left, rehearsing in New York with Winona Ryder as Lady Anne.

It has always been a dream of mine to communicate how I feel about Shakespeare to other people.

Al Pacino

Bottom left: Al Pacino gives an outstanding, restrained performance in the filmed extracts from *Richard III*.

Right: Pacino shares a joke with crew members while filming Richard III's death at the Battle of Bosworth Field.

You can't really label **Looking for Richard**. At one moment it is a gripping Shakespeare adaptation, then it turns into a *The Making of ...* documentary. You could also call it an educational guide to understanding and acting Shakespeare. The best approach is to throw away genre tags and celebrate it as a glorious one-off.

At the start of his enthusiastic narration, Pacino tells us: 'It has always been a dream of mine to communicate how I feel about Shakespeare to other people'. To do so, he returned to Richard III, a role he had already played on stage in Boston and on Broadway.

He considered filming the whole play 'straight', but cost – and the shadow of Olivier's film – deterred him. Instead, he and his chief collaborator, writer and actor Frederic Kimball, accumulated 80 hours of documentary footage – a three-year labour of love funded out of Pacino's own pocket, with the star returning to the project in between appearances in films such as *Carlito's Way*.

The pair's material has been edited into a freewheeling, unpretentious patchwork. They make a 'pilgrimage' to Shakespeare's birthplace and hit the streets of New York, asking ordinary people what they think about the Bard.

Shakespearean performers from both sides of the Atlantic are interviewed, with Kevin Kline, Kenneth Branagh and Vanessa Redgrave offering intelligent soundbites about iambic pentameters, or the difficulties Shakespeare holds for American actors. There are pithy contributions, too, from Peter Brook, director of the 1971 *King Lear*, as well as from two frustratingly unidentified English academics.

The interviews are intercut with footage of Pacino and Kimball scouting locations for filmed scenes from the play and rehearsing the cast in a high-rise office. The pair's occasional disagreements and Pacino's willingness to show his frustration at the complexity of *Richard III*'s language and plot are hugely endearing. After failing to explain a particularly intricate scene to co-producer Michael Hadge, Pacino says: 'It's very confusing. I don't know why we even bother doing this at all.'

Shakespeare as sport

Even more enjoyable are the sparely designed extracts. Despite the inevitable omission of numerous characters and incidents, Pacino's sportscast-style commentary ('Richard's in pretty good shape'; 'Richard needs to move fast.') means that prior knowledge of the play is not required.

His choice of ten pivotal scenes enables the plot to build to its climax just as effectively as in the Olivier or McKellen films. We see Clarence pleading for his life with the two murderers, a scene that gives Alec Baldwin the chance to show a subtle touch rarely seen in his Hollywood roles. Winona Ryder does the same as Lady Anne, in the grotesque seduction scene. We also watch the disintegration of the criminal alliance between Richard and Buckingham (Kevin Spacey at his sly, intelligent best), before Pacino meets a bloody end at Bosworth Field, stuck like a wild boar by Aidan Quinn's Richmond. A string of experienced if unfamiliar faces fill the supporting roles superbly.

To his immense credit, Pacino the director does not overindulge Pacino the star. His accent sometimes hovers somewhere between England and New York, but his trademarks – sudden rises in volume at odd points in a speech, frequent 'Hah!'s – are kept in check. This is quiet, irresistible villainy, not far removed from his celebrated performance as *The Godfather*'s Michael Corleone – like Richard, an attractive tyrant so ruthless he has his own brother executed.

Looking for Richard attracted universal acclaim. *The Village Voice* found it 'mesmerizing', while *Rolling Stone* called it 'outrageous fun'. 'Educational cinema at its most inventive and entertaining', said London's *Time Out*. Such praise wasn't going to make the film a box-office smash, although a US gross of $1.36 million was respectable for a documentary, and **Looking for Richard** remains popular on video in schools and colleges.

Perhaps the highest compliment which should be paid to this 'docu-drama type thing', as Pacino labels it, is that it leaves you longing to watch the cast perform *Richard III* in full.

ROMEO AND JULIET

Some shall be pardoned and some punished. For never was a story of more woe than this of Juliet and her Romeo.

Prince, *Romeo and Juliet*, Act V, Scene iii

Verona. A bloody street fight between members of the feuding Montague and Capulet clans forces Verona's prince to threaten lords Montague and Capulet with death if the violence resumes.

That night, Montague's son, Romeo, joins his cynical friend, Mercutio, and cousin, Benvolio, to gatecrash a masked party at Capulet's house. There, Romeo and Juliet, Capulet's 13-year-old daughter, fall instantly in love and immediately decide to get married.

The next morning, Romeo tells Juliet's devoted Nurse to send her to his confessor, Friar Laurence. The Friar weds the lovers in secret, hoping that the marriage may reconcile the two families.

Immediately after the ceremony, Juliet's hot-headed cousin, Tybalt, furious at Romeo's presence at the party, tracks him down and challenges him. When Romeo refuses to fight, Mercutio takes his place in the duel and is fatally wounded by Tybalt as Romeo tries to part them. In revenge, Romeo kills Tybalt and flees the scene. The Prince banishes him from Verona for life. After spending the night with Juliet, Romeo leaves for Mantua.

Juliet is ordered by her parents to marry Paris, a young Count, in two days' time, and the Nurse advises her to forget Romeo. In suicidal despair, she goes to Friar Laurence, who gives her a sleeping potion to take the night before the wedding which will make her appear dead for 42 hours. Laurence will summon Romeo to meet her as she wakes inside the Capulet tomb.

The plan works, and Juliet's shocked and grieving parents lay her in the tomb. But the friar carrying Laurence's explanatory letter to Romeo cannot reach Mantua. Believing Juliet is really dead, Romeo buys lethal poison and returns to Verona to die beside his wife. Paris tries to stop Romeo entering the tomb, they fight and Paris is killed. Once inside, Romeo kisses Juliet goodbye and swallows the poison. Juliet awakes, sees Romeo and, ignoring the Friar's pleas for her to leave, stabs herself. The lovers' deaths convince Capulet and Montague to make peace.

To gauge the universal appeal of *Romeo and Juliet*, you just have to scan the list of countries whose directors have adapted it for the screen: Brazil, Britain, Egypt, France, Germany, India, Israel, Italy, Spain and the US.

Some of these films use modern dialogue and localized, modern settings, and the age of the actors playing the star-crossed leads varies from 15 to at least 43, but the central focus is always the same: a young couple so in love they would kill themselves rather than be driven apart.

The play's story has 24-carat appeal for the teenagers and twentysomethings who have dominated the world's movie audiences for 30 years. It is no coincidence that the only Shakespeare play utterly dominated by a teenage love story has inspired cinema's three biggest Shakespearean hits: Franco Zeffirelli and Baz Luhrmann's *Romeo and Juliet* films and *Shakespeare in Love*.

The two lovers are not, of course, the only reason to see *Romeo and Juliet* on stage or screen – and when gushingly portrayed, they are the *last* reason to buy a ticket. For many viewers the play's greatest strengths lie elsewhere: in the Friar's good intentions, the Nurse's maternal loyalty to Juliet and, above all, in the crackling, unrestrained wit of Mercutio, whose murder leaves a gaping hole in the remainder of the action.

From the Mercutio-Tybalt duel onwards, the speed with which events spiral tragically out of control is well suited to energetic film-making. With strong performances and confident direction, audiences should be too caught up in the lovers' fortunes to question the sleeping potion finale, which stretches credulity to fairy-tale limits. After all, just what kind of experiments has Friar Laurence been conducting to establish that the dose he gives Juliet will work for precisely 'two-and-forty hours'?

Top left: Claire Danes, left, and Leonardo DiCaprio as the lovers in *William Shakespeare's Romeo + Juliet* (1996), directed by Baz Luhrmann.

Right: Richard Beymer as Tony, left, bids farewell to Natalie Wood as Maria in the Oscar-winning *West Side Story* (1961), which moved *Romeo and Juliet* to New York.

The first, silent, film version was directed in France by Clement Maurice in 1900 and film-makers in the US, Britain, Germany and Italy followed suit. Rival American versions from 1916, now lost, were among the longest silent Shakespeares ever made, at 50 and 80 minutes.

The production design for George Cukor's **Romeo and Juliet** (1936) established a lavish black-and-white benchmark later exceeded by the colourful Italian locations used by Renato Castellani (1954) and Zeffirelli (1968). **West Side Story** (1961) and the 1996 Luhrmann adaptation both brought the story to modern-day America.

Alongside these five films, all covered in this chapter, lesser-known screen adaptations include a 1964 Italian picture whose frantic, action-packed approach is attributable to director Riccardo Freda's previous experience – on low-budget 'spear-and-sandals' gladiator pictures. On the small screen, the BBC produced the play roughly once a decade between 1947 and 1978, the last version boasting a young Alan Rickman as Tybalt.

Old story, new words

Even before **West Side Story**, some film-makers were already choosing what, in commercial terms, may be the best option: keeping Shakespeare's plot, but adding their own dialogue and, sometimes, new characters. Among the more unusual of these adaptations is André Cayette's *Lovers of Verona* (France, 1949), reviewed by Britain's *Star* newspaper as 'a tender piece of romanticism'.

Angelo (Serge Reggiani), a young glassblower, and Georgia (Anouk Aimée), daughter of a former Fascist mayor, fall in love when they become stand-ins for the stars of a *Romeo and Juliet* film. Georgia's family are persuaded by her fiancé to shoot Angelo, and she kills herself. The couple die on the film studio set of Juliet's tomb. .

Two directors gave the play a Cold War spin – and a happy ending. In Anthony Asquith's *The Young Lovers* (UK, 1954), winner of a BAFTA award for Best Screenplay, Anna Sobek, the daughter of a minister from an unspecified communist state, falls for Ted Knight, who works in the code room of the American Embassy in London. They keep their affair and Anna's pregnancy secret and their eventual escape from Britain by sea was dubbed 'agonizingly moving' by the *Daily Express*.

Peter Ustinov's comedy, *Romanoff and Juliet* (US, 1961) reverses *The Young Lovers*' East-West divide. In the imaginary Eastern Bloc country of Concordia, Igor Romanoff (John Gavin) is smitten by Juliet Moulsworth (Sandra Dee), daughter of the American ambassador. Despite the interference of a Tybalt-like KGB agent, and the Moulsworth parents' attempt to wed Juliet to her wimpish ex-boyfriend, the couple end up married. Shakespeare would have found the switch from tragedy to comedy easier to understand than the film's mockery of contemporary nuclear hysteria, in a sub-plot involving a small boy who builds an Atom bomb with a toy chemistry set.

More recently, Brazilian television's *Romeu e Julieta* (1980) set Shakespeare's story among rival student groups at a

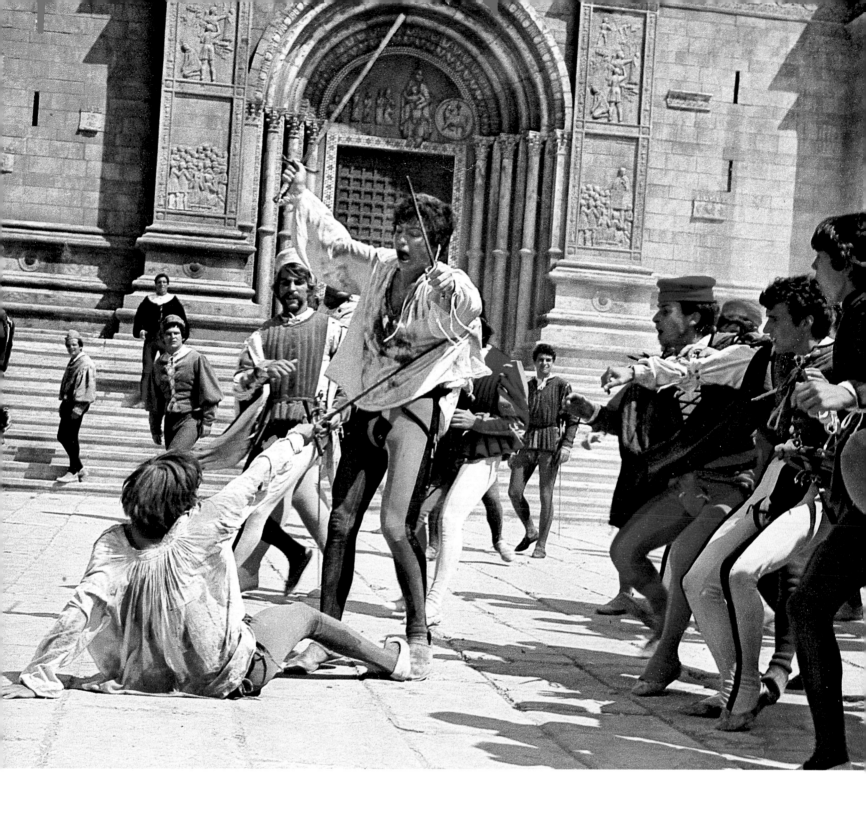

university in Ouro Preto, a mining town. In the 1990s, a number of films have concentrated on the racial divide highlighted in **West Side Story**: *Henna* (India, 1992), paired a Pakistani Muslim girl with an Indian Hindu boy; the lovers in *Torn Apart* (1990) were an Israeli soldier (Adrian Pasdar) and an Arab girl (Cecilia Peck, daughter of Gregory).

Inevitably, there have also been spoofs, with the balcony scene parodied in countless film and TV revue sketches. Popeye the Sailor had six minutes in which to woo Olive Oyl with his best Romeo impression in the cartoon short, *Shakespearian Spinach* (1940).

The ultimate insult to Shakespearean artistry came in 1995, when America's Troma Pictures, specialists in brainless, low-budget splatter movies, delivered *Tromeo and Juliet* (US, 1995), a tediously outrageous feast of body-piercing, mutilation, dismemberment and soft-core, kinky sex.

Juliet is the sexually abused daughter of a New York porn tycoon and the Nurse is a tattooed lesbian cook. 'Parting is such sweet sorrow', says Juliet. 'It totally sucks', replies Tromeo. Producer/director Lloyd Kaufman, tongue presumably in cheek, insisted that Shakespeare would have loved it: 'I've put in all the car crashes and decapitations he really wanted'.

ROMEO AND JULIET (1936)

US 123 MINS B/W

CAST	LESLIE HOWARD (Romeo), NORMA SHEARER (Juliet), REGINALD DENNY (Benvolio), JOHN BARRYMORE (Mercutio), BASIL RATHBONE (Tybalt), EDNA MAY OLIVER (Nurse), HENRY KOLKER (Friar Laurence), C. AUBREY SMITH (Lord Capulet), VIOLET KEMBLE (Lady Capulet), RALPH FORBES (Paris)
DIRECTED BY	GEORGE CUKOR
PRODUCED BY	IRVING G. THALBERG
ADAPTED BY	TALBOT JENNINGS
PHOTOGRAPHY	WILLIAM DANIELS
MUSIC	HERBERT STOTHART

Right: Leslie Howard as Romeo, left, bidding farewell to Norma Shearer's Juliet after their wedding night.

MGM's **Romeo and Juliet** was Hollywood's first feature-length adaptation of a Shakespeare tragedy. Producer Irving G. Thalberg pronounced it 'a cultural undertaking of importance', and the studio pulled out all the stops.

In the quest for 'authenticity', months of research went into the vast sets, and the 1,200 costumes designed by Oliver Messel and Adrian. William Strunk Jnr, Professor of English at Cornell University, was hired as literary adviser to ensure, he said, 'that no injustice was done' to Shakespeare. It cost $2 million – perhaps $80 million today – and MGM deserved 11 out of 10 for effort. The finished product rates less highly.

The age of the stars was the fatal flaw. Shakespeare's pivotal characters – Juliet, Romeo, Tybalt and Mercutio – were entrusted, respectively, to Norma Shearer (35), Leslie Howard (43), Basil Rathbone (44), and John Barrymore (54). Once they were chosen, the film unquestionably had star power, but could not hope to capture the play's tragic spirit: impetuous, *young* lives cut short.

Howard and Shearer (whose casting was not unconnected to her being Thalberg's wife) move in a spectacular world of romantic luxury, with Herbert Stothart's arrangements of Tchaikovsky's *Romeo and Juliet* as appropriately grand theme music. The magnificently choreographed ballet during the Capulet ball is a breathtaking highlight: Howard's Romeo watches Juliet rejecting a dozen masked suitors before dancing with Ralph Forbes's muscular Paris.

Once admiration turns to conversation, however, Howard and Shearer seem overwhelmed by an obligation to deliver Shakespeare's verse with more reverence than feeling. Cukor and his stars forget that however ornate the language of the balcony or wedding-night scenes, the words come to life only in the mouths of flesh-and-blood characters. Howard and Shearer fall short of that description.

Howard had suggested in a tie-in book that making Romeo interesting was 'a task to frighten any actor', and it proves beyond him. Perhaps inevitably, given his age, this self-absorbed Romeo would be more at home playing Hamlet.

Above: John Barrymore as Mercutio, front left, fights a fatal duel with Basil Rathbone's Tybalt, watched by Leslie Howard as Romeo, centre.

Left: Leslie Howard and Norma Shearer as the lovers – beautiful but bland – and both too old for their roles.

Better off without him ...

Only when Romeo has been banished can Shearer lift Juliet clear of a chaste, Snow White persona (she is first seen feeding deer in the Capulet garden!). There is real pain when she defies her father (gruff C. Aubrey Smith) and silently renounces the Nurse (shrill-voiced Edna May Oliver) – scenes which helped earn her a Best Actress Oscar nomination.

Set against these leads and the one-dimensional, though Oscar-nominated, villainy of Rathbone's Tybalt, Barrymore's hammy Mercutio is refreshing. He fleetingly brings some *joie de vivre* to Cukor's Verona, then dies cursing the Capulet and Montague clans with absurd politeness – a characteristic that deadens the film. By the time the lovers have died prettily, the energy of the opening scene (a massed swordfight broken up by the prince's cavalry charge) seems a distant memory.

Critical opinion generally praised the film's production values ahead of its performances, with *The New York Times* suggesting that the 'expansive' sets had 'gloriously released the play from the limitations of the stage'. *The New York Sun* mourned the absence of tragedy: 'It does not wring the heart, nor stir tears of sweet sympathy or bitter resentment.'

Thalberg lived just long enough to absorb this response to a project he had nurtured for ten years, but not his Best Picture Oscar nomination: aged 37, he died of pneumonia in September 1936, three weeks after **Romeo and Juliet**'s première.

It eventually grossed almost $2 million, yet the huge print and marketing costs left MGM with a loss of $900,000 and it was that relatively poor performance which contributed to Hollywood's refusal to tackle the Bard for another 17 years, until MGM re-entered the arena with *Julius Caesar*.

Cukor himself, looking back on **Romeo and Juliet** in 1971, conceded that his lovers had been 'too stodgy'. He went on: 'It's one picture that if I had to do over again, I'd know how. I'd get the garlic and the Mediterranean into it.'

11

ROMEO AND JULIET (1954)
ITALY/UK 138 MINS COLOUR

CAST	LAURENCE HARVEY (Romeo), SUSAN SHENTALL (Juliet), BILL TRAVERS (Benvolio), ALDO ZOLLO (Mercutio), ENZO FIERMONTE (Tybalt), FLORA ROBSON (Nurse), MERVYN JOHNS (Friar Laurence), SEBASTIAN CABOT (Capulet), LYDIA SHERWOOD (Lady Capulet), NORMAN WOOLAND (Paris)
DIRECTED BY	RENATO CASTELLANI
PRODUCED BY	SANDRO GHENZI
PHOTOGRAPHY	ROBERT KRASKER
MUSIC	ROMAN VLAD

Renato Castellani loved filming stories about young people struggling against a hostile society, so it was no surprise that when he turned to Shakespeare he chose *Romeo and Juliet*.

Like many post-war Italian directors, Castellani also loved his work to look as realistic as possible and so the bulk of **Romeo and Juliet**'s seven-month shoot was spent at medieval locations in Siena, Venice, Verona and Montagnana.

Robert Krasker, the cinematographer who shot Olivier's *Henry V* so brilliantly, was on hand to capture sunlit stone walls, scarlet canopies on market stalls and cloudless blue skies. The trouble is that Castellani was seduced by local colour and forgot drama.

Posters promised that Laurence Harvey, then 25 and a rising star with the Royal Shakespeare Company, would bring 'new fire and excitement to Romeo'. If only. He went on to provide a compelling presence in hard-edged, contemporary British dramas like *Room at the Top*, but as the Montague romantic he appears to love himself, his poetry and his poses, with Juliet in fourth place.

His voice, so smooth that it makes James Mason's sound as coarse as sandpaper, over-emphasizes every rhyme, smothering the life out of Shakespeare's verse. As for the 'fire-eyed fury' that drives Romeo to kill Tybalt and Paris, here it is more like mild irritation.

Shentall's Juliet has the lighter, unaffected touch you'd expect from an 18-year-old Derbyshire girl making her acting debut. With the beauty of a prim, English version of Grace Kelly, she had been plucked from secretarial college.

Opposite such an unresponsive Romeo, she has little opportunity to suggest teenage ardour (the pair hardly even kiss), but makes the most of her scenes with a furious father (blustering, operatic Sebastian Cabot) and her chilling speech before taking the sleeping potion. She married soon after shooting ended, and never returned to screen acting.

What a waste
The flat love story might be tolerable if the mood were lifted by livelier characters. Yet Castellani trims the Nurse's part to the bone, makes Friar Laurence an irritating ditherer and, unforgivably, reduces the play's most remarkable creation, Mercutio, to the tiniest of cameos. Any sense of a deep friendship between

Romeo and Mercutio vanishes and, after the latter's murder you feel that Tybalt might just as well have killed a total stranger.

The man cast as Mercutio, Aldo Zollo, was a Veronese architect, not a professional actor. Several other parts were filled by Italian amateurs (Montague was played by Giulio Garbinetti, a Venetian gondolier, and the Prince by Giovanni Rota, a novelist). This was a regular Castellani tactic in his quest for 'realism', although here it adds nothing.

While the plot's major incidents survive, so much of the play's finest dialogue is absent that the characters' behaviour sometimes seems confusingly unmotivated. It is easy to agree with the *New Statesman* reviewer who felt that no other screen adaptation left Shakespeare's text 'so hacked, patched and insensitively thrown away'.

Castellani's cuts allow him more time for pretty images rather than urgent action, so the film drags. In the interior scenes, figures appear in neat, static poses with the edge of the screen acting like a picture frame; the costumes and production design were heavily influenced by Renaissance artists like Raphael and Bellini. If he was attempting to match the beauty of Shakespeare's poetry with his screen imagery, Castellani succeeds only in providing rich material for art historians, and leaves most viewers starved of involvement. *The Nation* felt 'the tragedy collapses and is swept away in a visual flood', although *Variety* praised 'a combined treat for the eye and ear', which was 'wholly absorbing, frequently moving'. Remarkably, the Jury at the 1954 Venice Film Festival gave Castellani its Grand Prix, ahead of *On the Waterfront*.

British cinemagoers who may have come away disappointed could at least relax at home with the film's exclusive promotional accessories: couples could sit back on a couch covered in 'The Romeo and Juliet Fabric'; women could ease their tired feet into a pair of 'Juliet Slippers' available in black, red or emerald suede at 39 shillings a pair.

> The tragedy collapses and is swept away in a visual flood. The Nation

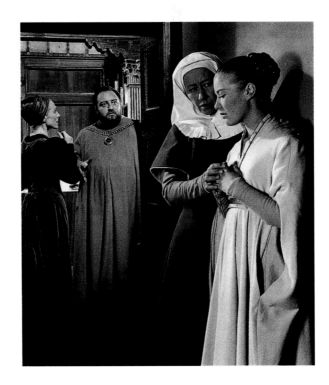

Left: Susan Shentall as Juliet, far right, is comforted by Flora Robson as Nurse. Sebastian Cabot, second left, and Lydia Sherwood play Lord and Lady Capulet.

Right: Laurence Harvey as Romeo, in the Capulet tomb with Susan Shentall as the 'dead' Juliet. It was Shentall's one and only screen appearance.

WEST SIDE STORY (1961)

US 153 MINS COLOUR

CAST	RICHARD BEYMER (Tony), NATALIE WOOD (Maria), RUSS TAMBLYN (Riff), GEORGE CHAKIRIS (Bernardo), RITA MORENO (Anita), NED GLASS (Doc), JOSE DE VEGA (Chino), SIMON OAKLAND (Lt Schrank), WILLIAM BRAMLEY (Officer Krupke)
DIRECTED BY	ROBERT WISE/JEROME ROBBINS
PRODUCED BY	ROBERT WISE
SCREENPLAY	ERNEST LEHMAN
BOOK	ARTHUR LAURENTS
MUSIC	LEONARD BERNSTEIN
LYRICS	STEPHEN SONDHEIM
PHOTOGRAPHY	DANIEL L. FAPP

Something amazing happens in **West Side Story**: 16th-century theatrical genius inspires a 20th-century film masterpiece. *Romeo and Juliet* is relocated to 1950s New York and Shakespeare's dramatic energy and rich verse become the wit and longing of Stephen Sondheim's lyrics, Leonard Bernstein's pulsating music, and the poetry of Jerome Robbins' choreography.

As in the original stage musical, which triumphed on Broadway in 1957, gangs of white American Jets (Montagues) take on Puerto Rican Sharks (Capulets). Romeo becomes Tony, who works for the elderly Doc (the Friar Laurence figure), in his soda shop, leaving Riff (Mercutio), who co-founded the Jets with Tony, to run the gang alone.

Maria (Juliet) works in a bridal shop after being brought from Puerto Rico by her volatile brother, Bernardo (Tybalt and Capulet combined). Bernardo runs the Sharks, dates Anita (who fills the Nurse's shoes as Maria's confidante) and wants Maria to marry Chino (Paris). Racist police Lieutenant Schrank and ineffectual Officer Krupke take on the Prince's legal role, arriving at the end of the film's dazzling opening 'fight', in which Jets and Sharks trade dance steps instead of blows.

Romeo and Juliet's great love poetry is matched by the duets and solos for Tony (the handsome, anodyne Richard Beymer) and Maria (Natalie Wood, giving a devastating portrayal of innocence betrayed). Dubbed by Jimmy Bryant and Marni Nixon, their songs include the tingling anticipation of Maria's 'I Feel Pretty',

the dazed joy of Tony's 'Maria' and the lovers' shared hope in 'Tonight', during their 'balcony' scene on a fire escape.

Their hesitant intimacy is played off against the overwhelming vitality of the Jets' 'Gee, Officer Krupke' (a mocking, 'Don't-blame-us-for-being-delinquents' lament), and the Sharks girls' equally ironic view of immigrant life, 'America' – an incomparable rooftop stomp led by Rita Moreno's fiery Anita and George Chakiris's brooding Bernardo.

Musical youth

These arm-thrusting, pelvis-tilting ensembles are a delight to watch. Crucially, the songs make you care about *all* of the singers, from the very sexy relationship between Moreno and Chakiris, down to the most junior Jet. It is here that **West Side Story** departs most strikingly from a play in which only the lovers and Mercutio are likely to move us.

Here, the focus on youth never wavers (Doc, Schrank and Krupke make just a handful of appearances, Maria's parents remain unseen) and the racial prejudice which divides these blue-collar kids is a more disturbing and convincing motor for the plot than the motiveless feud that separates *Romeo and Juliet*'s blue-blooded families.

Admittedly, nobody in 1961 thought the elaborately choreographed violence or the Jets' hip, sanitized street talk were an accurate portrayal of gang culture. The singing and dancing lift

West Side Story one step away from reality and Robert Wise pushes it further, occasionally surrounding Tony and Maria with dream-like optical effects. Yet none of this stops you believing in the story totally, and the ending is shockingly real – without relying on Shakespeare's potions, fateful bad timing and suicides.

After the 'rumble' in which Bernardo kills Riff and Tony kills Bernardo, Anita is almost raped by the Jets while trying to deliver a message from Maria to Tony. Enraged, she tells the Jets that Chino has killed Maria. Tony goes looking for Chino, who shoots him, and he dies in Maria's arms. As Tony's body is carried away by Jets and Sharks, nobody says – or sings – a word.

That stunned silence is an extraordinary conclusion to a film which became a critical and box-office sensation. *Saturday Review* hailed a 'triumphant work of art' and Britain's *Daily Express* announced: 'To call this a song and dance film would be to mock it'.

Such verdicts should have eased the hurt felt by Robbins, deviser and director of the Broadway show, who was dismissed mid-way through filming on the $5 million production (about $65 million today), studio executives having decided his co-directing partnership with Wise was not working.

Further consolation came when Robbins and Wise collected Best Director Oscars. Moreno and Chakiris were among those also honoured, as the Academy gave **West Side Story** ten awards – an apt haul for the greatest film musical ever made.

Left: Richard Beymer as Tony, left, gets ready to 'rumble' with George Chakiris as Bernardo. Chakiris won an Oscar as Best Supporting Actor.

Right: Rita Moreno as Anita, centre, launches the Shark girls' roof-top rendition of 'America', a deeply ironic view of immigrant life.

ROMEO AND JULIET (1968)
ITALY/GB 152 MINS COLOUR

CAST	LEONARD WHITING (Romeo), OLIVIA HUSSEY (Juliet), JOHN MCENERY (Mercutio), MICHAEL YORK (Tybalt), PAT HEYWOOD (Nurse), MILO O'SHEA (Friar Laurence), BRUCE ROBINSON (Benvolio), PAUL HARDWICK (Capulet), NATASHA PARRY (Lady Capulet), ROBERTO BISACCO (Paris), ROBERT STEPHENS (Prince)
DIRECTED BY	FRANCO ZEFFIRELLI
PRODUCED BY	ANTHONY HAVELOCK-ALLAN AND JOHN BRABOURNE
SCREENPLAY	FRANCO BRUSATI AND MASOLINO D'AMICO
PHOTOGRAPHY	PASQUALE DE SANTIS
MUSIC	NINO ROTA

Franco Zeffirelli sowed the seeds of his box-office triumph with **Romeo and Juliet** eight years before the film was released. In 1960, the Italian director's first stage Shakespeare was *Romeo and Juliet* at London's Old Vic theatre. He cast John Stride, then 23, and Judi Dench, 25, as arguably the most youthful star-crossed lovers ever seen in the West End, and the production was a huge hit.

In 1967, immediately after his success with *The Taming of the Shrew* (*see* pages 140–1), Zeffirelli returned to *Romeo*, hoping to transfer onto film the passion generated at the Old Vic. He felt confident of attracting a vast international audience, but most studios reckoned that the Bard was a poor commercial prospect. Eventually, Paramount Studios agreed to put up $800,000, much less than Zeffirelli wanted.

Believing that 'the kids in the story are like teenagers today', he chose actors almost as young as their characters: Leonard Whiting was 17, Olivia Hussey, chosen ahead of 350 hopefuls, just 15. Casting these total unknowns was a major gamble.

Following the precedent set by Renato Castellani in the 1954 *Romeo*, Zeffirelli filmed as much as possible at Italian locations: much of the three-month shoot was spent in small towns in Tuscany and Umbria (Verona now looked too modern), with additional interiors recreated at Cinecittà Studios in Rome.

Shakespeare's action unfolds in medieval churches, sun-drenched piazzas and shady side-streets, as Zeffirelli fills the screen with handsome, athletic boys in colour-coded tights and codpieces (garish red-and-yellow for Capulets, discreet blue for Montagues).

From the opening, frenzied brawl to the final procession of Capulet and Montague mourners, the whole film, as Richard Burton said to Zeffirelli after seeing some early footage, 'looks sensational'. Yet Burton also cautioned: 'You've got problems with the verse'. Whiting and Hussey were the chief culprits.

As intended, their youth makes the lovers' infatuation more credible than in Cukor or Castellani. Their beauty is beyond question (the nudity in the wedding-night scene caused a minor stir), and every intimate moment is lushly underscored by Nino Rota's love theme (later to become a hit record). Yet the pair's struggle to convey the meaning of Shakespeare's verse is painfully obvious – even though Zeffirelli had cut more than half the text.

Hussey fares marginally better when speaking and when silent. Her face conveys memorable dread as the story spirals towards her suicide. Whiting's London-accented Romeo remains more lovestruck wimp than desperate, fate-driven hero – an impression reinforced because Zeffirelli (unlike Cukor and Castellani) does not jeopardize audience sympathy by showing Romeo killing Paris.

Neither star ever had another such high-profile film role, although Hussey played the Virgin Mary for Zeffirelli in *Jesus of Nazareth* in 1977, and continues to appear regularly on screen.

Angry, crude and cynical
Among the strong supporting cast, Michael York overdoes the blazing-eyed fury of Tybalt, Pat Heywood's Nurse chatters away with splendid vulgarity and Robert Stephens makes an imperious Prince. Best of all, John McEnery delivers cinema's finest Mercutio – a cynical live wire whose death hits you hard, exactly as Shakespeare intended.

The Benvolio of Bruce Robinson (destined for fame in the 1980s as director of cult comedy *Withnail and I*) was among several British cast members whose performances suffered from poorly re-recorded dialogue. The same was true for the dubbed Italian actors playing Paris and Lord Montague, even though the latter's voice was provided by Laurence Olivier, who also delivered the Prologue.

When the film opened in Britain, the *Evening News* said Zeffirelli had 'murdered' the play and the *New Statesman* felt he 'might just as well have jettisoned the Bard altogether'. Yet *The People* welcomed a 'ravishing, civilized entertainment', and the *Evening Standard* felt that cinema had finally delivered Shakespeare with real passion: 'poetry made flesh'. For *The New York Times*, this was a 'lovely, sensitive, friendly, popularization' and *Time* hailed 'one of the handful of classic Shakespeare films'.

The visual splendour brought Oscars for cinematographer Pasquale de Santis and costume designer Danilo Donati, with nominations for Best Picture and Best Director (*Oliver!* won both). **Romeo and Juliet** enjoyed its greatest success on the bottom line: a world-wide gross of $48 million made it the biggest Shakespeare hit of all time. As Zeffirelli put it in his autobiography: 'From the Bronx to Bali, Shakespeare was a box-office hit.'

The first version of the play we have seen in which verse-speaking is infused with physical passion. Evening Standard

extravagant imagery makes perfect sense as a hymn to the hallucinatory pill Mercutio gives Romeo to get him in the mood for the Capulets' fancy-dress ball.

At this wildly extravagant event, the movie's frantic mood peaks, as Mercutio struts and mimes to the symbolic disco anthem 'Young Hearts Run Free'. Then, magically, everything calms down, as Romeo, in medieval armour, and Juliet, wearing angel's wings, glimpse each other through the waters of a tropical fish tank. Time stands still, and love at first sight has never seemed more convincing

The lovers breathlessly swear undying love in Juliet's pool, enlist the help of Miriam Margolyes's plump, Hispanic-accented Nurse (forever calling out 'Hooliet, Hooliet!') and are married by Pete Postlethwaite's Father Laurence, a mystic figure with a Celtic Cross tattooed on his suntanned back.

Danes, just 16 when the film was made, displays that elusive 'wiser-than-her-years' quality that the part demands, emerging as the first screen Juliet whose speeches sound like spontaneous expressions, not finely crafted jewels. Surprise, desire and terror jostle for position on her eager features.

By contrast, DiCaprio's throwaway and sometimes inaudible treatment of the poetry is – for those not inclined to swoon uncritically at his beauty – the movie's weakest link. He is far less assured with the dialogue than Danes or British stage veterans Margolyes and Postlethwaite, and only comes into his own after Mercutio's death scene (operatically filmed, with a requiem on the soundtrack). At the end of a high-speed car chase, Romeo screams with rage and frustration before blowing Tybalt away. By now, Luhrmann has reverted to high-speed mode – and the pace never slackens again.

Father Laurence's letter explaining Juliet's faked death goes undelivered because Romeo is out when the messenger from a courier service with the mock-Shakespearean name of 'Post Post

Above: Leonardo DiCaprio as Romeo, centre, Jesse Bradford as Benvolio, second from right, and Harold Perrineau as Mercutio, extreme right, showing off the Montague boys' firepower.

Left: Leonardo DiCaprio as Romeo, blasting his way into the church where Juliet has been laid to rest.

An eye for detail

Every aspect of the production design, down to the tiniest prop, seems geared towards making Shakespeare's dense language more digestible for teenage moviegoers, without actually changing the words. For example, in one of the lively beach scenes, Harold Perrineau's black, transvestite Mercutio (probably gay and, as Shakespeare makes clear, *definitely* in love with Romeo) denounces idle dreams in the 'Queen Mab' speech. Here the

Above: Claire Danes as
Juliet, about to fall for
Romeo through the waters of
a tropical fish tank. Love at
first sight has never seemed
more convincing.

Haste' calls at his Mantua trailer park. His pal Balthasar brings the bad news that sends DiCaprio driving back to Verona.

It is a pity that in an essentially faithful adaptation, Luhrmann allows his Romeo to shoot his way into the church, as police cars and helicopters close in, but cuts out the killing of Paris with a typical Hollywood reluctance to show heroes in too poor a light. Still, after that frenzied build-up, the silence inside the kitschly decorated church is astonishing. Cinematographer Donald McAlpine's shimmering camerawork is at its best as Romeo makes his way down an aisle lined with neon crosses, to where Juliet lies, surrounded by hundreds of candles.

In an inspired departure from Shakespeare, Luhrmann shows Juliet waking up a couple of seconds *before* Romeo drinks the poison. She is too dopey to reach out and stop him, so he drinks it and dies, aware that she is alive. She shoots herself with his gun, and then it is back to the TV newsreader for the Epilogue and a fade to black.

Many critics in Britain and the US were swept away by what *The Independent* called this 'rampantly cinematic' vision. The *Financial Times* headlined its review 'Artistic GBH to revitalize a masterpiece' and *Newsday* even nominated DiCaprio and Danes as 'the best actors of their generation'.

The detractors spoke just as loudly. The *Village Voice* attacked Luhrmann as 'a one-note vulgarian' who had 'obliterated' the text. The *Evening Standard* concluded: 'The talents involved in this campy extravaganza don't give a damn for Shakespeare'.

A very palpable hit

Twentieth Century Fox laughed all the way to the bank. They had spent a fortune on advertising the film on MTV and in teen publications and the $17 million production budget was turned into an international smash, taking $46 million in America and a further $98 million in the rest of the world – more than any other Shakespeare movie (though inflation-adjusted figures would put Zeffirelli's 1968 *Romeo* back into the number one spot). Luhrmann's soundtrack, which made telling use of songs by Radiohead, The Cardigans and others, spawned not one but two hit albums.

Before Luhrmann is praised, his debts to earlier adaptations of the play must be acknowledged. He followed Zeffirelli's 1968 example and cast very young leads. He followed *West Side Story*, which had transplanted the action from Italy to a modern America. The rest of the credit belongs to Luhrmann, Pearce and production designer Catherine Martin.

They pepper Verona (actually Mexico City and Vera Cruz) with Catholic imagery (ranks of Madonnas in Juliet's bedroom) and fleeting nods to the Bard (glimpses of the Shylock Bank and a billboard for Prospero Whiskey). These slightly alienating touches give us a sense that the story is unfolding in what Luhrmann called 'a created world' – and that phrase is the key to this adaptation.

Even though the dialogue is Shakespeare's, you have to let the director write his own dramatic rules, as you would in, say, a science-fiction film. If, as several movie critics did, you stop to wonder why the teenagers are allowed to carry guns like Wild West cowboys, or why Prince, the black police captain, doesn't gaol Romeo for Tybalt's murder instead of banishing him, the magic will not work.

This huge success very nearly didn't happen. Luhrmann was 'hot' after his box-office triumph with 1992's *Strictly Ballroom*, and Fox executives liked the idea of the modern setting. But they had major reservations about keeping Shakespeare's dialogue and were more inclined to greenlight another director's more traditional version of the play, with Ethan Hawke as Romeo. Only when Luhrmann showed them video extracts of DiCaprio as Romeo did they approve his project.

Fox funded a research trip that allowed Luhrmann and Pearce to spend three months in Miami where they met politicians and businessmen, rode with the local police and interviewed teenagers about their views on sex and drugs, gathering valuable material that would feed into their screenplay.

'We wanted', said Luhrmann, 'to look at how Shakespeare would've made a movie if he were here today'. The Bard, he argued, was 'a relentless entertainer' who used lots of different devices without ever losing control of his narrative, so modern film-makers should be free to be 'as outrageous and mad as you like, as long as there's clarity'. His **Romeo + Juliet** is outrageous *and* clear. Audiences left cinemas dazed, but not confused.

Below: Claire Danes with Leonardo DiCaprio in the candlelit church where the lovers commit suicide. The film overflows with Catholic imagery.

Thou must be married to no man but me, For I am ... born to tame you, Kate. Petruchio, *The Taming of the Shrew*, Act II, Scene i

12 THE TAMING OF THE SHREW

Padua. Wealthy nobleman Baptista Minola reminds Gremio and Hortensio, rivals for his beautiful younger daughter Bianca's hand, that she cannot marry until Katharina, his man-hating elder child, finds a husband.

Hortensio convinces his friend Petruchio, a wild-tempered bachelor in search of a wealthy wife, to woo Katharina. Meanwhile, Lucentio, a young bachelor, has fallen instantly in love with Bianca. Aided by his servant, Tranio, he disguises himself as a tutor and secretly woos Bianca, who falls for him.

Despite Katharina's fury at her first meeting with Petruchio, Baptista consents to their marriage. After the ceremony, Petruchio takes Katharina back to his country home and 'tames' her by depriving her of food and sleep for days.

In Padua, Baptista agrees to let Bianca marry Lucentio (really Tranio in disguise). Lucentio's father, Vincentio, arrives to find he is being impersonated by a stranger (hired by Lucentio to support the marriage), but the deceptions are swiftly forgiven.

At a celebratory banquet, Petruchio wagers Lucentio and Hortensio (who has married a widow) that Katharina will prove the most dutiful new bride. He wins when Katharina declares that wives must show unquestioning obedience to their husbands.

FILM BACKGROUND

From 1930s 'screwball' movies like *Bringing Up Baby* to 1989's *When Harry Met Sally*, it is one of the cardinal rules of romantic comedy: a screen couple who bicker and fight when the audience first encounters them will be in each other's arms when the end credits roll. The same principle served Shakespeare well in 1594 in *The Taming of the Shrew*.

Today, a Hollywood executive would identify the play as 'date movie' fare, since watching couples are bound to argue over its outrageously one-sided view of the battle of the sexes. Petruchio's treatment of Katharina has probably disgusted as many people as it has delighted, and her final speech remains the most notorious piece of male chauvinism in all Shakespeare. If audiences relish this slapstick-heavy clash on stage, they would surely enjoy it on screen, too.

Most film-makers have done away with Shakespeare's inherently theatrical Induction, in which drunken tinker Christopher

Sly is duped into thinking that he is a Lord, and watches the *Shrew* as a play-within-a-play. Many versions push the tiresome sub-plot involving Lucentio's pursuit of Bianca into the background, preferring to concentrate on Katharina and Petruchio as first-class star vehicles.

That approach has never been more apparent than in **The Taming of the Shrew** (1929), with Douglas Fairbanks and Mary Pickford. Its riotous view of the Bard was lampooned the following year in a skit written by a certain Alfred Hitchcock for a British variety film revue, *Elstree Calling*.

In addition to the 1929 **Shrew** and the other three films discussed in this chapter – **Kiss Me Kate** (1953), Franco Zeffirelli's **The Taming of the Shrew** (1967) and **10 Things I Hate About You** (1999) – there have been 'straight' feature film versions made in Italy (1942), Spain (1955) and Russia (1961), with Andrei Popov (Iago in the 1955 *Othello*) as Petruchio.

During the silent era, the play was filmed in Britain, France, Italy and America, with D.W. Griffith, founding father of the US movie industry, responsible for one of the earliest. On the small screen, the BBC produced the play in 1939, 1952 (with Petruchio played by Stanley Baker, Richmond in Olivier's *Richard III*) and 1980 (*see* page 193). The BBC even produced a sequel, *The Tamer Tamed* (1956), in which Petruchio finds that Katharina may not have been tamed after all. American television cast Charlton Heston as Petruchio in a modern-dress version in 1950, and in 1956 an NBC adaptation allowed the lead couple to meet in a boxing ring.

The play has inspired numerous movies about bachelors 'taming' wild women, such as the musical comedy *You Made Me Love You* (UK, 1933) and *Second Best Bed* (UK, 1938), and although few people would associate John Wayne with the Bard, he twice appeared in Petruchio-and-Katharina-style double-acts.

In John Ford's *The Quiet Man* (1952), Wayne was ex-boxer Sean Thornton, who returns to Ireland and marries his neighbour Will's fiery sister, Mary Kate (Maureen O'Hara), after winning a fist-fight with Will to secure her dowry. Then, in 1963's *McLintock!*, Wayne's cattle baron sparred with his tempestuous wife, Katherine (O'Hara again). The poster's tagline asked 'He tamed the West, but could he tame her?'

Left: Richard Burton as Petruchio, left, planting a 'clamorous smack' of a kiss on the lips of Elizabeth Taylor as Katharina in *The Taming of the Shrew* (1967).

Right: Tom Walls, right, tames his fiery bride, played by Jane Baxter, in *Second Best Bed* (1938).

Far right: Thelma Todd, left, and Stanley Lupino in the *Shrew*-inspired musical comedy, *You Made Me Love You* (1933).

CAST	MARY PICKFORD (Katharina), DOUGLAS FAIRBANKS (Petruchio), DOROTHY JORDAN (Bianca), EDWIN MAXWELL (Baptista), GEOFFREY WARDWELL (Hortensio), JOSEPH CAWTHORN (Gremio), CLYDE COOK (Grumio)
DIRECTED BY	SAM TAYLOR
PRODUCED BY	PICKFORD CORPORATION/ELTON CORPORATION
PHOTOGRAPHY	KARL STRUSS

A vastly extravagant burlesque of Shakespeare. Variety

In 1927, *The Jazz Singer* had marked Hollywood's transition from the silent to the sound eras, and in 1929 Sam Taylor's **The Taming of The Shrew** became the first feature-length, 'all talking' Shakespeare movie.

It brought together for the one and only time two of silent cinema's brightest stars: Mary Pickford, the blonde whose 'Cinderella' roles had earned her the nickname 'America's Sweetheart', and Douglas Fairbanks, swashbuckling hero of *The Thief of Bagdad*. They were America's most famous married couple, so audiences could watch the Shakespeare tale in which, as the posters hollered, 'a cave man woos and wins an Amazon', and wonder whether this battle resembled the Pickford-Fairbanks rows hinted at by gossip columnists.

It took a budget of $500,000 (around $18 million today) to cover the couple's vast pay cheques and the construction of

enormous Padua sets on what was then the world's largest sound stage. What emerged, as *Variety* pointed out, was 'a vastly extravagant burlesque' of Shakespeare, which grossed $1.1 million (it would have done better had it not been released after the Wall Street Crash hit Americans' spending power).

This is Shakespeare reinvented as 'The Doug'n'Mary Show'. Apart from an early glimpse of Bianca embracing a handsome suitor, nothing remains of scenes not featuring either Katharina or Petruchio. Clyde Cook's squeaking, hangdog Grumio is the only character allowed occasionally to deflect the spotlight from the stars.

Pickford's Katharina is a five-foot firebrand, blessed with one of cinema's great entrances. Pots and chairs crash into the hall of Baptista's home as servants dive for cover. Finally we see her, dressed in black, a long whip at her side, glowering at the camera.

She growls her lines; the piratical Fairbanks bawls his, like a circus ringmaster. Yet with so little of Shakespeare's text retained, there are regular stretches of two or three minutes in which no one says a word. The film could – and did – run as a silent, with title cards distributed to many cinemas.

Doctoring the Bard

Taylor had made a handful of snappy modern alterations to the script, earning himself an 'additional dialogue' credit which inspired an American newspaper cartoon showing a bust of Shakespeare being removed from the Library of Congress, and replaced by one of Taylor. But what Taylor really cared about is crash-bang-wallop comedy, of which, to be fair, there is plenty in the play. The great difference is that here it is the be-all and end-all of the action.

Pickford wallops and whips Fairbanks when they first meet. He forces her to say 'I do' by stomping on her foot during the wedding ceremony (a scene, incidentally, which is one of the earliest screen set pieces created from an incident that Shakespeare describes, in a fine speech by Gremio, but does not show).

At Petruchio's house, Pickford initially pretends to have been tamed after overhearing Fairbanks telling his huge dog how he plans to subdue his bride (a pro-Katharina moment not found in Shakespeare). Then the tit-for-tat mayhem resumes in the couple's bedroom. Peace finally arrives after Pickford brains her husband with a well-aimed stool. Cradling her poor, wounded boy, she flings her whip into the fire and agrees to swear the moon is the sun if Petruchio says so.

Cut to Baptista's house, where Pickford is politely telling the dinner guests how wives must honour their husbands as lord, king and governor – only to aim a 'Don't think I believe this baloney!' wink at Bianca, and ensure that America's womenfolk wouldn't be *too* offended by Elizabethan chauvinism.

Although some critics admired Pickford's performance, she deeply regretted taking on a Shakespeare talkie, revealing in her autobiography: 'My confidence was completely shattered, and I was never again at ease before the camera or microphone'. She made only two more features before retiring from the screen in 1933 – although time must eventually have healed the wounds. In 1966, not long before the première of Franco Zeffirelli's *Shrew*, she spent $100,000 having the original print of her version restored and re-released.

Left: Douglas Fairbanks as Petruchio, centre, with Mary Pickford as Katharina during the lavish, farcical wedding scene.

Right: Douglas Fairbanks and Mary Pickford, real-life husband and wife, confront each other in Petruchio's bedroom.

KISS ME KATE (1953)

US 106 MINS COLOUR

CAST	HOWARD KEEL (Fred Graham/Petruchio), KATHRYN GRAYSON (Lili Vanessi/Katharina), ANN MILLER (Lois Lane/Bianca), TOMMY RALL (Bill Calhoun/Lucentio), RON RANDELL (Cole Porter), KEENAN WYNN (Lippy), JAMES WHITMORE (Slug)
DIRECTED BY	GEORGE SIDNEY
PRODUCED BY	JACK CUMMINGS
SCREENPLAY	DOROTHY KINGSLEY
MUSIC AND LYRICS	COLE PORTER
BOOK BY	SAM AND BELLA SPEWACK

A pair of New York gangsters suddenly burst into song and tap-dance down an alley, celebrating the Bard's value in chat-up routines:

'Brush up your Shakespeare, start quoting him now

Brush up your Shakespeare, and the women you will wow'.

It is a showstoppingly bizarre scene from *Kiss Me Kate*, the musical in which Cole Porter's genius refreshes the livelier parts of *The Taming of The Shrew*, and energetic backstage comedy replaces its duller segments. All in garishly coloured 3D.

Produced five years after the stage version became a Broadway smash, the film opens as Porter (Ron Randell) is helping blazered actor/director Fred Graham to persuade his fierce-tempered ex-wife, Lili Vanessi, to star in Porter's new show, *Kiss Me Kate*, as 'a perfect shrew'. Bianca will be played by Fred's current squeeze, Lois Lane (Ann Miller).

We cut to opening night, a while before the curtain rises to leave the main plot strands dangling. Bill Calhoun, Lois's on-off boyfriend and the show's Lucentio, has lost $2,000 to a gangster, Hogan, in a crap game, and signed his IOU in Fred's name. Hogan's henchmen, Lippy (dapper Keenan Wynn) and Slug (a numbskulled James Whitmore), turn up in Fred's dressing room demanding payment. Lili, meanwhile, appears devoted to her cattle baron fiancé, Tex, but suspects that Fred wants her back.

The performance begins with the four principals as 'Shakespearean portrayers' launching into a musical version of the *Shrew*. This play-within-a-play device acknowledges Shakespeare's Induction, and the Spewacks use small chunks of his dialogue to carry the plot from one number to the next.

The songs that dispose, briefly, of the Bianca sub-plot exist to showcase Miller's supercharged dancing (one critic called her 'a Greek statue struck into action by lightning'), whereas in the numbers featuring Petruchio and Katharina, Porter's inimitable humour adds brilliant polish to what, by Shakespeare's standards, is fairly crude raw material.

One of Petruchio's most famous lines, 'I Come To Wive It Wealthily In Padua', becomes an appropriately rousing opening number for Keel, who combines an emphatic baritone, uncomplicated charm and a strapping physique. The newly married

Left: Howard Keel, left, Ann Miller, centre, and Kathryn Grayson play the stars of the musical-within-the-film, an adaptation of the *Shrew*.

Right: Richard Burton in a daze as Petruchio, left, with Elizabeth Taylor as Katharina. Taylor gives one of the weakest performances of her career.

Below: Elizabeth Taylor as Katharina, centre, kneels obediently before her husband in the film's closing scene. Bice Valori as Widow, left, and Natasha Pyne as Bianca reluctantly do likewise.

10 THINGS I HATE ABOUT YOU (1999)

US 97 MINS COLOUR

CAST	JULIA STILES (Katarina 'Kat' Stratford), HEATH LEDGER (Patrick Verona), LARRY MILLER (Walter Stratford), LARISA OLEYNIK (Bianca Stratford), JOSEPH GORDON-LEVITT (Cameron James), DAVID KRUMHOLTZ (Michael Eckman), ANDREW KEEGAN (Joey Donner)
DIRECTED BY	GIL JUNGER
PRODUCED BY	ANDREW LAZAR
SCREENPLAY	KAREN MCCULLAH LUTZ, KIRSTEN SMITH
PHOTOGRAPHY	MARK IRWIN

This high-school take on *The Taming of the Shrew* achieves a remarkable double. It is a 1990s teen comedy with a brain, and a Shakespeare adaptation that is wittier and more enjoyable than its source – thanks largely to a good-natured script which follows the *Shrew*'s plot as faithfully as Hollywood conventions and political correctness allow.

Cameron, a new pupil at Padua High, Seattle, is the Lucentio figure who instantly falls for Bianca, a beautiful, vapid sophomore: 'I burn, I pine, I perish', he exclaims, borrowing a Lucentio line from the *Shrew*. The trouble is that Bianca's father will not let her date until her older sister, Kat, does too. Since bookish, university-bound Kat is 'a heinous bitch' with a reputation for assaulting boys, Cameron's chances seem slim.

His nerdish friend, Michael (David Krumholtz, a cross between Woody Allen and Billy Crystal), assumes the Tranio role and dedicates himself to Cameron's pursuit of Bianca. First, Cameron helps her with her French, echoing Lucentio's disguise as Cambio the Latin tutor, but while that ruse is all it takes to win Bianca in the *Shrew*, **10 Things** makes Cameron work harder.

The plot gets into gear once the impossibly vain Joey Donner (Hortensio and Gremio rolled into one), sets his sights on Bianca. Michael and Cameron convince Joey that he can only reach Bianca by hiring a boyfriend for Kat, and Pat Verona, the school's Australian-accented wild man, is enrolled, for $100 per date.

Below: Andrew Keegan as the obnoxious Joey Donner, right, asking for a date from Larisa Oleynik as Bianca.

He soon realizes that macho tactics won't work on Kat, so the *Shrew*'s hopelessly outdated sexual politics take on a 'caring, sharing' 1990s slant: in order to tame the shrew, the hero tames himself. Assisted by inside information from Bianca, he adapts to suit Kat's tastes. He stops smoking, pretends to enjoy feminist prose and looks after Kat when she gets drunk at a wild house party (still an obligatory component for a teen movie, even one with 16th-century roots).

Kat is finally won over by the best of the film's silly set pieces: Pat's show-stopping rendition on the sportsfield of 'Can't Take My Eyes Off You', accompanied by the school band. He, naturally, has genuinely fallen for her.

Accompanied by Bianca, who has rejected the obnoxious Joey in favour of Cameron, Kat meets Pat at the Prom. But when she overhears Joey remonstrating with him over the 'cash-for-dating' scam she rushes out, furious. Back at school on the following Monday he convinces her that he really cares and they are reconciled.

A touch bizarre
From start to finish, experienced sitcom director Gil Junger generates laughs without resorting to 'gross-out' jokes (sadly, with more of these the film would probably have made more than its impressive worldwide take of $63 million). There are some original touches thanks to Padua High's eccentric teachers and bizarre student cliques, although not every Shakespeare link comes off, for example, one of Kat's female friends has a deeply contrived obsession with the Bard.

Heath Ledger's Jim-Morrison looks and abundant charm should serve him well for years, while Stiles' sharp-witted performance immediately earned her two more Shakespearean roles: Ophelia in Michael Almereyda's *Hamlet*, and Desdemona in *The One*, the reworking of *Othello*.

She does well during the scene in which Kat attributes her boy-hatred to her shame at having lost her virginity to the preening Joey three years earlier. That is a more convincing motive than Katharina's resentment at Baptista's favouritism towards Bianca in the *Shrew*, and the Stratfords' father is equipped with an equally moral, PC reason for his 'no dating' rule: he is an obstetrician desperate for his daughters not to end up pregnant.

The significance of the film's title? It is revealed in the penultimate scene. Kat's hip, black English teacher has instructed his class to write a Shakespearean sonnet. Kat's poem replaces Katharina's 'honour thy husbands' speech, with a tearfully written list of Pat's ten greatest flaws, the last of which is:

'I hate the way I don't hate you
Not even close, not even a little bit, not even at all.'

A sonnet as the emotional climax of a teen comedy? The Bard would have approved.

Below: Heath Ledger as Patrick Verona, left, with Julia Stiles as Kat at the Padua High School prom. Both actors have genuine star quality.

12

In the months following the end of World War II, 22-year-old Franco Zeffirelli was desperately trying to decide what to do with his life. Having narrowly escaped death while fighting for the Italian partisans, he was struggling to adjust to a peacetime routine built around his architectural studies in Florence.

Then, in September 1945, he went to the city's Odeon cinema to see Laurence Olivier's *Henry V*. He was entranced by the drama and colourful pageantry and went home absolutely certain: 'Architecture was not for me; it had to be the stage. I wanted to do something like the production I was witnessing.'

As described in his autobiography, it was that experience which set Zeffirelli on the road to an exceptionally successful career as a designer and director, much of it dedicated to popularizing Shakespeare's work. His film versions of *The Taming of the Shrew*, *Romeo and Juliet* and *Hamlet* won him few friends among academics, who could not bear to see Shakespeare's texts so heavily edited, while many critics argued that poetry and subtlety had been sacrificed in favour of spectacle. Opera critics accused Zeffirelli of similar crimes when he filmed Verdi's version of *Othello*, *Otello*.

Such attacks apparently never bother him. He cares far more about paying customers than salaried experts defending the 'sanctity' of great drama. In 1990, summing up his approach to filming Shakespeare, he said: 'With the cinema, you have to make up your mind whether you do a film for a small number of people who know it all – and it's not very exciting to work for them – or really make some sacrifices and compromises but bring culture to a mass audience.' His success in achieving the latter is beyond doubt.

Zeffirelli's Shakespearean education began in the 1930s. He was born in February 1923, the illegitimate son of a philandering Florentine cloth merchant who refused to acknowledge him. His mother, a dressmaker, died when he was six and for the next few years he was brought up by his father's secretary, an elderly English spinster named Mary O'Neill, and other members of the *scorpioni*, Florence's famously sharp-tongued, expatriate Englishwomen.

When he was nine or ten, Franco and O'Neill began to read Shakespeare together, and he fell in love with *Romeo and Juliet*. The devotion of the *scorpioni* would be lovingly dramatized in his autobiographical comedy-drama, *Tea With Mussolini* (Italy/UK, 1998), with the O'Neill figure played by Olivier's widow, Joan Plowright. 'Those spinsters', said Zeffirelli, 'made me what I am today.'

After the war, his good looks and charm convinced film producer Helen Deutsch to offer him a five-year Hollywood acting contract, but he turned her down and instead commenced a personal and professional relationship with the great Italian director Luchino Visconti. They lived together for several years, and he assisted Visconti on stage productions, including an *As You Like It* in Rome, before designing the sets on three Visconti

Above: Zeffirelli takes a break during the making of *Hamlet* (1990), his third film of a Shakespeare play.

You have to make up your mind whether you do a film for a small number of people or bring culture to a mass audience. Franco Zeffirelli

films, including *Senso* (Italy, 1954), where his work contributed to a lush, Technicolor vision of 1860s Italy.

Visconti had a profound influence on Zeffirelli, convincing him that a story's setting should be rendered in the most precise detail possible. It was an influence he carried into his Shakespeare films, although it first emerged in the mid-1950s, as he designed and directed operas at La Scala in Milan, in Rome, New York and at Covent Garden.

He made his theatre debut in 1960 with *Romeo and Juliet* at the Old Vic, and, although deeply nervous at 'presuming to do Shakespeare in the land of his birth', followed his instincts and set out to abolish the middle-aged approach to the play that had made George Cukor's 1936 film so bland. His use of a young, passionate cast, headed by John Stride and Judi Dench, was savaged by most critics, but *The Observer*'s Kenneth Tynan

called it 'a revelation ... perhaps a revolution' and that transformed it into a major success.

The stage production's youthful leads set the tone for Zeffirelli's film of *Romeo* and in 1965 his sexy, boisterous *Much Ado About Nothing* for the National Theatre introduced two more ingredients that would soon contribute to his Shakespeare films – Nino Rota's lively music and reworked text to simplify the most obscure language.

Having always believed that theatre and opera work were 'somehow only a preparation' for cinema, he finally made the transition by pairing Richard Burton and Elizabeth Taylor in *The Taming of the Shrew* (*see* page 140). When he followed that with the immense international success of *Romeo and Juliet* (*see* page 128), Zeffirelli had completed the swiftest, most profitable Shakespearean 'double' in screen history. The *Shrew* established

Above: Zeffirelli, centre, directs Natasha Pyne as Bianca, second from left, as they rehearse the opening sequence of *The Taming of the Shrew* (1967). On the extreme right is Michael York, as Lucentio.

him as a movie director; *Romeo* brought him an Oscar nomination and made him rich.

Both films look wonderful, sharing the opulence and authentic period detail of his opera productions, although he dismisses critics who suggest that his work is more impressive visually than dramatically, stating in his autobiography: 'I don't believe that millions of young people throughout the world wept over my film of *Romeo and Juliet* just because the costumes were splendid.'

Nevertheless, as he fills the screen with beautiful, hand-picked youths for the Capulet and Montague brawls, or the undergraduate parade that opens the *Shrew*, the contrast with the Shakespeare films of Kozintsev or Kurosawa could not be greater. In their screen visions, every peasant, servant or soldier deepens our understanding of the world in which the principal characters exist; in Zeffirelli's, the extras usually seem like mere decoration.

Both films also demonstrated his willingness to tamper with Shakespeare's text, by not only replacing Elizabethan words with 'simpler' alternatives but introducing additional lines, some of them indefensibly crass. During *Romeo*'s duel between Tybalt and Mercutio, for example, an impatient Capulet boy cries: 'Make haste, Tybalt, we can't wait all day!' a contribution as redundant as it is unShakespearean. Zeffirelli once responded to criticism of his approach: 'We must make [the audience's] lives easy without betraying the author.' Sometimes he appears to cross the line dividing customer service and author betrayal.

Romeo might have been followed by a film musical of *Much Ado About Nothing*, with a Nino Rota score. Zeffirelli travelled to New York in 1973 to ask Liza Minnelli, with whom he had 'a great rapport', to play Beatrice. She declined.

Convinced that 'when you concentrate on one medium, you wear out easily', Zeffirelli kept himself fresh by juggling opera assignments in Europe and the US with film and television work. His devout Catholic faith, which had deepened after he survived a near-fatal car crash in 1969, fed into his direction of *Jesus of Nazareth*, the six-hour mini-series starring Robert Powell as Christ, which took two years to make and was seen by hundreds of millions of viewers worldwide in 1977.

Next came *The Champ* (US, 1979), a sentimental drama about a down-and-out boxer played by Jon Voight (whom Zeffirelli talked to about making a film of *Hamlet*), and *Endless Love* (US, 1981), a saccharine, modern-day *Romeo and Juliet* story that grossed $70 million worldwide. He made a marvellous film of Puccini's *La Traviata* in 1982, followed by the $10 million *Otello* (1986), the most expensive opera film ever made. Placido Domingo played the Moor with immense power and magnetism. As usual, Zeffirelli ensured that his studio interiors matched the splendour of his exterior locations (Barletta Castle, Italy, and a Venetian fortress on Crete) and, as usual, he ran into trouble for cutting a classic work.

Critics were incensed by his removal of almost half an hour of Verdi's music, including Desdemona's 'Willow Song'; he defended himself with his trademark self-confidence: 'I'm sure Verdi would understand what I have done, as certain things work in theatre and not on film.' Indeed, *Otello* is Zeffirelli's best Shakespearean work, because it relies less than *Othello* on language (Verdi's librettist, Boito, reduced 3,500 lines of Shakespeare to 800 lines of much simpler Italian).

Zeffirelli's flamboyant and, frankly, operatic style as a director is better suited to the sublimely passionate blend of orchestra and voices in Verdi than it is to the Bard's long, psychologically intricate speeches. A double-bill of *Otello* and Zeffirelli's massively abridged *Hamlet* (*see* page 30) would vividly illustrate his strengths and weaknesses in transferring these two contrasting forms to the screen.

Since directing Mel Gibson as the Dane, he has represented Sicily as a senator for the Forza Italia party, and made three more films: *The Sparrow* (1993), another tale of illicit, juvenile love (this time involving a novice nun), a solid adaptation of *Jane Eyre* (1996), and *Tea With Mussolini*.

Although he turned 77 in 2000, there might yet be more Shakespeare from the Italian who has brought classical drama to millions who might never otherwise have seen it. Promoting *Hamlet*, he promised an American interviewer: 'As long as I live, I'll give my blood to keep these great works alive.'

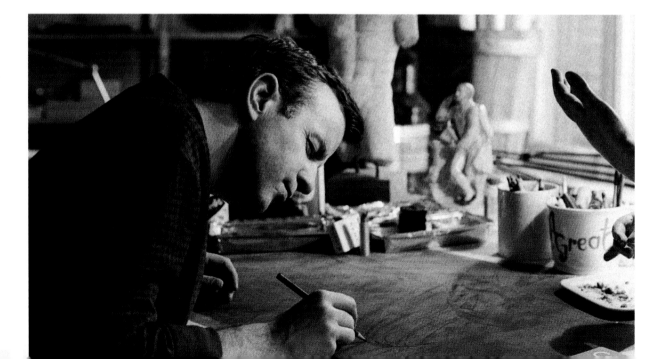

Top right: Zeffirelli, left, with 'star-crossed lovers' Olivia Hussey and Leonard Whiting during production of *Romeo and Juliet* (1968), the movie that made Zeffirelli rich.

Right: Zeffirelli, left, directing Placido Domingo in the title role of *Otello* (1986), his film of Verdi's opera. Critics attacked Zeffirelli for cutting half an hour of Verdi's music.

Left: Zeffirelli at work in his Rome studio in 1965. He began his career as a set designer in the 1950s.

THE PLAY

Prospero, deposed Duke of Milan, lives on a remote island with his teenage daughter, Miranda, and his servants: Caliban, a monstrous savage, and Ariel, a spirit.

Prospero's studies have given him magical powers and he summons a storm to wreck the ship carrying Antonio, the brother who deposed him. Among those also cast ashore are Alonso, King of Naples, his son, Ferdinand, his brother, Sebastian, and Gonzalo, the councillor who helped Prospero to flee from Milan. Trinculo, a jester, and Stephano, a drunken butler, are washed up on another part of the island.

Miranda and Ferdinand fall in love at first sight. Antonio and Sebastian try to kill Alonso. Caliban urges Stephano and Trinculo to kill Prospero. But Prospero foresees both plots and sends Ariel to foil them.

After blessing Miranda and Ferdinand's marriage with a Masque, Prospero rounds up his enemies. But he chooses not to take revenge on his brother and Caliban, and resolves to abandon magic. He sets Ariel free and prepares to return home with the other Neapolitans.

FILM BACKGROUND

Cinema loves taking audiences to far-off islands to watch marooned characters adapt or perish. Just think of *Robinson Crusoe*, *Lord of the Flies*, even *The Blue Lagoon*. *The Tempest* had supplied this fundamental template – and much more besides, back in 1612.

The action unfolds in real time (taking place during four hours of one day), which should make for fast-moving film treatment. In Prospero, we have the wronged, vengeful hero familiar from countless movies, but one whose last-minute forgiveness delivers what Hollywood would call a first-class 'feel-good' ending. His magical control of the elements and a small army of spirits, nymphs and goddesses, should, like the fairy world of *A Midsummer Night's Dream*, lend itself to film's box of audio-visual tricks.

In short, *The Tempest* has rich cinematic potential. It was first tapped in the silent era, which saw several versions made in America and Europe. British director Percy Stow's 1908 film, regarded as one of the finest Shakespeare silents, has a moving simplicity. Using painted rocky backdrops and English countryside to represent the island, it covers most of the plot in just eight minutes, and boasts some delightful special effects (a jump-cut turns Ariel, played by a young girl, into a monkey).

The four best-known feature adaptations of the play are the focus of this chapter: MGM's sci-fi adventure, **Forbidden Planet** (1956), Derek Jarman's idiosyncratic **The Tempest** (1979), Paul Mazursky's modernized **Tempest** (1982) and Peter Greenaway's extravagant **Prospero's Books** (1991).

Television *Tempest*s include four from the BBC, made between 1939 and 1980, and the NBC network's 1960 American production, with Lee Remick as Miranda and Richard Burton as Caliban. Peter Fonda was the most recent small-screen Prospero, in a 1998 film which relocated the story to the Mississippi bayou during the American Civil War.

William Wellman's Western, *Yellow Sky* (1948), incorporates elements of the play, as a band of outlaws led by Gregory Peck end up in a desert ghost town, whose only inhabitants are a Prospero and Miranda-like pair: an elderly prospector and his tomboyish granddaughter. The town, like Prospero's island, becomes a place where men reveal their true colours.

Perhaps the most intriguing treatment is one that never made it to the screen. Michael Powell, a director whose mastery of screen magic fills pictures like *A Matter of Life and Death*, always longed to adapt *The Tempest*. For his first, abortive attempt, in the 1950s, he wanted John Gielgud to play Prospero, with ballerina and actress Moira Shearer as Ariel.

Then in 1970, after making *Age of Consent* (a *Tempest*-like tale of a painter, played by James Mason, in self-imposed exile on a tiny Australian island), Powell resurrected the plan. He had a formidable cast lined up: Mason, Topol, Michael York and Mia Farrow. Powell wrote a screenplay and tried for several years to find backers in Britain, Greece and Egypt, but he could never raise sufficient funding. Perhaps Powell would have become the first *Tempest* film director convincingly to represent the exotic setting *and* do full justice to the play's fantasy and humanity.

Left: Heathcote Williams as Prospero in Derek Jarman's *The Tempest* (1979), a gloomy, low-budget vision of the play.

Bottom left: Unknown actors playing Prospero, left, and Miranda in *The Tempest* (1908), directed by Percy Stow. This simple, affecting film is regarded as one of the finest Shakespeare silents.

FORBIDDEN PLANET (1956)
US 96 MINS COLOUR

CAST	WALTER PIDGEON (Doctor Morbius), ANNE FRANCIS (Altaira), LESLIE NIELSEN (Commander Adams), WARREN STEVENS (Lt 'Doc' Ostrow), JACK KELLY (Lt Farman), EARL HOLLIMANN (Cook), ROBBY THE ROBOT
DIRECTED BY	FRED MCLEOD WILCOX
PRODUCED BY	NICHOLAS NAYFACK
SCREENPLAY	CYRIL HUME
PHOTOGRAPHY	GEORGE FOLSEY
MUSIC	LOUIS AND BEBE BARRON

'Shakespeare takes a journey into space.' That headline above the review of **Forbidden Planet** in London's *Evening Standard* neatly sums up this hugely enjoyable – and influential – science-fiction transformation of *The Tempest*. The *Evening Standard's* Alan Brien believed that scriptwriter Cyril Hume had 'produced the most rumbustiously enjoyable of all Hollywood planetary melodramas, apparently by dressing *The Tempest* in space suits'.

Forbidden Planet's $1 million-plus budget made it, at the time, the most expensive sci-fi movie ever made and, although MGM would never have jeopardized that investment by letting dusty old Shakespeare appear in publicity for the film, *The Tempest* has left its mark all over the storyline.

In 2257AD, a Universal Planets Cruiser skippered by unflappable Commander J.J. Adams (Leslie Nielsen), lands on planet Altair IV to search for survivors from the Belerophon, a spaceship that lost contact with Earth 20 years earlier.

Adams and his senior officers, Lt Farman and Doc, meet the film's Prospero figure, Dr Morbius, the only survivor from the Belerophon, now living happily with his beautiful daughter, Altaira (a mini-skirted Anne Francis), who, like Miranda, has 'never known any human being except her father'. The pair are served by the film's Ariel: Robby the Robot, an electronic Jeeves who can speak 187 languages and manufacture everything from hors-d'oeuvres to emeralds ('It's the housewife's dream', quips Nielsen).

Flirting with danger

Adams instantly follows Ferdinand's lead in *The Tempest* by falling for Altaira, as does Farman, and she canoodles innocently with both in scenes so crassly written that you understand why the review in *The New Yorker* said it was a pity Hume's screenplay 'didn't lift some of Shakespeare's language'.

Back at the ship, the cruiser's bourbon-swilling cook assumes the low-life comedy role filled by Stephano, the drunken butler in *The Tempest*, but humour and cheesy romance are soon pushed aside by the return of the terrible, incomprehensible force that Morbius claims wiped out the Belerophon's crew. A vast, invisible monster, immune to laser blasts, twice attacks the ship, killing Farman and three other crewmen.

Morbius reluctantly shows Adams and Doc the vast machine created 500,000 years ago by the planet's original inhabitants, the Krel, a race infinitely superior to man – at which point William Shakespeare gives way to pure sci-fi hokum. Doc takes a Krel 'brain boost', realizes that the invisible foe is a 'monster from the Id', then dies. That leaves Adams to convince Morbius that the creature responsible for destroying the Belerophon's crew was the product of his own subconscious, and that it is now attacking again.

As this monster bashes its way into the Krel lab to attack Adams and Altaira, Morbius – just like Prospero – renounces vengeance, killing off his 'evil self' – at the cost of his own life.

Above: Earl Holliman as the spaceship's Cook greets Robby the Robot – the Ariel-like servant to the film's Prospero figure, Dr Morbius.

The film ends with Altair IV blown to smithereens by a Krel chain reaction, as Adams, Altaira and Robby fly back to Earth.

Regardless of its *Tempest* parallels, **Forbidden Planet** is great fun. The soundtrack of 'electronic tonalities' (perhaps high-pitched equivalents to the 'sounds and sweet airs' of Prospero's island) and the painted planetary backdrops now seem decidedly primitive, but some of the Oscar-nominated special effects, notably the cavernous Krel lab, are still very impressive.

Robby remains a terrific creation. Built like a steel Michelin man, with the voice of a staid 1950s radio announcer, he was the first movie robot to become a hero in own right, appearing again in *The Invisible Boy* in 1957, and is the 'grandfather' of metallic

stars such as C-3PO and Robocop. *The Guardian* even awarded Robby **Forbidden Planet**'s 'acting honours' – a fairly damning verdict on wooden performances by Pidgeon, Baxter and, especially, Nielsen, whose unvarying, deadpan style points the way to his appearances in the *Naked Gun* films.

The Id monster (which proves that this *Tempest* has no Caliban) was an intelligent alternative to the bug-eyed creatures that dominated 1950s sci-fi. Irving Block, author of the story on which **Forbidden Planet** was based, said he devised the Id idea because 'there are real monsters and demons inside each one of us, without our knowing': something Shakespeare knew 400 years earlier.

Above: Anne Francis as Altaira, left, with Leslie Nielsen as heroic Commander Adams preparing to fly back to earth in the final scene.

13

THE TEMPEST (1979)

UK 96MINS COLOUR

CAST	HEATHCOTE WILLIAMS (Prospero), TOYAH WILCOX (Miranda), DAVID MEYER (Ferdinand), KARL JOHNSON (Ariel), JACK BIRKETT (Caliban), CHRISTOPHER BIGGINS (Stephano), PETER TURNER (Trinculo), NEIL CUNNINGHAM (Sebastian), RICHARD WARWICK (Antonio), PETER BULL (Alonso), KEN CAMPBELL (Gonzalo)
DIRECTED BY	DEREK JARMAN
PRODUCED BY	GUY FORD, MORDECAI SCHREIBER
SCREENPLAY	DEREK JARMAN
PHOTOGRAPHY	PETER MIDDLETON
MUSIC	BRIAN HODGSON, JOHN LEWIS

Right: Blind performance artist Jack Birkett as a whining Caliban with a taste for raw eggs.

Even in 1979 a budget of £150,000 could not buy much screen magic. With so little to spend, Derek Jarman was never going to sprinkle **The Tempest** with dazzling effects. Emotion and entertainment, on the other hand, are less expensive movie commodities, but Jarman delivers little of either. His intimate, housebound vision of the play might have worked superbly on stage: on screen it feels monotonous and alienating.

In 1978, Jarman had directed *Jubilee*, an outlandish film in which Queen Elizabeth I is transported from 1578 to the heyday of Punk, along with a magician and his assistant, called Ariel. It was a short step from these characters to *The Tempest*, which, Jarman wrote, 'obsessed' him.

After writing a script that reorders scenes without altering Shakespeare's plot, he set out to film 'an island of the mind', with production design and camerawork all calculated to focus on the characters' thoughts, not their environment.

Prospero and Miranda live in the cold, high-ceilinged rooms of a stately home (Stoneleigh Abbey in Warwickshire). Faces, if visible at all, seem illuminated only by firelight or candles and a static camera is trained on characters delivering their lines from the middle distance. The handful of exterior scenes, in which the shipwrecked Neapolitans walk along sand dunes, are shot through a blue filter, suggesting a perpetual dusk or dawn, and the all-pervading gloom is deepened by two performances fatally shorn of feeling.

Heathcote Williams' waistcoated magician looks 20 years younger than most stage Prosperos, and has a touch of the Romantic poet about him, shaggy dark curls framing a stubbled face. He barely raises his voice above a whisper and the richly contrasted emotions of Shakespeare's hero, notably pride in his magic and fury at Antonio, are all absent. A graph charting Williams' portrayal would show a numbing flatline.

Ariel shares similar, depressive tendencies. Wearing white boiler-suit, shoes and gloves, Karl Johnson's palour and drab speech suggest a careworn ghost rather than Shakespeare's 'gentle spirit'. You wait in vain for sparks of tension or affection in his relationship with Prospero.

Beauty and the beast

More effective is Toyah Wilcox, bringing robust sexual energy to Miranda, whose sheltered innocence can seem vacuous on stage. Caliban, played by the hulking Jack Birkett (a bald, blind performer also known as 'The Incredible Orlando'), is suitably repellent, distinguished by his whining North of England accent, maniacal laugh and taste for raw eggs.

His tattered overcoat and Miranda's ragged ball gown are typical of eclectic costumes which draw on 400 years' worth of fashions, leaving the action out of time and in tune with Jarman's desire to make 'a dream film'. It is a dream in which the director's homosexuality – a powerful force throughout his work – counterbalances the supremely heterosexual imagery of Shakespeare's Miranda/Ferdinand scenes.

Stephano (Christopher Biggins) is hysterically camp, and when brightness symbolically floods the screen for the penultimate scene, Jarman brings in 20 pretty sailors from Alonso's ship, who pair up, dance a hornpipe and greet a naked Trinculo with a chorus of wolf whistles. He then replaces *The Tempest*'s masque, a supernatural celebration of male/female fertility, with jazz diva Elisabeth Welch, singing 'Stormy Weather' in punning tribute to the play's title.

This rousing finale cannot erase the overriding tedium of a movie inferior in every respect to Jarman's unconventional, riveting 1991 film of *Edward II*, a play by Shakespeare's great contemporary, Christopher Marlowe. *Variety* criticised **The Tempest** for 'generally limp control of the narrative', and *The New York Times* branded it 'almost unbearable'. That review, Jarman wrote in his journal for 1979, 'destroyed' **The Tempest**'s American prospects; a more favourable reception in Britain (London's *Time Out* called it 'a major achievement') enabled it to finish 'a moderate success'.

In the same journal, Jarman noted: 'The only audience I worry about is my collaborators on the film'. Provided his cast and crew liked the finished result he was happy. Such unashamed disregard for the paying public may explain why, for many, watching this version of *The Tempest* is an ordeal.

Left: Toyah Wilcox bringing laughter and vitality to the role of Miranda.

Far left: Jazz diva Elisabeth Welch as the goddess who sings 'Stormy Weather' in a surprising and very camp finale.

TEMPEST (1982)
US 134 MINS COLOUR

CAST	JOHN CASSAVETES (Phillip), MOLLY RINGWALD (Miranda), SAM ROBARDS (Freddy), SUSAN SARANDON (Aretha), RAUL JULIA (Kalibanos), VITTORIO GASSMAN (Alonzo), GENA ROWLANDS (Antonia), JACKIE GAYLE (Trinc), ANTHONY HOLLAND (Sebastian)
DIRECTED BY	PAUL MAZURSKY
PRODUCED BY	PAUL MAZURSKY
SCREENPLAY	PAUL MAZURSKY, LEON CAPATANOS
PHOTOGRAPHY	DONALD M. MCALPINE
MUSIC	STOMU YAMASHTA

Tempest devises easy-to-spot 1980s equivalents for *The Tempest*'s principal characters and plot. The trouble is that the parallels in Paul Mazursky and Leon Capetanos's script only skim the surface of Shakespeare's play, without reaching its soul – leaving **Tempest** as a very pale imitation.

The opening, early morning scene establishes a Greek island setting and introduces its four inhabitants: the Prospero and Ariel figures, Phillip (John Cassavetes) and Aretha (Susan Sarandon), Phillip's petulant teenage daughter, Miranda (Molly Ringwald, three years away from 'Brat Pack' fame) and Kalibanos, a sex-starved goat-herd, energetically portrayed by Raul Julia as a lascivious caricature.

A series of leisurely flashbacks then take us back to New York, 18 months earlier, and we learn that Phillip is an architect, deep in mid-life crisis and sick of designing Atlantic City casinos for property magnate Alonzo. When he discovers that his actress wife, Antonia (played by Cassavetes's wife, Gena Rowlands), is sleeping with Alonzo, adultery replaces the coup which deposes Prospero and Phillip flees to Athens with Miranda. There he begins an affair with Aretha, a twice-divorced American cabaret singer. When Alonzo and Antonia track them down, Phillip, Miranda and Aretha take a boat to the island and meet Kalibanos.

Copying a masterpiece

Apart from an island scene showing Kalibanos emulating Caliban by trying to snatch Miranda's virginity, the storyline up to this point has less in common with Shakespeare than with any number of American dramas about middle-aged professionals. You wonder why Mazursky has restricted himself by copying *The Tempest* – and inviting inevitable comparisons with a masterpiece – when he could have written an original screenplay about a disenchanted architect.

Where Prospero is endearingly noble, Cassavetes (in a role originally offered to Paul Newman) makes Phillip unappealingly selfish and unfathomable. Sarandon is as spirited and attractive as ever, but Aretha's behaviour has to be awkwardly shoehorned

to fit the Ariel mould. Likewise, Alonzo is improbably devoted to an elderly stand-up comedian, Trinc, purely to create an equivalent for Trinculo.

Tellingly, the only scene in which **Tempest** briefly matches *The Tempest* comes when, instead of just finding superficial equivalents for Shakespeare's characters, the script closely imitates his poetry. Phillip almost drowns Kalibanos as punishment for assaulting Miranda, and the goat-herd furiously retorts that he has been poorly rewarded for helping Phillip. 'I show you the olive and the fig and the sweet water!' he yells, echoing Act I, Scene ii of the play, when Caliban angrily reminds Prospero how he was shown the island's 'fresh springs, brine-pits, barren place and fertile'.

Only in the last 40 minutes, when Alonzo's yacht cruises past the island, carrying Antonia, Alonzo, his staff and his teenage son, Freddy, does the action begin directly to copy the play. Phillip spots Alonzo's party heading ashore and *seems* magically to conjure a violent thunderstorm which capsizes their speedboat (since Kalibanos has forecast bad weather, Mazursky chickens out of suggesting that it is *really* Phillip's doing). Freddy, meanwhile, has met Miranda while swimming and the pair are instantly attracted.

The capsized visitors escape drowning, and resolution follows swiftly. Aretha tells Phillip that 'it's time to forgive' Antonia and Alonzo, so he does. The next day Phillip, Antonia and Miranda set off happily for New York. What a gulf there is between this pat conclusion and the audience satisfaction which can be generated by the climax of *The Tempest*.

Ultimately, **Tempest** works neither as adaptation nor as pastiche, and a *New York Times* review labelling it as 'an overblown, fancified freak of a film' was typical of critical reactions that ensured commercial failure. Mazursky would later suggest those reviews left him 'devastated'. Perhaps he wished his first idea for filming *The Tempest* had come off. He had approached Mick Jagger to appear as 'an androgynous Ariel' in a film that would have resembled 'a Marx brothers musical'. Just imagine the outlandish treatment Shakespeare would have received, if only Jagger had said 'Yes'.

Above: Left to right are Raul Julia, Susan Sarandon, John Cassavetes and Molly Ringwald as the four inhabitants of *Tempest*'s Greek island.

Right: Cassavetes as Philip, the film's Prospero figure, an American architect deep in mid-life crisis and shaken by his wife's adultery.

PROSPERO'S BOOKS (1991)
UK/NETHERLANDS/FRANCE/ITALY 120MINS COLOUR

CAST	JOHN GIELGUD (Prospero), ISABELLE PASCO (Miranda), MARK RYLANCE (Ferdinand), ORPHEO, PAUL RUSSELL, JAMES THIERREE and EMIL WOLK (Ariel), MICHAEL CLARK (Caliban), MICHAEL ROMEYN (Stephano), JIM VAN DE WOUDE (Trinculo), KENNETH CRANHAM (Sebastian) TOM BELL (Antonio), MICHEL BLANC (Alonso), ERLAND JOSEPHSON (Gonzalo)
DIRECTED BY	PETER GREENAWAY
PRODUCED BY	KEES KASANDER
SCREENPLAY	PETER GREENAWAY
PHOTOGRAPHY	SACHA VIERNY
MUSIC	MICHAEL NYMAN

Watching Peter Greenaway's extraordinary vision of *The Tempest* is infuriating. Shakespeare's profound human drama and John Gielgud's captivating Prospero are swamped by a torrent of live action and animated imagery. 'The play', said the *Financial Times*, 'becomes not so much a great, pure morality fable as a blank cheque for Greenaway's imagination'.

His inspiration is the magnificent speech in which Prospero tells Miranda how his exile was eased by Gonzalo's kindness:

'Knowing I loved my books, he furnished me
From mine own library with volumes that
I prize above my dukedom.'

This led Greenaway to create 24 books, dealing with science, mythology and other subjects Prospero might have used to transform himself into a magician. The books are also viewed as the source of *The Tempest*'s poetry, because Greenaway, like many scholars, sees Prospero as Shakespeare's alter ego: in his last play, the Bard said goodbye to the stage with a hero who bids farewell to creative powers. Greenaway equates Shakespeare with Prospero by having Gielgud provide all the characters' voices (airy tones for Ariel, a distorted growl for

Caliban). Prospero is sometimes shown writing their speeches in exquisite calligraphy.

As each book becomes relevant — the *Book of Water* when Prospero summons the storm, the *Book of Games* when Miranda and Ferdinand play chess — its pages come to life. Through a vivid combination of computer animation (using the revolutionary Quantel Paintbox program) and high-definition video, text writes itself, diagrams rotate, and bodily fluids splash onto the screen. A plummy (and uncredited) male voice-over comments on each volume and seals the 'Prospero is Shakespeare' concept in the final moments: Gielgud has been filling the last pages of Book 24 — *Thirty-Six Plays*, by William Shakespeare.

In addition to this dazzling but dramatically useless visual trickery, Greenaway fills his elaborate sets (designed by a Dutch team in an Amsterdam studio) with hundreds of mostly naked extras, representing Prospero's spirits and nymphs. Agonizingly slow tracking shots show Gielgud alongside marching and dancing figures — young, old, male, female, thin, fat. A typically insistent score from Michael Nyman, Greenaway's regular composer, adds to the monotony.

Losing the plot
Somewhere, trying vainly to grab the audience's attention, is the plot of *The Tempest*, although even viewers familiar with the play could be confused. It takes a while to adjust to an Ariel played by four different actors (aged between about five and 35), although there's no mistaking the naked Caliban, played with crab-like physicality by English dancer Michael Clark.

On the rare occasions when we can watch and listen to 87-year-old Gielgud in full flow, *The Tempest* comes movingly into focus. He shows absolute mastery of a role he had played in three stage productions, with Prospero's acute sense of his own mortality and tender concern for Miranda paramount.

Greenaway's refusal to let the other actors use their own voices until the penultimate scene makes it impossible to talk about 'performances' from an accomplished international cast: Britain's Tom Bell, Kenneth Cranham and Mark Rylance, France's Isabelle Pasco and Michel Blanc, Sweden's Erland Josephson. They are just elegantly dressed pawns in an elaborate game — like the characters in earlier, equally heartless Greenaway films such as *The Draughtsman's Contract*.

Greenaway suggested that **Prospero's Books** 'needs to be seen several times' to be fully appreciated — a prospect to frighten most critics and cinemagoers (although a $1.8 million American gross was adequate for such rarefied fare). 'As daring and eye-dazzling as anything achieved by a British film-maker, and as cold to the touch as an iceberg', said *The Times*. The *Independent* condemned 'a meticulous cancellation of Shakespeare's imaginative world'.

The *Village Voice* attacked the 'compulsive embellishment' that reflects Greenaway's art-college background and love of European painting. Viewers armed with a solid grasp of art history — or, better still, the illustrated screenplay — can spot references to Antonello da Messina (Prospero's study), Rembrandt (the Neapolitans' costumes), Botticelli and many others. Such allusions go to the heart of what's wrong with **Prospero's Books** — it turns *The Tempest* into a multi-media art exhibition.

Left: John Gielgud as the wise, humane Prospero. He had already played the role in four stage productions.

Top right: This flashback scene, based on a painting by Veronese, shows the Neapolitan conspirators preparing for the coup that deposes Prospero.

Far right: Dancer Michael Clark plays Caliban as half-man, half-amphibian creature.

The play becomes not so much a great, pure morality fable as a blank cheque for Greenaway's imagination. Financial Times

⑬

ANTONY AND CLEOPATRA (1972)

SPAIN/SWITZERLAND/UK 160 MINS COLOUR

CAST	CHARLTON HESTON (Antony), HILDEGARD NEIL (Cleopatra), ERIC PORTER (Enobarbus), JOHN CASTLE (Octavius), JANE LAPOTAIRE (Charmian), FREDDIE JONES (Pompey), FERNANDO REY (Lepidus), JULIAN GLOVER (Proculeius)
DIRECTED BY	CHARLTON HESTON
PRODUCER	PETER SNELL
SCREENPLAY	CHARLTON HESTON
PHOTOGRAPHY	RAFAEL PACHECO
MUSIC	JOHN SCOTT, AUGUSTO ALGUERO

Charlton Heston's screen love affair with Shakespeare's Mark Antony reached a rocky conclusion in this overlong, underbudgeted epic. It is more impressive than the earlier Roman collaboration between Heston and producer Peter Snell's – *Julius Caesar* (1970) – but this is not saying much.

After playing Mark Antony in the 1949 and 1970 films of *Caesar* (*see* pages 52 and 58), Heston had become obsessed with filming *Antony and Cleopatra*, which he considered Shakespeare's finest play (never previously filmed at feature length).

After writing a screenplay that sensibly removed many minor characters, Heston assumed directing duties only after Orson Welles turned him down. Had Welles accepted, he would surely not have allowed Shakespeare's plot, with its inherently cinematic criss-crossing between Alexandria, Rome, Syria and Athens, to progress as sluggishly as Heston's movie. Nor would Welles have embellished Shakespeare's language with gratuitous background action, such as the bout between two gladiators during a crucial early scene.

Yet even Welles might have failed to overcome the twin handicaps that defeated Heston – a $1 million budget (about $14 million today) too small to accommodate major battle sequences and, in South African actress Hildegard Neil, a Cleopatra incapable of mastering one of Shakespeare's most demanding roles.

The budgetary constraints are not immediately apparent, however, as lushly photographed exteriors in southern Spain double convincingly for elegant Roman villas and the sun, sea and sand of Egypt. Although paltry compared to the gargantuan splendour of *Cleopatra* (US, 1963), the sets built for the Egyptian queen's Alexandrian palace are fine.

The problems of scale arise when Heston's Antony abandons his vapid new wife, Octavia (Carmen Sevilla), and rushes back to Cleopatra, thereby breaching his alliance with Octavia's brother, the powerful, priggish Octavius (John Castle).

Disaster at sea

For the battle between Antony and Octavius's forces at Actium, a naval clash that Shakespeare could only allude to as off-stage 'noise of a sea-fight', Heston wanted massive spectacle. Financial constraints obliged him to splice together original footage of Antony's flagship ramming one of Octavius's galleys with outtakes of warships from *Ben Hur*. The resulting montage – close-ups of vast, sturdy replica ships intercut with long shots of tiny, flimsy models – is laughable, ruining the pivotal moment when Cleopatra betrays Antony by withdrawing her fleet.

The later battle, when Cleopatra's second betrayal helps Octavius's cavalry to overwhelm Antony's troops, is more effective but still falls far short of Hollywood epic standards. Yet Heston cannot resist over-indulging his own, epic image, so we watch Antony fighting his way through Roman horsemen with apparently superhuman strength.

Even if it had been staged on a grander scale, the suspicion is that all this action might still muffle **Antony and Cleopatra**'s impact as a tragic love story, and in any case, the performances leave the central couple's relationship fatally lop-sided. As the *Sunday Express* noted, there is 'sensitivity, integrity and great love' in Antony as played by Heston, for once not overreliant on his trademarks (steely gaze, clenched jaw and expansive laughter), and there is a genuine sense of loss when his second defeat drives him to suicide. Would that the ravishingly beautiful Neil could have hinted at Cleopatra's 'infinite variety'.

Perfect cheekbones and lipgloss do not compensate for a nondescript personality and insensitive handling of the verse, particularly in the tense build-up to Cleopatra's suicide; she is embarrassingly outacted by her lady-in-waiting, Charmian (the seductive and moving Jane Lapotaire, a fine Cleopatra for the BBC in 1981).

Right: Charlton Heston as Antony and Hildegard Neil as Cleopatra. There was precious little chemistry between the stars and, to Heston's dismay, the movie flopped.

It is Lapotaire and the other British actors with plenty of experience of stage Shakespeare who are the strongest members of a multinational supporting cast: Freddie Jones as a grizzled, wine-guzzling Pompey; Julian Glover (Heston's double during technical rehearsals) as a dignified Proculeius, and Eric Porter as a memorably cynical Enobarbus, the loyal lieutenant driven to a cliff-top suicide after his final desertion of Antony. Only Castle's oddly disinterested Octavius disappoints.

Antony and Cleopatra always stands or falls by its stars, and when the film opened in Britain negative criticism of Neil's performance confirmed Welles's preproduction warning to Heston that 'if you don't have a great Cleopatra, you can't do this play'.

Lousy reviews ruined the movie's chances of wide distribution in the US, and, writing in his autobiography, Heston was forced to lament: 'The film I cared more about than any I've made was a failure.'

Right: Hildegard Neil as Cleopatra, left, with Monica Peterson as Iras, the servant who kills herself in the Egyptian queen's monument.

A PETER SNELL PRODUCTION

CHARLTON HESTON
HILDEGARD NEIL
AS **ANTONY AND CLEOPATRA**

TECHNICOLOR ®   FILMED IN TODD AO 35m/m

14

LOVE'S LABOUR'S LOST (2000)

UK/FRANCE/US 93 MINS COLOUR

CAST	KENNETH BRANAGH (Berowne), NATASCHA MCELHONE (Rosaline), ALESSANDRO NIVOLA (King), ALICIA SILVERSTONE (Princess), MATTHEW LILLARD (Longaville), CARMEN EJOGO (Maria), ADRIAN LESTER (Dumaine), EMILY MORTIMER (Katherine), NATHAN LANE (Costard), TIMOTHY SPALL (Armado)
DIRECTED BY	KENNETH BRANAGH
PRODUCED BY	DAVID BARRON, KENNETH BRANAGH
SCREENPLAY	KENNETH BRANAGH
PHOTOGRAPHY	ALEX THOMSON
MUSIC	PATRICK DOYLE

Love's Labour's Lost is a delight, hailed by *The Sunday Telegraph* as Kenneth Branagh's 'most endearing film', and bursting with what *Variety* called 'silly, charming and always honest entertainment'. That doesn't necessarily make it good Shakespeare.

Branagh updates the story to 1939, cuts almost 75 per cent of an exceptionally wordy text and transforms a rarely staged play (filmed only once before, by the BBC in 1985) into an old-fashioned musical, featuring 1930s standards from Irving Berlin, Cole Porter and the Gershwins.

His $13 million film has the studio sheen, heightened colours and escapist spirit of Fred Astaire/Ginger Rogers classics like *Top Hat* (US, 1935), and leaves you humming its tunes, or replaying the dance routines. That's a cherishable and, since the 1960s, elusive cinema experience – although very mixed reviews (including *The Guardian*'s 'slipshod and leadenly unfunny') contributed to a disappointing British box-office gross of $410,000. The problem with **Love's Labour's Lost** as Shakespeare is that it is difficult to recall any scenes as written by the Bard.

Witty, Movietone-style newsreels (plummily voiced by Branagh) summarize missing scenes, and the first of these introduces us to the college at which the King of Navarre (serene Nivola) and his companions – Longaville (preppy Lillard), Dumaine (suave Lester) and Berowne (Branagh at his most relaxed) – are beginning three years' study.

Gathered in a circular, domed library (part of Tim Harvey's superb, 'fantasy Oxbridge' production design), they sign an oath renouncing female company and then suddenly drop their pentameters and launch into 'I'd Rather Charleston'. It's a gasp-inducing moment, promptly topped by Timothy Spall's absurdly pompous, 'Spaneesh'-accented Don Armado, expressing his love for statuesque country wench Jaquenetta (Stefania Rocca) with his hilarious rendition of 'I Get A Kick Out of You', as a music video.

The plot moves into gear once the Princess of France arrives, in a dreamy night-time sequence, to discuss a France-Navarre financial settlement. She is accompanied by three ladies-in-waiting, Rosaline, Maria and Katherine, and instant, mutual attraction turns the story into 'Four Brides for Four Students': Princess matched with King, Rosaline with Berowne; Maria with Longaville, Dumaine with Katherine.

During the badinage, eavesdropping and mock rejections that ensue, Branagh reinvents Shakespeare's comic characters. The desperately boring male pedant, Holofernes, becomes a whimsical female tutor, Holofernia (Geraldine McEwan); Costard, the innuendo-prone clown becomes Nathan Lane's vaudeville comic, although neither they, nor Spall, have much to do as Branagh goes all out for romance.

Sung from the heart

The lovers deliver seven of the ten songs, chosen because Branagh believed they equalled Shakespeare in conveying 'how silly, wonderful, stupid and agonizing' love is. Thus Berowne's long speech in praise of love does a *segue* into 'Cheek to Cheek', and as he sings 'Heaven, I'm in heaven' the boys fly up to the library ceiling on invisible wires. The girls sing 'No Strings (I'm Fancy Free)' while performing a synchronized-swimming homage to Busby Berkeley (loosely equivalent to their deer-shooting expedition in the play) and join their paramours for a pulsating, sexy 'Let's Face the Music and Dance'.

All of this is captivating, despite some slightly amateurish – and oddly endearing – edges to the singing and dancing from everyone except award-winning stage musical stars Lester and Lane (who sings 'There's No Business Like Showbusiness'). A greater problem arises from the shifts out of simple lyrics or newsreel commentary back into lofty Shakespearean metaphor. By the time you've readjusted, the next song may be seconds away; Shakespeare is reduced to filler material.

Such verse as remains is handled well by everyone except the miscast Silverstone, who is outshone by the *Vogue*-like grace of McElhone's Rosaline and left breathless by the Princess's lines. She struggles most with the speech following the announcement of the death of her father, the King, during which she insists that after hasty beginnings she and Navarre must spend a year apart before marrying.

Her companions follow suit, so the couples drive off for a bittersweet airfield farewell that pays tribute to *Casablanca*. It's a perfect finale – spoiled by Branagh's sentimental epilogue: a newsreel montage of the characters' heroic contributions to World War II, ending with a joyful, VE-Day reunion. Following 90 minutes of featherlight fantasy with a three-minute war is a dreadful way to turn Shakespeare's ending into 'Love's Labour's Won'.

Left: Left to right are Kenneth Branagh, Matthew Lillard, Alessandro Nivola and Adrian Lester as the four bachelors who swear a short-lived oath renouncing female company.

Above left: Natascha McElhone as Rosaline, far right, and Kenneth Branagh as Berowne, second right, lead the four pairs of lovers in one of the film's dance routines.

Left: Alicia Silverstone, miscast as the princess of France. Shakespeare's verse leaves the *Clueless* star breathless.

(14)

MUCH ADO ABOUT NOTHING (1993)
UK/US 111 MINS COLOUR

CAST	KENNETH BRANAGH (Benedick), EMMA THOMPSON (Beatrice), RICHARD BRIERS (Leonato), MICHAEL KEATON (Dogberry), DENZEL WASHINGTON (Don Pedro), ROBERT SEAN LEONARD (Claudio), KEANU REEVES (Don John), KATE BECKINSALE (Hero)
DIRECTED BY	KENNETH BRANAGH
PRODUCED BY	STEPHEN EVANS, DAVID PARFITT AND KENNETH BRANAGH
SCREENPLAY	KENNETH BRANAGH
PHOTOGRAPHY	ROGER LANSER
MUSIC	PATRICK DOYLE

A travesty, but oh what a lovely one … You get mugged by its magic. Financial Times

Much Ado About Nothing has the most dazzling opening sequence of any Shakespeare comedy. On a sunny Italian hillside, the leisurely picnic enjoyed by Emma Thompson's Beatrice and her companions is spectacularly interrupted. The sight of Don Pedro and his gallant brothers in arms galloping back from distant conflict sends the women sprinting to noble Leonato's villa, with both groups captured in slow motion and accompanied by Patrick Doyle's brassy score.

The women hurriedly shower and change into white cotton dresses even cleaner than the ones they've just discarded; the soldiers strip off, plunge into fountains to scrub away the trail dust and emerge with their leather trousers and cream tunics looking as good as new. Like opposing armies, the two groups march into a courtyard in formation – and the battle of the sexes can commence.

It's exuberant, economical film-making: in five minutes, Branagh has established the location and tone of a comedy that will prove 'fresh, unaffected and rumbustious' (*The Guardian*), introduced its principal characters and hooked his audience.

He had visualized this sequence while playing Benedick on stage in 1988, and at about the same time also decided that *Much Ado* (previously filmed in East Germany, in 1963, and twice in Russia, in 1956 and 1973) would come most vividly to life in a lush landscape, a view triumphantly vindicated by the results of his decision to shoot in Tuscany instead of Messina, on Sicily (the play's location).

A sunny outlook

All but a handful of scenes take place in the landscaped gardens and grounds of the 14th-century Villa Vignamaggio in the Chianti region, either beneath perfect blue skies or on balmy nights filled with masked revelling. It's an irresistible combination: beautiful scenery, beautiful weather and (mostly) beautiful people caught up in a flimsy plot that hinges on *five* cases of eavesdropping and is over almost before it's begun.

Its main strand involves a pair of the blandly gorgeous young lovers to be found in so many Shakespeare comedies, in this case Kate Beckinsale, as Leonato's daughter, Hero, and Robert Sean Leonard as Claudio. Don John, Pedro's bastard brother, deceives Claudio into believing that Hero has slept with another man and then flees after Claudio denounces her as a whore during their abruptly terminated wedding ceremony.

Leonato (Briers at his most benevolent) and his brother, Antonio (Brian Blessed, all lusty, theatrical guffaws), pretend that Hero is dead and Beatrice asks Benedick to kill Claudio for slandering her cousin. However, conflict is swiftly averted once Dogberry, the idiotic constable given to ludicrous misuse of words, extracts confessions from Don John's accomplices, Borachio and Conrad. Don John is captured, Claudio and Hero married, and Benedick, the sworn bachelor, and Beatrice, the confirmed spinster, who have been tricked into falling in love, will get married.

It's the 'merry war' between this pair that has ensured *Much Ado*'s lofty reputation amongst the comedies, and Branagh and Thompson, still husband and wife at the time, enjoy their verbal jousts. Branagh could be less self-conscious in his soliloquies, but there's no faulting Thompson, who balances 'clear intelligence and deep vulnerability' (*Daily Mail*) to suggest Beatrice's pleasant, spirited nature and her fear of being left on the shelf.

Only Denzel Washington among the Americans matches Thompson for star quality, delivering a typically regal portrayal as Pedro. Keanu Reeves's wooden performance as Don John, happily a man 'not of many words', can partly be excused as he's playing a cardboard villain, but Branagh made an inexcusable error in overindulging Michael Keaton's grotesque Dogberry. With greasy hair, foul teeth and a scarcely intelligible accent – Welsh-Irish-American, with a dash of Long John Silver – Keaton leers, gurns and, like Ben Elton's equally absurd deputy, Verges, runs around pretending to ride an invisible horse.

As *The Times* noted, 'the film stops dead whenever Keaton appears', although – happily – his four, excruciating appearances put only a small dent in the surrounding joy, good humour and sexual energy that won over even those critics who thought that Branagh had overdone the thigh-slapping jollity. The *Financial Times* encouraged readers to 'get mugged by its magic'; *Variety* found it 'continuously enjoyable'.

Much Ado was a smash, recouping its budget in the UK alone – where it grossed around $10 million (£5.4 million) – and taking a further $22 million in America where it was the most successful British film of 1993.

Right: Kenneth Branagh as Benedick with Emma Thompson as Beatrice, united at the end of the couple's 'merry war'. Off screen the stars were still husband and wife.

Below: From second left to right are Kenneth Branagh as Benedick, Robert Sean Leonard as Claudio, Denzel Washington as Don Pedro and Keanu Reeves as Don John.

CAST	ANTHONY HOPKINS (Titus), JESSICA LANGE (Tamora), HARRY LENNIX (Aaron), ALAN CUMMING (Saturninus), JONATHAN RHYS MEYERS (Chiron), MATTHEW RHYS (Demetrius), ANGUS MACFADYEN (Lucius), COLM FEORE (Marcus), LAURA FRASER (Lavinia), JAMES FRAIN (Bassianus)
DIRECTED BY	JULIE TAYMOR
PRODUCED BY	JODY PATTON, CONCHITA AIROLDI, JULIE TAYMOR
SCREENPLAY	JULIE TAYMOR
PHOTOGRAPHY	LUCIANO TOVOLI
MUSIC	ELLIOT GOLDENTHAL

Rape, murder, mutilation and cannibalism – *Titus Andronicus* contains so many horrors that some critics dismiss it as a juvenile gore-fest, unworthy of Shakespeare's name. Julie Taymor's devastating **Titus** shows that there's much more to the play than mere violence.

Only the second screen version of Shakespeare's bloodiest tragedy (following the BBC's 1985 production), **Titus** shares the dazzling invention displayed by Taymor's award-winning direction of the Disney stage musical *The Lion King*. She bravely retains a time-bending concept originally developed for her 1994 off-Broadway staging of *Titus Andronicus*, so while Shakespeare's plot is set in Rome, AD 400, Taymor uses ancient ruins, Dante Ferretti's stunning production design and Milena Canonero's Oscar-nominated costumes to straddle the 5th and 20th centuries.

Titus opens as a young boy is magically transported from the present day to the Coliseum in Rome and watches Anthony Hopkins's grizzled Titus lead his army in a stylized victory parade,

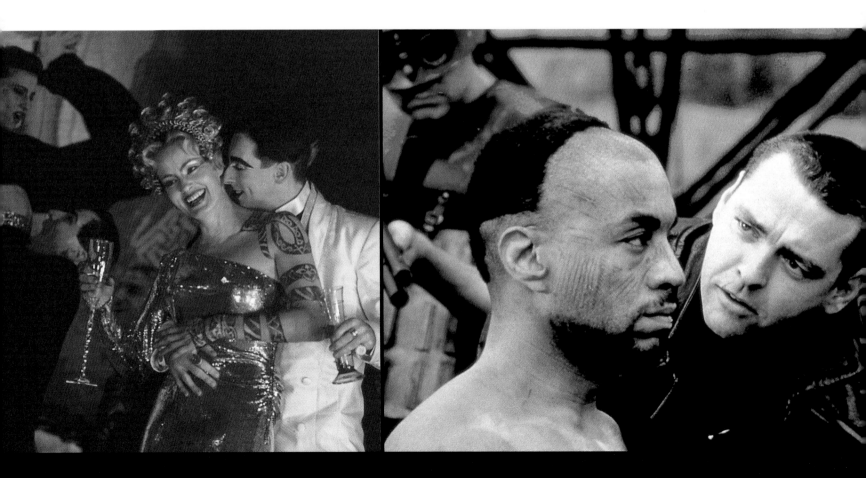

Above: Jessica Lange as Tamora, centre, the tattooed Goth queen, embraced by Alan Cumming as Saturnius,

Above right: Harry Lennix as Aaron, centre, the villainous Moor captured and interrogated by Angus

Titus Andronicus speaks directly to a time whose audience feeds daily on tabloid sex scandals

with chariots followed by tanks and motorbikes. Titus has lost 21 of his 25 sons in conquering the Goths and capturing their tattooed Queen, Tamora (Jessica Lange). He initiates a terrible cycle of killings with the ritual sacrifice of Tamora's eldest son – in the first of several jarring special-effects sequences that push us into what *The New York Times* called 'a surreal, time-collapsed dream world, a murderously supercharged virtual reality'.

Vowing revenge, Tamora, her surviving sons, Chiron and Demetrius, and Aaron the Moor (Harry Lennix), her slave and secret lover, seize their opportunity after the queen marries Rome's corrupt new emperor, Saturninus (Alan Cumming), who is headquartered in Mussolini's former government centre and protected by 1930s-style Blackshirts.

On Aaron's instructions, Chiron and Demetrius kill Bassianus, the emperor's brother. They then rape his wife, and Titus's only daughter, Lavinia (doe-eyed Laura Fraser), abandoning her in a swamp after cutting off her hands and tongue; mercifully, Taymor shows only the attack's heart-rending aftermath.

Gore and laughter

Two of Titus's sons, Quintus and Martius, are framed for Bassianus's murder by Aaron, an Iago prototype played by Lennix with chilling menace and a nice line in to-camera soliloquies. He deceives Titus into cutting off his own hand to 'save' his condemned children from execution, and Taymor deftly fuses horror with hilarity: Titus's severed hand is driven away from his villa by Aaron in a sports car, and his sons' severed heads are promptly delivered by messenger van. This pushes Titus towards Lear-like madness, and Hopkins is almost unwatchably moving as a man who starts off so blindly devoted to Rome that he unhesitatingly kills one of his sons, Mutius, for disobeying the emperor, only to find his faith shattered by the realization that 'Rome is but a wilderness of tigers'.

Lucius, Titus's last son (and father of the boy from the opening scene), raises a Goth army against Saturninus, and captures Aaron, who has fled Rome with the child Tamora has born him in secret. Titus lures Chiron and Demetrius to his villa, slits their throats, bakes their flesh into a pie (Taymor unwisely has Hopkins repeat Hannibal Lecter's cannibalistic slurping from *The Silence of the Lambs*) and feeds it to Tamora at a dinner that swiftly becomes a massacre.

Titus ends Lavinia's misery by breaking her neck, then kills Tamora. Saturninus kills Titus and, as Lucius shoots Saturninus, a breathtaking freeze-frame transplants the dinner guests into the Coliseum, now filled with spectators in 1990s dress. Their rapt attention is a potent reminder of the Coliseum's killing-as-entertainment origins; according to Taymor's persuasive argument, it also shows *Titus Andronicus* 'speaking directly to our times; a time whose audience feeds daily on tabloid sex scandals, teenage gang rape, high school gun sprees'.

Despite strong reviews, **Titus** was too harrowing to break into the mainstream, as demonstrated by an American gross of $1.9 million. Its daring fusion of periods, fantasy and graphic reality, not to mention accents (American, Scots, Irish and Welsh), might have been an incoherent mess. Yet Taymor gives it absolute clarity by decisively separating the opposing sides.

The Goths and Saturninus relish an obscenely decadent existence (Jazz-age parties and a Roman orgy), matched by extravagant performances: Cumming strikes camp, leering poses; Lange, clad in figure-hugging gold, is vampishly seductive; Jonathan Rhys Meyers and Matthew Rhys play Tamora's savage sons as hysterical, video game-addicted punks. By contrast, Titus's family lives modestly, and Hopkins, Angus Macfadyen, as Lucius, and Colm Feore, as Titus's brother, Marcus, adopt the credible acting style you might expect from a conventional stage production. Their dignity helps Taymor to make a powerful case for *Titus Andronicus* to be treated with respect and ensures that the relentless brutality of **Titus** is moving and thought-provoking, rather than numbingly empty.

Left: Anthony Hopkins as Titus, face and armour caked with clay in the stylized victory parade at the start of the film.

TWELFTH NIGHT (1996)
UK/US 133 MINS COLOUR

CAST	IMOGEN STUBBS (Viola/Cesario), TOBY STEPHENS (Orsino), HELENA BONHAM CARTER (Olivia), STEVEN MACKINTOSH (Sebastian), NIGEL HAWTHORNE (Malvolio), BEN KINGSLEY (Feste), RICHARD E. GRANT (Sir Andrew Aguecheek), MEL SMITH (Sir Toby Belch)
DIRECTED BY	TREVOR NUNN
PRODUCED BY	STEPHEN EVANS, DAVID PARFITT
SCREENPLAY	TREVOR NUNN
PHOTOGRAPHY	CLIVE TICKNER
MUSIC	SHAUN DAVEY

Trevor Nunn's record as one of British theatre and television's finest directors of Shakespeare led to great expectations for **Twelfth Night**, his first attempt at transferring the Bard to the big screen. Those hopes were not fulfilled by a movie that is consistently intelligent, attractive and well-spoken, but only fitfully entertaining. After gathering generally poor reviews, its UK gross of $1 million was a sad return on a $5 million budget.

Nunn regards *Twelfth Night* as a 'perfect work of art' and reworked it to meet cinema's demands only with great reluctance. He updated the story to the 1890s, wrote in an explanatory verse prologue and, sensibly clarifying the background to the plot, devised an elaborate opening sequence showing the shipwreck that precedes the start of the play. Shakespeare's identical twins, Viola and Sebastian, are cross-dressing entertainers on board a cruise ship capsized by a violent storm, and are washed ashore separately on the coast of Illyria, each believing the other drowned.

Illyria is represented by autumnal Cornwall, with much of the action set against a picturesque, cobbled fishing village or spectacular cliff-tops, with St Michael's Mount doubling as the castle of Duke Orsino, with whom Viola finds service, disguised as a man, Cesario.

A double life
Viola's acting skills are vital in Orsino's men-only, military court, which has a strong *Prisoner of Zenda* feel, and the Orsino/Cesario strand of the story comes alive much more effectively than on stage, with Nunn chopping up Shakespeare's scenes to keep the pair's relationship more consistently in view, and the excellent Imogen Stubbs (Nunn's wife) making Viola's cross-dressing both tense and amusing: she must fence, smoke cigars and play billiards – activities that might blow her cover.

Orsino, whom Stephens makes appropriately self-pitying and vain, sends Cesario as his go-between to woo the countess Olivia (Bonham Carter, as comfortable as ever with 19th-century manners). Olivia has become a virtual recluse in her elegant country mansion and gardens (Prideaux Place and the National Trust house at Lanhydrock), mourning the deaths of her father and brother. She cannot return Orsino's affection but is instantly smitten by Cesario; Viola falls in love with Orsino, who becomes more affectionate towards Cesario than he might wish.

In another part of Illyria, the liner's captain, Antonio (Nicholas Farrell), is clearly in love with Sebastian, whom he rescued from the wreck, but all the romantic and sexual confusions of Shakespeare's most gender-conscious play accumulate at a disappointingly even pace, which, noted *The Daily Telegraph*, has 'no real rhythm or flow'.

Nor is there much zip to some 'dreadful hamming' (*Sight and Sound*) from Richard E. Grant as the blond, foppish Andrew Aguecheek, who is hopelessly in love with Olivia, and a

Left: Left to right are Helena Bonham Carter, Stephen Mackintosh, Imogen Stubbs and Toby Stephens, celebrating the double wedding that ends the film.

Far left: Richard E. Grant gives an irritating performance as the foppish Sir Andrew Aguecheek.

Above: Nigel Hawthorne as Malvolio, reading the forged letter that invites him to dress up in yellow stockings to delight the countess Olivia.

bewhiskered Mel Smith as her Falstaffian cousin, Sir Toby. They conspire with Olivia's maid, Maria (Imelda Staunton), to dupe the conceited steward, Malvolio (Nigel Hawthorne), into believing that Olivia loves him, and, most famously, wants to see him capering about in yellow stockings. They then lock him up for his apparently lunatic behaviour, at which point Hawthorne's marvellous performance echoes his torments in *The Madness of King George*.

Mostly, the cast raise smiles rather than laughter, and the film comes alive only in the last half-hour. Sebastian turns up at Olivia's at the same time as his sister, causing some chaotic and enchanted mistaken-identity comedy, and ends up married to Olivia five minutes after meeting her, leaving Viola to reveal her true identity and marry Orsino.

Nunn then emphasizes, more strongly than most stage productions, that it's only the twins and their spouses who end happily: we see Malvolio striding away from Olivia's household to plot his revenge; Toby and Maria riding off together to a marriage founded on convenience, not love, and Shakespeare's jester, Feste, whom Ben Kingsley has played with a haunting, melancholy edge, wandering along the cliffs to find fresh employment.

This was not the first screen *Twelfth Night*. Russia's Lenfilm studio made a colour feature version in 1955; West Germany produced a black-and-white feature in 1962, and British television has filmed the play six times. The best example, made for commercial television in 1969, paired Alec Guinness as Malvolio with Ralph Richardson as Sir Toby.

14

This section gives details of significant film and/or television versions of the Shakespeare plays that have yet to be turned into English-language feature films designed for cinema release. Throughout, 'BBC Shakespeare' refers to the complete cycle of Shakespeare plays produced by the BBC and Time-Life between 1978 and 1985.

All's Well That Ends Well

Regarded as one of the most 'difficult' of the comedies, charting the uneasy marriage between Bertram and Helena, *All's Well That Ends Well* has been televised twice by the BBC: a record of John Barton's RSC production in 1968, and the BBC Shakespeare version (1981).

The Comedy of Errors

A silent version of the tale of mistaken identities, involving twin masters (the two Antipholuses) and servants (the two Dromios), was released in America in 1908. The only feature-film adaptation is *The Boys from Syracuse* (US, 1941), based on the Rodgers and Hart musical, *Boys from Syracuse*, which had freely adapted Shakespeare's play and was a hit on Broadway in 1938. The film keeps Shakespeare's ancient setting but uses 20th-century language and is packed with light-hearted jokes and anachronisms, such as a metered, taxi-style chariot. Its screenwriting credit states: 'After a play by Shakespeare ... long, long after!'

A BBC production in 1954 dressed its cast in Jane Austen-era costumes and combined speech, recitative and songs with live accompaniment from a 12-piece orchestra. The BBC screened the play twice more, first adapting an RSC production from 1964, which featured Diana Rigg and Janet Suzman, and then in 1984, when trick photography allowed Roger Daltrey, lead singer of The Who, to double impressively as the two Dromios; Hammer Horror star Ingrid Pitt played the courtesan. ITV's 1978 version had Judi Dench and Francesca Annis as the female leads.

Coriolanus

Shakespeare's account of the general brought down through his arrogance and dependence on his domineering mother is the least-performed of the three Roman plays, and has had minimal screen treatment. In 1951, American television produced a one-hour adaptation, set in Mussolini-era Rome, and in 1963, *Coriolanus* was incorporated into the BBC's epic *Spread of the Eagle*, a nine-part mini-series that adapted the Roman plays into a continuous narrative. Alan Howard played the title role for the BBC Shakespeare in 1984.

Italy produced the only big-budget cinema adaptation in 1964, with *Coriolano, eroe senza patria* (literally, 'Coriolanus, hero without a country', but marketed internationally as *Thunder of Battle*). Loosely based on the play, it was dismissed by *Monthly Film Bulletin* as 'colourless' and 'unexciting'.

Cymbeline

Set in Roman Britain, with a wildly improbable, genre-defying plot, and a marvellously resilient heroine, in Imogen, *Cymbeline* had its first screen outing in Edwin Thanhouser's 1913 American silent. This ran for 41 minutes, boasted impressive crowd scenes and exterior action shots, and is regarded as one of the finest silent Shakespeares. The next notable screen adaptation did not emerge for 70 years: the 1983 BBC Shakespeare version, with Helen Mirren as Imogen.

Henry VI Parts I, II and III

Never adapted for the cinema, all three parts of this history cycle were filmed by the BBC in 1960, 1965 (within the RSC's Wars of the Roses cycle) and, most recently, for the BBC Shakespeare in 1982, when Brenda Blethyn, Oscar-nominated star of *Secrets and Lies* (UK/France, 1996), played Joan of Arc.

Henry VIII

Actor-manager Sir Herbert Beerbohm Tree played Cardinal Wolsey in a silent British *Henry VIII* in 1911 (now lost) and, in 1912, America's Vitagraph company released a 10-minute production with impressively shot court scenes. The BBC Shakespeare *Henry VIII* (1979) was shot on location at two castles and a stately home, all in Kent, with John Stride (Ross in Polanski's *Macbeth*) as the king, and Claire Bloom as Katharine of Aragon.

Right: Francesca Annis as Luciana, left, alongside Judi Dench as Adriana in the British television version of *The Comedy of Errors* (1978), based on a Royal Shakespeare Company production.

Below right: Helen Mirren as Imogen, heroine of the BBC Shakespeare production of *Cymbeline* (1983).

King John

In September 1899, King John became the first Shakespeare play ever filmed, thanks to Sir Herbert Beerbohm Tree. Shot in the open air at the Biograph company's studio in London, the film originally depicted four scenes from Tree's production of the play at a West End theatre, Her Majesty's, and is believed to have run for four minutes.

The only fragment still in existence runs for just one minute and is taken from the final scene of the play. Wearing a white robe, King John (Tree) sits in a chair in front of a painted backdrop, writhing in pain and clutching his chest, much to the distress of his son, Prince John (played by a young actress, Dora Senior), and two actors in period armour, playing Lord Bigot and the Earl of Pembroke. Released on the day that Tree's stage production opened, this landmark film may well have been conceived more as a 'trailer' for the play than as entertainment in its own right.

In 1952, the BBC filmed *King John* with legendary actor-manager Donald Wolfit (the model for 'Sir' in 1983's *The Dresser*) in the title role. Shortly before his death in 1984, Leonard Rossiter, much-loved star of British sitcoms *Rising Damp* and *The Fall and Rise of Reginald Perrin*, played King John for the BBC Shakespeare.

Above: Derek Jacobi as Richard, left, with John Gielgud as John of Gaunt in the BBC Shakespeare's *Richard II* (1978).

Left: Ermete Novelli as Shylock, centre, in the trial scene from *The Merchant of Venice* (1910), an Italian silent directed by Gerolamo Lo Savio.

Measure for Measure

Regarded as one of Shakespeare's 'problem plays', the gripping drama set in Vienna and examining the nature of justice was produced by West German television in 1963 and for the BBC Shakespeare in 1978, with Canadian actress Kate Nelligan as the novice heroine, Isabella.

The Merchant of Venice

The notorious and uneasy comedy of Portia's suitors and Shylock's demand for a pound of flesh was very popular in the silent era, and *The Merchant of Venice* was filmed in Britain, France, Germany, Italy and the US between 1908 and 1923. The hour-long German silent, *Der Kaufmann von Venedig* (1923), was a loose adaptation, featuring Werner Krauss (Shylock) and Henny Porten (Portia), both national superstars at the time.

The BBC has produced the play four times, in 1947, 1955, 1972 (with Frank Finlay as Shylock and Maggie Smith as Portia) and 1980, when director Jonathan Miller cast Warren Mitchell, best known as objectionable Alf Garnett in the sitcom *'Til Death Us Do Part*, as Shylock for the BBC Shakespeare. Miller's Edwardian-era production for the National Theatre was filmed for television in 1969, preserving one of Laurence Olivier's finest performances, as a bespectacled, elegantly dressed Shylock (it was shown in the US in 1974).

The Merry Wives of Windsor

The comedy surrounding Falstaff's farcical attempt to bed Mistresses Ford and Page was filmed in the US in 1910 and adapted as *Falstaff* for a 1911 French silent. The BBC's 1952 production was transmitted live, with Robert Atkins as Falstaff, and the cast of the 1982 BBC Shakespeare included Richard Griffiths as Falstaff and Ben Kingsley as Ford.

Pericles, Prince of Tyre

The seldom-performed late romance, centred on the shipwrecked prince, his devoted wife, Thaisa, and long-lost daughter, Marina, was filmed for the BBC Shakespeare in 1984.

Richard II

This play, which some critics consider better read as poetry than watched as drama, became the first Shakespeare history to receive full-length television treatment with the 1950 BBC production. NBC's Hallmark Hall of Fame series cast its regular leading man, Maurice Evans, as Richard, with Sarah Churchill, daughter of Winston, as the Queen, in a lavish production transmitted live to 55 US cities in 1954.

The BBC has twice filmed the play, in 1960, as part of the Age of Kings cycle (which adapted eight history plays into eight

60–90-minute episodes), and in the first season of the BBC Shakespeare, in 1978, with Derek Jacobi as Richard, Jon Finch (Polanski's Macbeth) as the usurper, Bolingbroke, and John Gielgud as his father, John of Gaunt.

Timon of Athens

Rarely staged in the theatre, the blackly comic story of Timon, the deeply misanthropic Greek, was screened in the BBC Shakespeare in 1981, with Jonathan Pryce in the title role.

Troilus and Cressida

The Trojan War tragedy was directed by Jonathan Miller in 1981 for the BBC Shakespeare, with Jack Birkett (Caliban in Jarman's *The Tempest*) as the 'deformed and scurrilous' Greek, Thersites.

Two Gentlemen of Verona

This early romantic comedy, centred around Proteus's love for Julia and Valentine's for Silvia, was filmed for West German television in 1963 and for the BBC Shakespeare in 1983.

The Winter's Tale

Silent films of the late romance of Othello-like jealousy and the healing power of time were produced in the US (1910), Germany (1914) and Italy (1914; with an actor dressed as Shakespeare serving as narrator).

In a BBC production from 1962, Leontes was played by Robert Shaw and in 1968, Frank Dunlop's Edinburgh Festival stage production was recorded and released as a feature film, starring Laurence Harvey as Leontes and Jim Dale of *Carry On ...* fame as the Bohemian rogue, Autolycus. Jane Howell directed the BBC Shakespeare (1981) with Robert Stephens as Polixenes on some very stylized sets, involving giant white cones.

Above: Robert Atkins as Falstaff, centre, with Mary Kerridge as Mistress Page, left, and Betty Huntley-Wright as Mistress Ford, right, in the BBC's 1952 production of *The Merry Wives of Windsor*.

In 1989, Kenneth Branagh transformed the Bard from cinema's forgotten man into one of its most popular writers. His *Henry V* was only the second English-language Shakespeare feature to have been produced since 1972; in the decade after it became a hit, British and American directors produced 17 Shakespeare movies.

The company behind *Henry V* was called Renaissance Films — and a renaissance is just what it started. 'Branagh opened it all up with *Henry V*. That was just an explosion', declared Al Pacino, director and star of *Looking for Richard*, in 1996. 'We learned that people could appreciate and enjoy these plays. Now you say "Shakespeare" in Hollywood and people listen.'

Branagh did not simply start the revival and then walk away. Although he has set Shakespeare aside to direct a mainstream thriller, an ensemble comedy and an overblown horror movie, he has kept returning to the plays, to film *Much Ado About Nothing*, *Hamlet* and *Love's Labour's Lost*.

In artistic terms, he occupies middle ground, between cinema's other most prolific Shakespeareans: Franco Zeffirelli, Laurence Olivier and Orson Welles. Like Zeffirelli, Branagh is committed to making Shakespeare accessible to the largest possible audience, but does so without resorting to the textual compromises favoured by the Italian — as can be seen from his determination to film *Hamlet* uncut, at more than twice the length of Zeffirelli's 1990 version. Until *Love's Labour's Lost* (*see* page 160), when the lyrics of 1930s love songs took precedence, Branagh had always given Shakespeare's language pride of place.

Like Olivier and Welles, Branagh plays the leading roles in his Shakespeare films, yet his performances never dominate as Olivier dominates his *Richard III*, or Welles dominates *Chimes at Midnight*. Alongside those two gigantic personalities, Branagh appears a comparatively selfless servant of Shakespeare, actors and cinemagoers, particularly those with little knowledge of the Bard.

Many teenagers and adults have written to Branagh over the years, explaining how *Henry V* or *Much Ado* helped them to 'get into Shakespeare', and those letters sustain a passionate belief in popularism which stems from Branagh's working-class background and, specifically, his parents. 'They used to come along and watch me in plays and say they enjoyed it, but they wouldn't know', he said early in 2000. 'My parents are the reason I wanted to make Shakespeare available to ordinary people.'

Staging posts

Branagh was born in Belfast in December 1960, the son of a Protestant joiner who when the Troubles flared in 1969 moved his wife and three children to a safer environment, Reading, near London. To fit in at school, Branagh gradually erased his Ulster accent. At the age of 15, he went to see Derek Jacobi as Hamlet

in Oxford and, as he later wrote, 'the damage was done. I began to read more of Shakespeare. I resolved to become an actor.'

Encouragement from his drama teacher helped him overcome his parents' reticence over his stage ambitions and he won a place at the Royal Academy of Dramatic Art (RADA). Its principal, Hugh Cruttwell, became a major influence, helping, as Branagh put it, 'to convert the school show-off into an honest actor'. Later, Cruttwell could be found as a 'production consultant' on the sets of his former student's Shakespeare films, trying to ensure that Branagh's directing duties did not weaken his performance.

Branagh graduated from RADA in 1982, after winning its highest honour, the Bancroft Gold Medal, and immediately made his West End debut, in the public school drama, *Another Country*, earning Most Promising Newcomer awards from the Society of West End Theatres and *Plays and Players* magazine. Cast as Henry V for the RSC in 1984, he demonstrated the chutzpah that has always served him well. He requested and was granted an audience with Prince Charles at Kensington Palace and asked the heir to the throne if he was right to portray Henry as a man isolated by his royal responsibilities. Charles agreed. *Henry V* was a hit, and its director, Adrian Noble, deserves credit for the subsequent success of *Henry V*, which retained the stage production's unglamorous depiction of kingship and conflict.

Above: Branagh as Berowne in his musical version of *Love's Labour's Lost* (2000), the least faithful and, in Britain, least successful of his four Shakespeare adaptations.

Branagh opened it all up with *Henry V*. That was just an explosion. Now you say 'Shakespeare' in Hollywood and people listen. Al Pacino

Above: Branagh, right, directs Michael Maloney, left, and Kate Winslet in the grounds of Blenheim Palace, Oxfordshire, during the filming of *Hamlet* (1996).

Right: Branagh giving an Oscar-nominated performance as the troubled king in *Henry V* (1989).

14

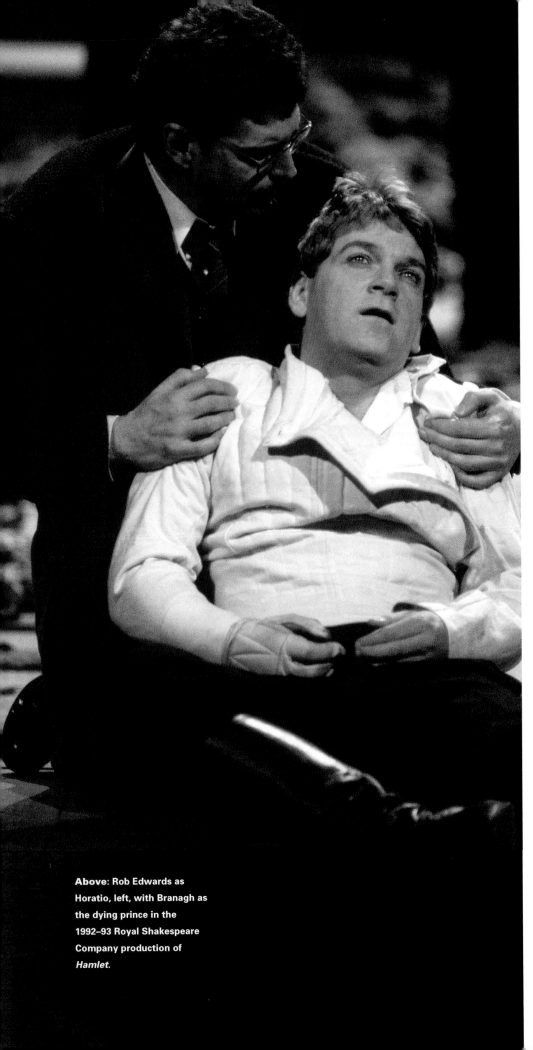

Above: Rob Edwards as Horatio, left, with Branagh as the dying prince in the 1992–93 Royal Shakespeare Company production of *Hamlet*.

After the RSC *Henry V*, Branagh's major breakthrough came in 1987. Millions watched his engaging performance as a left-leaning 1940s idealist, Guy Pringle, in the BBC drama, *Fortunes of War*, alongside Emma Thompson, and when the co-stars married in 1989, the media turned them into 'Ken and Em', the golden couple of British acting (they endured unpleasant tabloid reporting when the marriage ended in 1995).

Soon after filming *Fortunes of War*, Branagh teamed up with actor David Parfitt and launched the Renaissance Theatre Company with the première of *Public Enemy*, his semi-autobiographical play about a James Cagney-obsessed Ulster youth. The pair put together a programme of Shakespeare on stage, with Branagh persuading his boyhood hero, Derek Jacobi, to direct him as Hamlet, and Judi Dench to direct him as Benedick in *Much Ado About Nothing*. The emphasis in this Renaissance season was on clear, realistic acting, designed, as Branagh's Shakespeare films would be, to entertain people who had little or no prior knowledge of the plays.

Audiences in London and on Renaissance's regional tour responded very positively, although Renaissance was still short of funds, and to boost its fortunes, Branagh wrote an autobiography, *Beginning*. It was lively and unpretentious, but he was promptly attacked for writing his life story at the grand old age of 28, by the same British newspapers that a year earlier had hailed him as 'the new Olivier'.

That label seemed rather lazy at first, given the vast differences between Olivier – the electrifying idol of the 1930s – and Branagh's calmer, less physically striking presence on stage and screen; he described himself in *Beginning* as 'a short-assed, fat-faced Irishman'. By filming *Henry V*, however, Branagh ensured that comparisons with Olivier would be both inevitable and valid – and boldly made a movie that withstood them all.

That film established the Branagh 'family': collaborators who have continued to work with him regularly on both sides of the camera. The list is headed by Tim Harvey (production designer on all eight of Branagh's films to date), Patrick Doyle (composer for six), Richard Briers (roles in seven) and Russell Jackson of the Shakespeare Institute in Stratford-upon-Avon (text adviser on all four Shakespeare films). That consistency of personnel reflects Branagh's stated desire to generate on a film set the same company atmosphere that he enjoys in stage production, 'so that the whole movie will have that theatrical quality'.

Breaks from the Bard

When Shakespeare is not involved, Branagh has tackled various genres, with extremely variable results. His first non-Shakespearean project was *Dead Again* (US, 1991), an enjoyably preposterous homage to Hitchcock thrillers that briefly hit number one at the US box office. Branagh played a jaunty Los Angeles private eye falling in love with an amnesiac woman (Emma Thompson), who was haunted by black-and-white flashbacks of her past life as a 1940s concert pianist, murdered by her German composer husband (Branagh again). His next project, *Peter's Friends* (UK, 1992), resembled a crudely inferior British remake of Lawrence Kasdan's classic ensemble comedy-drama, *The Big Chill* (US, 1983): both focused on former university friends reunited for a weekend of soul-searching at a large, isolated house.

After directing his first short film, *Swan Song*, an Oscar-nominated Chekhov adaptation starring John Gielgud, and hitting the box-office jackpot with *Much Ado*, Branagh received BAFTA's Michael Balcon Award for outstanding British contribution to cinema. That run of acclaim was followed by the $44 million *Mary Shelley's Frankenstein* (US, 1994), which suffered a remarkably ferocious critical mauling and yet still grossed more than $100 million worldwide. Although more faithful to the book than previous screen adaptations, it was frenetic without being thrilling, and hampered by the mis-match between Branagh's unconvincing Frankenstein and Robert De Niro's fearsome, affecting monster.

In all three of his genre pictures, Branagh never seems as fully in control of his material as he is with Shakespeare, or with the *Hamlet* production *In The Bleak Midwinter* (*see* page 184), and tends to overindulge his own performances, for example playing Frankenstein bare-chested or allowing himself a truly embarrassing drunk scene as Andrew, the disillusioned movie director, in *Peter's Friends*. He is a more sensitive and sympathetic actor as Henry V or Hamlet than he is in those films or in sub-standard Hollywood fare such as the John Grisham adaptation, *The Gingerbread Man* (US, 1998) or the dreadful *Wild Wild West* (US, 1999).

There is an equivalent, though less significant, weakness in three of his Shakespeare films: not self-indulgence, but inconsistency. His tendency to cast American movie stars alongside more experienced British Shakespeareans has obvious box-office appeal, but has repeatedly thrown the films off balance; as has his occasionally poor handling of crucial set-pieces. *Much Ado* was handicapped by the presence of Michael Keaton and Keanu Reeves, *Hamlet* was undermined by its numerous Hollywood star cameos and an absurd, earth-shattering encounter between Hamlet and the Ghost, and *Love's Labour's Lost* was weakened by a miscast Alicia Silverstone and a badly misjudged ending.

As Branagh contemplates his next Shakespeare move, the hope must be that he will eventually repeat the consistency of *Henry V*, the only one of his Shakespeare films in which every performance and directorial stroke sits comfortably within an absolutely coherent whole.

Even if *Love's Labour's Lost* were to be Branagh's last Shakespeare, his place in the history of Shakespeare on screen is secure. Other directors, notably Baz Luhrmann, with *William Shakespeare's Romeo + Juliet*, and Richard Loncraine, with *Richard III*, may have made more vibrant and original contributions to the 1990s revival. Without Branagh and *Henry V*, they wouldn't have had their chance.

Below: Branagh behind the camera, directing his second Shakespeare film, *Much Ado About Nothing* (1993), on location at a villa in Tuscany.

All the world's a stage, And all the men and women merely players. *Jacques, As You Like It*, Act II, Scene vii

SHAKESPEARE IN OTHER MOVIES

Right: Lenny Henry as black actor Miles Pope, right, who understudies Othello and disguises himself as white to avoid the Mafia in *True Identity* (1991).

Left: Jack Benny as Joseph Tura, right, the Polish actor playing Hamlet in *To Be or Not To Be* (1942) with Carole Lombard, left, as his wife.

FILM BACKGROUND

The Old Actor (US, 1912) is a ten-minute silent about an elderly Shakespearean who is fired by a theatre manager, consoles himself with quotations from *As You Like It* and *Macbeth*, disguises himself as a beggar and eventually regains his job. It's a sentimental tale but important nonetheless as probably the earliest title on a long list of films about actors that have made use of Shakespeare's plays.

Scriptwriters who show thespians rehearsing and performing Shakespeare invariably work from the same artistic principles. They hope that his verse will add a poetic touch of class to their contemporary prose, however well-written, and since the Bard expresses almost every conceivable human emotion, there is bound to be a scene or soliloquy that can be extracted to reflect a leading character's emotional crisis or comic misadventures.

This mini-genre of films ranges widely, from staging the Bard in India (**Shakespeare Wallah**), through an abandoned London auditorium (**Theatre of Blood**) to an English village (**In The Bleak Midwinter**). The actors in Tom Stoppard's **Rosencrantz and Guildenstern Are Dead** are at work inside *Hamlet*, and in the Elizabethan London of **Shakespeare in Love**, the young Will acts as well as writes.

The films listed above and featured in this chapter stage Shakespeare's work with vigour and commitment, but the formula can sometimes seem laboured, as in the comedy-thriller *True Identity* (US, 1991) which roped in *Othello* to bolster its would-be profound 'message' about racial attitudes. Lenny Henry plays Miles Pope, a black American actor who, with the aid of some impressive make-up, disguises himself as white to avoid the Mafia, who want to silence him after his accidental discovery that leading mafioso Frank Luchino (Frank Langella) has faked his own death. Under a new identity, Luchino turns up as producer of the *Othello* in which Miles is understudying the Moor. The twist is designed to equate Shakespeare's exploration of racism with numerous scenes in which Miles is treated with greater respect as a 'white' man than he ever was when black, but it's far too contrived to succeed.

Arguably the most disastrous example of the 'putting on Shakespeare' genre is writer-director Stephen Poliakoff's *Food of Love* (UK, 1997). Carrying strong echoes of **In The Bleak Midwinter**, it starred Richard E. Grant as a jaded City banker who persuades a group of friends to join him in an idyllic English village for a shambolic recreation of the open-air *Twelfth Night* that they had triumphantly staged there as students. Released in late 1999, two years after it was completed, this $4 million mess left the *Evening Standard* 'dazed by the unbelievable badness' of script, acting and direction, and swiftly disappeared from cinemas.

As for the Bard's own appearances on screen, those critics who suggested that **Shakespeare in Love** was his first were wrong. The hour-long British comedy silent, *Old Bill 'Through The Ages'* (UK, 1924), shows the time-travelling dream of World War I soldier, Old Bill (Syd Walker), and includes a sequence in which he goes to Stratford-upon-Avon and meets Shakespeare (Austin Leigh). The Bard dictates a sonnet to a room full of typists and then bores Queen Elizabeth and her courtiers to sleep with readings from *Hamlet* and other plays.

The Immortal Gentleman (UK, 1935) had the Bard meeting fellow playwright Ben Jonson and poet Michael Drayton at a tavern in Southwark, whose customers remind him of characters from *Romeo and Juliet*, *The Merchant of Venice* and other plays, prompting some appallingly acted excerpts. The time-travel premise reappeared in *Time Flies* (UK, 1944), as cheeky Tommy (radio comedian Tommy Handley) and friends were whisked back to the 1590s for a series of comic encounters with famous Elizabethans, including one in the Globe with Shakespeare, who is struggling to write the balcony scene in *Romeo and Juliet*.

Finally, attention must be paid to Ernst Lubitsch's classic *To Be or Not to Be* (US, 1942), the blackly comic, tense and moving story of a company of Polish actors bravely resisting the Nazis in occupied Warsaw. Their leader, vain, hammy Joseph Tura (Jack Benny) plays Hamlet with excruciating pomposity, prompting a Gestapo officer's notorious quip: 'What Tura did to Shakespeare, we are now doing to Poland'. Mel Brooks took on the Benny role in the brasher, colour remake (US, 1983), and both versions occupy a special niche in the history of Shakespeare on screen, as the only movies to mock both *Hamlet* and Hitler.

SHAKESPEARE WALLAH (1965)

INDIA 124 MINS B/W

CAST	FELICITY KENDAL (Lizzie Buckingham), SHASHI KAPOOR (Sanju), GEOFFREY KENDAL (Tony Buckingham), LAURA LIDDELL (Carla Buckingham), MADHUR JAFFREY (Manjula), J.D. TYTLER (Bobby), JENNIFER KAPOOR (Mrs Bowen)
DIRECTED BY	JAMES IVORY
PRODUCED BY	ISMAIL MERCHANT
SCREENPLAY	RUTH PRAWER JHABVALA, JAMES IVORY
PHOTOGRAPHY	SUBRATA MITRA
MUSIC	SATYAJIT RAY

Shakespeare Wallah is the episodic, superbly played story of a group of itinerant English actors falling on hard times in 1950s India. Written and directed with great delicacy, its intimate drama of disenchantment and first love doubles as a vivid history lesson, and it deservedly garnered outstanding reviews, with *Time* praising its 'moments of brilliance and grace' and *The Daily Telegraph* suggesting that 'writing, acting and picture can seldome have been combined so happily'.

Middle-aged Tony and Carla Buckingham (husband and wife Geoffrey Kendal and Laura Liddell) and their innocent, only child, 18-year-old Lizzie (the real-life couple's younger daughter, Felicity) perform the Bard's work at theatres, boarding schools, gentlemen's clubs – anywhere that will hire their tiny troupe, The Buckingham Players. The cast is completed by the elderly, ailing Bobby (an elegant J.D. Tytler) and two young Indian actors. The Kendal parents are playing themselves, since they led their touring company, 'Shakespeariana', around India in 1947, the year of Indian independence, and it is Geoffrey's tour diary that inspired **Shakespeare Wallah**.

At first, when the company performs *Antony and Cleopatra* at the palace of a melancholy maharajah, the scene evokes the *Hamlet* players arriving at Elsinore, although the maharajah's lavish hospitality will be the Buckinghams' only brush with Eastern luxury. From this point onwards their unglamorous existence is matched by Ivory's no-frills, almost documentary approach (necessitated by a budget of just $80,000). The grainy black-and-white photography of Subrata Mitra (regular cameraman for the great Indian director Satyajit Ray, who wrote the film's sitar-laced score) denies the locations, including Simla, Bombay and Lucknow, any of the colourful exoticism that Ivory conjures so well in another Anglo-Indian drama, *Heat and Dust* (UK, 1983).

When the troupe's van breaks down, they are rescued by Sanju (Shashi Kapoor), a handsome Indian playboy. He is instantly attracted to Lizzie, as she is to him, and he follows the group to their next destination, where independent India's growing indifference to Shakespeare becomes increasingly apparent.

A grand private school, which under the British Raj would always take six Shakespeare performances from the Buckinghams, now wants just one. This is *Hamlet*, with Carla as Gertrude, Lizzie as Ophelia and Tony playing the Prince, as Geoffrey did on the Shakespeariana tours, in a grand, old-fashioned and impressive style. The cancelled performances, however, are a serious financial blow, and, for Tony, a humiliating 'rejection of everything I am'.

Meanwhile Lizzie, her yearning for first-hand rather than Shakespearean romance vibrantly conveyed by Kendal, is blind to Sanju's selfishness (nicely concealed by Kapoor's ardent, charming veneer). She falls in love, not realizing that Sanju is also involved with a vain, temperamental film star, Manjula (Madhur Jaffrey's acidic debut, for which she won Best Actress at the Berlin Film Festival).

Culture clash

The implications of the gulf between the Buckinghams' drab, boarding-house accommodation and Manjula's pampered existence (waited on by a deaf-mute maid, and carried from a hillside film location like a princess) stretch beyond the leading characters, since it is Manjula's popularity in the song-and-dance extravaganzas produced by India's burgeoning movie industry that is killing the appeal of Shakespeare – literally in the case of Bobby, who suffers a fatal heart attack.

This cinema-versus-theatre battle is joined when Manjula, having discovered Sanju's dalliance with Lizzie, disrupts the Buckinghams' sold-out performance of *Othello* (an apt choice, since Sanju and Lizzie's interracial romance has an Othello/Desdemona flavour). Swanning into Sanju's stalls box during Act V, Manjula causes a great hubbub as the starstruck audience stands to catch a glimpse of her, interrupting Tony's growling Othello. The damage done, Manjula leaves, but a furious Sanju stays behind. That night, like Romeo to Juliet, he secretly goes to Lizzie's bedroom and they spend the night together.

Fittingly, Lizzie's performance in *Romeo and Juliet* provides the climax. When a man in the audience whistles obscenely at her, Sanju assaults him, starting a mini-riot that causes the show to be abandoned. He asks Lizzie how she can tolerate such disrespect. She says she adores acting, but would give it up if he asked her to; his mortifying silence finishes their affair. The film ends with Lizzie on board the liner taking her to England; leaving her parents to a bleak Indian future.

It is a much less hopeful outcome than the one experienced by the Kendals in real life, not least because their elder daughter, Jennifer, who appears as the boarding-house owner and who was the model for Lizzie, married her Indian boyfriend – none other than Shashi Kapoor.

Left: Felicity Kendal as Juliet, right, in the wedding scene from the Buckingham Players' production of *Romeo and Juliet*.

Above: Geoffrey Kendal as Tony Buckingham, removing his make-up after playing Othello in a disrupted performance at an Indian theatre.

Writing, acting and picture can seldom have been combined so happily. The Daily Telegraph

15

THEATRE OF BLOOD (1973)
UK 102 MINS COLOUR

CAST	VINCENT PRICE (Edward Lionheart), DIANA RIGG (Edwina Lionheart), IAN HENDRY (Peregrine Devlin), MILO O'SHEA (Inspector Boot), ERIC SYKES (Sergeant Dogge)
DIRECTED BY	DOUGLAS HICKOX
PRODUCED BY	JOHN KOHN, STANLEY MANN
SCREENPLAY	ANTHONY GREVILLE-BELL
PHOTOGRAPHY	WOLFGANG SUSCHITZKY
MUSIC	MICHAEL J. LEWIS

Coated in black humour and splattered with gore, **Theatre of Blood** is not just outrageously entertaining, it is also educational. As deranged actor Edward Lionheart systematically bumps off London's leading theatre critics, the film doubles as a handy 'Guide to Shakespearean Murder'.

The opening title sequence, showing bloody extracts from silent Shakespeare films, tells us what to expect, and Lionheart's first murder follows immediately. *Financial Times* critic and local housing association chairman, George Maxwell (Michael Hordern, gloriously pompous), fatally ignores his wife's *Julius Caesar*-like premonition ('I read your horoscope: March is a difficult month for you') and drives to a derelict building. The squatters he has come to eject hack him to shreds, like the conspirators assassinating Caesar, and a watching police constable reveals himself to be Lionheart.

Vincent Price is at his ripest as Lionheart, who has been presumed dead for the past year since his suicidal leap into the Thames from the penthouse belonging to Peregrine Devlin (a sombre Ian Hendry), chairman of the nine-member Critics' Circle that had just denied him its Best Actor award. Now, holed up in the abandoned Burbage Theatre (really London's Putney Hippodrome) he has set out to murder the critics by recreating deaths from the nine Shakespeare plays in his final repertory season.

Partners in crime
With help from his devoted, twentysomething daughter Edwina (Diana Rigg, frequently disguised as a male biker, in ginger wig and moustache) and the meths-drinking tramps who murdered Maxwell, he's always one step ahead of the police who are led by Milo O'Shea's plodding, pipe-smoking Inspector Boot and Eric Sykes's far from dogged Sergeant Dogge. Victim number two, Hector Snipe, dies like his heroic Trojan namesake in *Troilus and Cressida*, speared by Lionheart as Achilles, and his corpse is dragged around behind a galloping horse.

Then comes the film's most gruesomely hilarious sequence (several reviewers attacked the violence, notably the critics of *Time* magazine and the *Daily Mail*, which found it 'too gory to be funny'). In homage to the decapitation of Cloten in *Cymbeline*, a sleeping Horace Sprout (Arthur Lowe) is beheaded by Lionheart – in surgeon's outfit and accompanied by Rigg as the nurse supplying hypodermic and saw – with composer Michael J. Lewis supplying a melody better suited to a 1950s love scene.

The carnage continues: Trevor Dickman (Harry Andrews) has his heart cut out, giving Lionheart the pound of flesh denied Shylock in *The Merchant of Venice*; Oliver Larding (Robert Coote, Roderigo in Welles's *Othello*) is drowned in a barrel of red wine, like Clarence in *Richard III*. Solomon Psaltery (Jack Hawkins) is duped into believing that his voluptuous wife (Diana Dors) is having an affair and smothers her like Desdemona.

Above: Vincent Price as crazed Edward Lionheart, left, and Robert Morley as Meredith Merridew with the pie made from Merridew's beloved poodles – a culinary homage to *Titus Andronicus*.

Chloe Moon (played by Price's wife, Coral Browne) is electro-cuted by a rigged hairdryer (Joan of Arc burned at the stake in *Henry VI, Part 1*) and the impossibly camp Meredith Merridew (Robert Morley in a salmon-pink suit) is choked to death with a pie made from his beloved poodles (Tamora fed her own sons in *Titus Andronicus*).

Tossing in some macabre puns along the way, screenwriter Anthony Greville-Bell fashions a twisted morality tale (some of the critics have been given emblematic surnames), with Lion-heart exploiting each reviewer's dominant vice to lure them to their death: with Dickman, it's his lust for Edwina (disguised as a nubile actress); Larding's a boozer who can't pass up a free wine tasting, and so on.

The hacks are a caricatured bunch of malicious self-servers, and only Devlin, the least unsympathetic, escapes, rescued by the police just before having his eyes put out (Gloucester in *King Lear*) at the Burbage. Lionheart sets fire to the building and, after Edwina is killed by a tramp, climbs to the roof, carrying his daughter like Lear with Cordelia, and leaps to his death in the flames.

Despite the repetitive structure – alternating between murders and police investigation – the verve displayed by Douglas Hickox in the set pieces ensures that **Theatre of Blood** is never monotonous, as do enthusiastically over-the-top perfor-mances from a remarkable cast. Price rants his way through extracts from the plays in wigs and immense false noses, mangling the verse in those unmistakeable mid-Atlantic tones ('bosom' emerges as 'booze-um'), and ensuring that Lionheart's crimes against Shakespeare are even more horren-dous than his murders.

Above: Vincent Price in Lionheart's Shylock costume, centre, brandishes the knife with which he will claim 'a pound of flesh' from Harry Andrews as Trevor Dickman, left. Diana Rigg as Lionheart's daughter, right, looks on.

15

ROSENCRANTZ AND GUILDENSTERN ARE DEAD (1990)

UK 118 MINS COLOUR

CAST	GARY OLDMAN (Rosencrantz), TIM ROTH (Guildenstern), RICHARD DREYFUSS (The Player), IAIN GLEN (Hamlet), JOANNA MILES (Gertrude), DONALD SUMPTER (Claudius), JOANNA ROTH (Ophelia), IAN RICHARDSON (Polonius)
DIRECTED BY	TOM STOPPARD
PRODUCED BY	MICHAEL BRANDMAN, EMANUEL AZENBERG
SCREENPLAY	TOM STOPPARD
PHOTOGRAPHY	PETER BIZIOU
MUSIC	STANLEY MYERS

Rosencrantz and Guildenstern are like a Shakespearean Laurel and Hardy or Abbott and Costello.

Tom Stoppard

Below: Gary Oldman as Rosencrantz, left, and Tim Roth as Guildenstern in the closing scene that confirms the accuracy of the film's title.

Tom Stoppard's directorial debut plays witty, ironic and irreverent games with *Hamlet*, but unlike the best film versions of that great tragedy it never manages to jump clear of its theatrical origins.

Stoppard originally sold the screen rights to *Rosencrantz and Guildenstern are Dead*, the stage comedy that made his name, soon after its award-winning 1967 premières in the West End and on Broadway. He wrote a screenplay for MGM, but the project languished for 20 years until he bought the rights back and wrote a new scipt.

Shot in Yugoslavia, the film, like the play, views *Hamlet* entirely from the point of view of the prince's doomed friends, and asks: 'What do Rosencrantz and Guildenstern get up to while travelling to Elsinore, kicking their heels "offstage", and sailing to their deaths in England?' The answer is that Roth's irritable, sarcastic Guildenstern (who's not as clever as he thinks he is) and Oldman's garrulous, goofy Rosencrantz (who's not as dumb as he appears) do little and say a great deal.

They muse on why they've been summoned and how to plumb the madness of Iain Glen's mild-mannered, romantic prince. Rosencrantz considers mortality in a rambling, banal equivalent to the 'To be, or not to be' soliloquy and keeps asking who he is, since the film's most persistent running joke (spun from the moment in *Hamlet* when Gertrude reverses Claudius's 'Thanks, Rosencrantz and gentle Guildenstern') is that neither they, nor anybody else in Elsinore knows which one is which.

This shabby, oddly likeable, pair was likened by Stoppard to 'a Shakespearean Laurel and Hardy or Abbott and Costello', but Roth and Oldman's clipped, question-and-answer routines are more like the chatter of Vladimir and Estragon in Samuel Beckett's *Waiting for Godot*: beautifully timed, inconsequential and better suited to stage than screen. Stoppard's screenplay acknowledges that the duologues that worked beautifully in the theatre might not be enough to hold a cinema audience's attention and so adds a new running gag (initially delightful but then over-indulged) in which Rosencrantz casually makes 'scientific' breakthroughs, including the discovery of steam power, gravity and the hamburger.

Attempts are made to break the static mood by sending the pair from room to room in a suspiciously deserted castle, although no matter how many times they clatter up and down flights of wooden stairs, Stoppard's methods, as the *Independent on Sunday* noted, 'still reek of the stage'.

Play within a play

About 250 lines from *Hamlet* are retained, to show the duo quizzing the prince and to add a new layer of covert observation to a play already full of eavesdropping. Our heroes listen in on conversations involving Hamlet, Donald Sumpter's brusque Claudius, Ian Richardson's twittering Polonius and Joanna Roth's doll-like Ophelia. Stoppard's most outrageous stroke shows the pair inadvertently causing Polonius' death.

The better you know *Hamlet*, the more enjoyable such moments are likely to be and the same applies when the rather mysterious players whom Rosencrantz and Guildenstern meet *en route* to Elsinore briefly mime the play's opening and closing phases in the middle of the film.

There is captivating mime work and puppetry by these French and Eastern European actors, while a bearded, English-accented Richard Dreyfuss (a late replacement for Sean Connery) plays their flamboyant, all-knowing leader with gusto, delivering a droll running commentary on the rules of Shakespearean tragedy. Stoppard piles up layer upon layer of illusion – at one point you watch a puppet show within a dumb show within a play within a film – yet the essence of the tragedy is still crystal clear.

Stoppard places the players on the England-bound ship, to work one final, surreal twist on *Hamlet*. Rosencrantz reads aloud the letter ordering Hamlet's execution, the prince overhears this and replaces the letter with the order for his friends' deaths. After the pirate attack (the film's one genuinely cinematic sequence), Dreyfuss reads Hamlet's letter and on reaching England Roth and Oldman, still as baffled by their fate as they have been throughout, are strung up not by the English king, but by the players.

Although the film was greeted by very mixed reviews in Britain and the US, it won the Golden Lion at the Venice Film Festival in 1990, a triumph that provided a 'revenge' for Stoppard's heroes more ironic than anything even his brilliant imagination could devise. The previous British winner of the Golden Lion was Laurence Olivier's 1948 *Hamlet*, the movie that completely and notoriously cut Rosencrantz and Guildenstern out of *Hamlet*.

Above: Joanna Roth as Ophelia, left, and Iain Glen as Hamlet in the Shakespeare play-within-the-film.

15

IN THE BLEAK MIDWINTER (1995)

UK 98 MINS B/W

US TITLE: A MIDWINTER'S TALE

CAST	MICHAEL MALONEY (Joe Harper), JULIA SAWALHA (Nina), JOHN SESSIONS (Terry du Bois), RICHARD BRIERS (Henry Wakefield), HETTA CHARNLEY (Molly), JOAN COLLINS (Margaret d'Arcy), NICHOLAS FARRELL (Tom Newman), MARK HADFIELD (Vernon Spatch), GERARD HORAN (Carnforth Greville), CELIA IMRIE (Fadge)
DIRECTED BY	KENNETH BRANAGH
PRODUCED BY	DAVID BARRON
SCREENPLAY	KENNETH BRANAGH
PHOTOGRAPHY	ROGER LANSER
MUSIC	JIMMY YUILL

Cast in the same mould as the Mickey Rooney/Judy Garland, 'Let's do the show right here' musicals of the 1930s and 40s, with crude humour replacing the songs, **In The Bleak Midwinter** uses *Hamlet* as the canvas for an unashamedly sentimental, warts-and-all portrait of the lower end of the acting profession.

'A little, heartfelt number', was how Branagh described it and he committed $1 million of his own money to shoot the snappy script that he had written in less than a month, with a thirtysomething hero, Joe (Maloney, nicely capturing Branagh's indomitable enthusiasm), whose choice of career, like Branagh's, was made when he saw *Hamlet* at the age of 15.

After a year's unemployment, Maloney risks losing a lucrative part in a Hollywood sci-fi trilogy and the wrath of his agent (Collins at her most flamboyant) to play the prince and direct a no-budget, Christmas production of *Hamlet*. The venue is an ugly church in his home village, Hope, that his schoolteacher sister, Molly, is trying to save from demolition.

A montage of hilarious auditions (such as a half-crazed woman doing *Macbeth* with hand puppets), yield a predictably motley cast. Bigoted, seen-it-all veteran Henry (Briers, in irascible mode) will play Claudius opposite the drag Gertrude of Terry (Sessions), who is gay and exceedingly camp. Their Ophelia will be Nina (Julia Sawalha), a myopic, absent-minded novice, with the other roles shared between pretentious, self-obsessed Tom (the preening Farrell), the boozing Carnforth, and Vernon, the resident cynic. Celia Imrie's Fadge, the show's ethereal designer, announces that she gauges how things are going by the hardness of her nipples.

Rehearsal scenes in the church are dominated by the actors' innuendo-laden, bitchy digs at their colleagues' talents or complaints about their lines being cut. There are pratfalls, rows and line cock-ups. Terry, Henry and Fadge walk a tightrope between broad characterization and caricature, but there's plenty of laughter at the expense of what Joe calls 'all the normal insecurities and vanities' of actors.

Parts imitating life

The sentimentality starts creeping in via the individuals' connections to their parts. When Terry, as Gertrude, tells Hamlet that 'thou has cleft my heart in twain', he rushes out in tears because the speech reminds him of his own estranged son, the product of his one heterosexual encounter as a teenager. Nina's husband, a pilot, was killed in a mid-air crash and after singing Ophelia's mad lament for her dead father she too runs off distraught.

Naturally, the production looks like being a disaster: no ticket sales, the church's landlord threatening eviction and then Joe's sci-fi offer meaning he must reluctantly abandon the team and head for Hollywood. Molly is about to go on as understudy when, of course, Joe comes back just in time for his first lines.

The montage showing brief extracts from the performance blends the sublime (Hamlet's soliloquies) with the ridiculous (Marcellus firing a machine gun over the audience's heads in the opening scene). An audience of villagers starts off sceptical and becomes totally engrossed (precisely the transformation Branagh wants his Shakespeare films to produce in cinemagoers new to the Bard) and end up roaring their approval. Terry has a backstage reconciliation with his son (improbably tracked down and invited to the show by Henry). Joe and Nina end up in each other's arms and Tom gets the sci-fi gig, courtesy of a Hollywood producer (a wildly over-the-top Jennifer Saunders).

'Some will find the ending sentimental. It is. Actors are sentimental,' wrote Branagh, to forestall criticism in the introduction to the published screenplay. But some reviewers swooped on his 'deadeningly quaint' resolutions (*Village Voice*) and *The Sunday Times* lamented that the screen 'fogs over with fondness'.

Others were prepared to accept **In The Bleak Midwinter** on its own, modest terms as a small, energetic and unpretentious film that does what it sets out to do with good humour and provides 'undemanding but not entirely weightless fun' (*The Guardian*). It is made still more old-fashioned in appearance because of the black-and-white photography. Branagh's direction has a much lighter touch than he displayed in his other contemporary ensemble comedy, *Peter's Friends* (UK, 1992), perhaps because he had just a 21-day shoot and, for the first time in his film-making career, was not also burdened with acting duties. The film made around $450,000 in Britain and the cast received the Osello d'Oro award for ensemble acting, at the Venice Film Festival.

Right: John Sessions as Terry, the drag Gertrude, left, and Richard Briers as Henry, an irritable Claudius, in the church production of *Hamlet*.

Left: Michael Maloney as Joe, centre (standing), tries to win his cast's trust at the first *Hamlet* read-through.

SHAKESPEARE IN LOVE (1998)

US 122MINS COLOUR

CAST	JOSEPH FIENNES (William Shakespeare), GWYNETH PALTROW (Viola de Lesseps), COLIN FIRTH (Lord Wessex), IMELDA STAUNTON (Nurse), JUDI DENCH (Queen Elizabeth), BEN AFFLECK (Ned Alleyn), GEOFFREY RUSH (Philip Henslowe)
DIRECTED BY	JOHN MADDEN
PRODUCED BY	DAVID PARFITT, DONNA GIGLIOTTI, HARVEY WEINSTEIN, EDWARD ZWICK, MARC NORMAN
SCREENPLAY	MARC NORMAN, TOM STOPPARD
PHOTOGRAPHY	RICHARD GREATREX
MUSIC	STEPHEN WARBECK

With one foot in the 1590s and the other firmly in the 1990s, **Shakespeare in Love** offers something for everyone. There's comedy built from anachronism, wordplay, bedroom farce and crude knockabout; a feast for lovers of period drama, thanks to a tastefully squalid recreation of Elizabethan London; a passionate love story with a bitter-sweet ending, thanks to the *Romeo and Juliet*-like affair between Joseph Fiennes's Shakespeare and Gwyneth Paltrow's cross-dressing Viola.

The panache displayed by director John Madden in whisking these disparate ingredients together, coupled with the obvious, wholehearted enjoyment of an outstanding cast, drew rave reviews; *The Daily Telegraph suggested*: 'In its marriage of farce and sentiment there is an undeniable magic – a comic spirit that can fairly be called Shakespearean'.

The film became a phenomenon. Made for $25 million, it grossed $100 million in America, a further $190 million in the rest of the world, collected the BAFTA for Best Film and seven Oscars, including Best Picture and Best Actress, reward for Paltrow's exemplary English accent and radiant, if ingratiating performance. Millions of people will always picture the Bard as Fiennes plays him: wide-eyed, horny, energetic and not particularly bright.

The Oscar-winning screenplay, originally written by Marc Norman in 1993, with Julia Roberts and Daniel Day-Lewis slated to play the leads, was then 'doctored' by Tom Stoppard. It takes us to London, 1593, where young Will has promised his new comedy, *Romeo and Ethel, the Pirate's Daughter*, to the owner of the Rose Theatre, Philip Henslowe (Geoffrey Rush, on manic, BAFTA-winning form), who needs a hit to pay off a vicious loan-shark, Fennyman (the sneering Tom Wilkinson).

Will has writer's block and the play is stalled until he receives plot hints from his more successful rival, Christopher Marlowe (a typically languid cameo from Rupert Everett) and falls for a wealthy merchant's daughter, Viola de Lesseps, who's unhappily betrothed to the dastardly Lord Wessex (Colin Firth).

> In its marriage of farce and sentiment there is an undeniable magic – a comic spirit that can fairly be called Shakespearean.
>
> The Daily Telegraph

Since women are forbidden from acting, the stagestruck Viola boldly dresses as a young man, Thomas Kent, and is cast as Romeo. Once Will learns her true identity, they begin an affair, the verse suddenly flows from his quill and their illicit passion turns the comic *Romeo and Ethel* into the tragic *Romeo and Juliet*. Viola's lasciviously helpful nurse (Imelda Staunton) inspires Juliet's nurse; Wessex, about to take Viola to his Virginia tobacco plantation, inspires Tybalt and Paris.

Firth makes Wessex a subtly malevolent bad guy, his villainy underlined by the fact that he can't bear the theatre. This terrible failing is exploited by Judi Dench's Queen Elizabeth, who wagers him £50 that a play 'can show us the very truth and nature of love', and in just three brief appearances, Dench's imperiously caustic, Oscar-winning portrayal sums up the film's 'big questions', about love, duty and the power of art.

Must the show go on?

In the farcical rehearsal scenes at the Rose it's a joy to find 16th-century actors, led by Ben Affleck's swaggering Ned Alleyn, displaying the same vanity and sentimentality as their counterparts in 20th-century backstage comedies, and even less competence. Python-like anachronisms (Will visits a shrink) rub shoulders with 'hindsight' jokes that bear Stoppard's distinctive, literate hallmark; the best concern Marlowe's mysterious death and the bloodthirsty 12-year-old who hangs around the Rose: he's called John Webster, and is therefore destined to write gruesome Jacobean tragedies such as *The White Devil*.

When Webster reveals that Henslowe's company is harbouring a woman, the officious Master of the Revels, Tinley (Simon Callow) closes the theatre for 'immorality', setting up a classic, eleventh-hour crisis. Richard Burbage, exuberantly played by Martin Clunes, allows Henslowe's company to use his rival venue, the Curtain, and Will steps in as Romeo. Viola slips away to the Curtain after her wedding and, when the adolescent playing Juliet finds that his voice is breaking, takes over. *Romeo and Juliet*, reduced to a wondrous, ten-minute montage, driven forward by Stephen Warbeck's busy, romantic score, is a sensation.

As the play comes together so movingly, it becomes clear that despite their mockery of the Bard as a man, Madden and company's ultimate goal has been an all-out celebration of his work. The climax of **Shakespeare in Love** demonstrates that nothing beats Shakespeare on stage.

The queen, who's been watching in secret, is so impressed that she claims her £50 from Wessex, before insisting that Viola join him in the New World. That enables Madden to end on a dream-like shot of Paltrow after a shipwreck, striding along a vast American shore as Will begins to write *Twelfth Night* – another comedy with a cross-dressing Viola as its heroine.

Below: Judi Dench gives an Oscar-winning performance as Elizabeth I, who asks: 'Can a play show us the very truth and nature of love?'

Right: Gwyneth Paltrow as Viola, centre, and Joseph Fiennes as Shakespeare at the climax of the *Romeo and Juliet* performance.

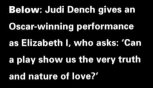

SHAKESPEARE IN LOVE (1998)

 **16**

SHAKESPEARE AT THE OSCARS

1935 *A Midsummer Night's Dream*

ACADEMY AWARDS
Cinematography Hal Mohr
Film Editing Ralph Dawson

NOMI·NATION
Picture Produced by Henry Blanke

1936 *Romeo and Juliet*

NOMINATIONS
Picture Produced by Irving G. Thalberg
Actress Norma Shearer
Supporting Actor Basil Rathbone
Art Direction Cedric Gibbons, Frederic Hope and Edwin B. Willis

1946 *Henry V*

SPECIAL AWARD
Laurence Olivier

NOMINATIONS
Picture Produced by Laurence Olivier
Actor Laurence Olivier
Art Decoration/Interior Decoration (colour)
Paul Sheriff and Carmen Dillon
Scoring of a Dramatic or Comedy picture
William Walton

1947 *A Double Life*

ACADEMY AWARDS
Actor Ronald Colman
Scoring of a Dramatic or Comedy Picture
Miklos Rozsa

NOMINATIONS
Direction George Cukor
Original Screenplay Ruth Gordon and Garson Kanin

1948 *Hamlet*

ACADEMY AWARDS
Picture Produced by Laurence Olivier
Actor Laurence Olivier
Art Direction/Set Decoration (b/w) Roger Furse/Carmen Dillon
Costume Design (b/w) Roger Furse

NOMINATIONS
Direction Laurence Olivier
Supporting Actress Jean Simmons
Scoring of a Dramatic or Comedy Picture
William Walton

1953 *Julius Caesar*

ACADEMY AWARD
Art Direction/Set Decoration (b/w) Cedric Gibbons and Edward Carfagno/Edwin B. Willis and Hugh Hunt

NOMINATIONS
Picture Produced by John Houseman
Actor Marlon Brando
Cinematography (b/w) Joseph Ruttenberg
Scoring of a Dramatic or Comedy Picture
Miklos Rozsa

1953 *Kiss Me Kate*

NOMINATION
Scoring of a Musical Picture André Previn and Saul Chaplin

1956 *Richard III*

NOMINATION
Actor Laurence Olivier

1956 *Forbidden Planet*

NOMINATION
Special Effects A. Arnold Gillespie, Irving Ries and Wesley C. Miller

1961 *West Side Story*

ACADEMY AWARDS
Picture Produced by Robert Wise
Direction Robert Wise and Jerome Robbins
Supporting Actor George Chakiris
Supporting Actress Rita Moreno
Cinematography (colour) Daniel L. Fapp
Art Direction/Set Decoration (colour) Boris Leven/Victor A. Gangelin
Costume Design (colour) Irene Sharaff
Sound Todd-AO Sound Department (Fred Hynes, sound director), and Samuel Godwyn Studio Sound Department (Gordon E. Sawyer, sound director)
Film Editing Thomas Stanford
Scoring of a Musical Picture Saul Chaplin, Johnny Green, Sid Ramin and Irwin Kostal

NOMINATION
Adapted Screenplay Ernest Lehman

1965 *Othello*

NOMINATIONS
Actor Laurence Olivier
Supporting Actor Frank Finlay
Supporting Actress Maggie Smith
Supporting Actress Joyce Redman

1967 *The Taming of the Shrew*

NOMINATIONS
Art Direction/Set Decoration Lorenzo Mongiardino, John DeCuir, Elven Webb and Giuseppe Mariani/Dario Simoni and Luigi Gervasi
Costume Design Irene Sharaff and Danilo Donati

1968 *Romeo and Juliet*

ACADEMY AWARDS
Cinematography Pasquale de Santis
Costume Design Danilo Donati

NOMINATIONS
Picture Produced by Anthony Havelock-Allan and John Brabourne
Direction Franco Zeffirelli

1985 *Ran*

ACADEMY AWARD
Costume Design Emi Wada

NOMINATION
Direction Akira Kurosawa
Cinematography Takao Saito, Masaharu Ueda and Asakazu Nakai
Art Direction Yoshiru Muraki and Shinobu Muraki

1989 *Henry V*

ACADEMY AWARD
Costume Design Phyllis Dalton

NOMINATIONS
Actor Kenneth Branagh
Direction Kenneth Branagh

1990 *Hamlet*

NOMINATIONS
Art Direction/Set Decoration Dante Ferretti/Francesca Lo Schiavo
Costume Design Maurizio Millenotti

1995 *Richard III*

NOMINATIONS
Art Direction/Set Decoration Tony Burrough
Costume Design Shuna Harwood

1996 *Hamlet*

NOMINATIONS
Adapted Screenplay Kenneth Branagh
Art Direction/Set Decoration Tim Harvey
Costume Design Alex Byrne
Original Dramatic Score Patrick Doyle

1996 *William Shakespeare's Romeo + Juliet*

NOMINATION
Art Direction/Set Decoration Catherine Martin/Brigitte Broch

1999 *Shakespeare in Love*

ACADEMY AWARDS
Picture Produced by David Parfitt, Donna Gigliotti, Harvey Weinstein, Edward Zwick and Marc Norman
Actress Gwyneth Paltrow
Supporting Actress Judi Dench
Original Screenplay Marc Norman and Tom Stoppard
Art Direction/Set Decoration Martin Childs and Jill Quertier
Costume Design Sandy Powell
Original Musical or Comedy Score Stephen Warbeck

NOMINATIONS
Direction John Madden
Supporting Actor Geoffrey Rush
Cinematography Richard Greatrex
Film Editing David Gamble
Make-up Lisa Westcott and Veronica Brebner
Sound Robin O'Donoghue, Dominic Lester and Peter Glossop

2000 *Titus*

NOMINATION
Costume Design Milena Canonero

SHAKESPEARE ON TV

Above: Judi Dench, left, and Ian McKellen as husband and wife in *Macbeth* (1979), one of the greatest television Shakespeares ever made.

At its worst, television turns a Shakespeare play into an interminable series of talking heads, set against studio backdrops that are trapped awkwardly between theatrical illusion and cinematic reality.

At its best, as in the five productions covered on the following pages, television can illuminate the poetry and psychology of Shakespeare's language more forcefully than either theatre or cinema. The small screen brings the Bard's characters into your living room and can involve you as intimately in Desdemona's agonies as in those of a betrayed soap opera wife. It can leave you more dismayed by Macbeth than you would be by a cop show's most corrupt detective.

TV Shakespeare comes in two varieties: theatre productions adapted for television (this chapter's **Antony and Cleopatra**, **Macbeth** and **Othello**) and versions conceived especially for the small screen (this chapter's **King Lear** and **The Taming of the Shrew**). The **Shrew** was one of the few outstanding adaptations in the BBC Shakespeare – the largest ever television project dedicated to the Bard's work. Devised by British producer Cedric Messina and part-funded by the Time-Life corporation, it involved the filming of all 37 plays at a combined cost of around

$15 million. They were screened in Britain and by the Public Broadcasting Service in the US between 1978 and 1985.

Direction, production design and performances for the series were intended to be readily accessible to the largest possible international audience, an approach that often led to accusations of bland conservatism from TV critics. Reviewers generally had more praise for the scale of the undertaking than its overall artistic achievement.

American Shakespeare enjoyed its small-screen heyday in the 1950s, thanks to NBC's Hallmark Hall of Fame series. In return for copious advertising, Hallmark, the Kansas-based greetings cards giant, invested heavily in well-made, respectable productions, budgeted (at today's prices) at around $2–3 million each.

Between 1953 and 1960, Hallmark Shakespeares invariably starred Maurice Evans. He was already 51 when he played Hamlet in the first production and appeared in six more, including *Richard II* and *Macbeth* (US television's first colour Shakespeare, in 1954). Average Hallmark audiences of between 8 and 18 million were well below those for top-rated sitcoms or game shows, but compared to combined attendances for Shakespeare at every theatre in the US, the figures were colossal.

ANTONY AND CLEOPATRA (1974)

UK 162 MINS COLOUR

CAST	RICHARD JOHNSON (Antony), JANET SUZMAN (Cleopatra), PATRICK STEWART (Enobarbus), CORIN REDGRAVE (Octavius), ROSEMARY MCHALE (Charmian), RAYMOND WESTWELL (Lepidus), TIM PIGOTT-SMITH (Proculeius)
DIRECTED BY	JON SCOFFIELD (TV) TREVOR NUNN (STAGE)
PRODUCTION COMPANY	ATV
MUSIC	GUY WOOLFENDEN

This adaptation of Trevor Nunn's acclaimed 1972 *Antony and Cleopatra* for the Royal Shakespeare Company is captivating and superbly acted. As *The Times* noted: 'Television lifted the production off the stage and into its own ethereal element.'

The actors are obviously in a studio throughout, yet you feel transported to Egypt and Rome, thanks to brilliantly suggestive production design and camerawork. In the Egyptian scenes, Janet Suzman's majestic Cleopatra, Richard Johnson's rugged Antony and their followers wear loose, multi-coloured robes, recline on vast cushions, wine cups in hand, or dance to fluttering Middle-Eastern woodwind. Figures are viewed through lace curtains, or an artificial heat haze, and the edge of the frame is often blurred, as if Antony's 'lascivious wassails' were too delightful to be real.

In Rome, Corin Redgrave's puritanical Octavius and his deputies wear white togas, stand in tight, stiff groups and are framed in sharp focus against an antiseptic, bright white background. These vivid contrasts alert our senses to the tension between Egyptian freedom and Roman discipline, while the sparkling verse and intelligent performances show that tension giving rise to tragedy.

The four principals, retained from the stage production, are outstanding. Suzman, tanned and husky-voiced, gives equal weight to all the queen's contradictory qualities: vanity, capriciousness, self-assurance and girlish vulnerability. Even while capable of betraying Antony, she is so deeply in love with him that she utters an unforgettable, primal scream when he dies. Johnson blends courage, unquenchable largesse and the agonized self-awareness of a man who knows that his passions will destroy him. Both actors capture the essence distilled by Shakespeare's language: godlike desires mingled with all-too-human failings.

Alongside them, Patrick Stewart's amiable, bearded Enobarbus is every inch the good soldier, torn by divided loyalties. Redgrave is icily convincing, making Octavius a ruthless politician who has never known a moment's joy. Scoffield and Nunn ensure that this extremely long and complicated play progresses at a healthy pace (helped by the omission of the Pompey subplot), although when it was shown on ABC in the US in 1975 the running time was extended by advertising. That prompted many angry viewers to write to *The New York Times*, complaining at the ludicrous clashes between poetic tragedy and dumb commercials for soft drinks, cough medicine and deodorant.

Right: Janet Suzman as Cleopatra, centre, kneeling at the feet of Richard Johnson as Antony after his defeat at the Battle of Actium.

MACBETH (1979)
UK 146 MINS COLOUR

CAST	IAN MCKELLEN (Macbeth), JUDI DENCH (Lady Macbeth), JOHN WOODVINE (Banquo), BOB PECK (Macduff), GRIFFITH JONES (Duncan), ROGER REES (Malcolm), IAN MCDIARMID (Ross/Porter)
DIRECTED BY	PHILIP CASSON (TV) TREVOR NUNN (STAGE)
PRODUCED BY	TREVOR NUNN
MUSIC	GUY WOOLFENDEN

Below: Judi Dench as Lady Macbeth. *The Scotsman* said her sleepwalking scene 'will be remembered as long as acting is honoured'.

'You'll never see a better television production of Shakespeare.' That was how *The Guardian* greeted the Royal Shakespeare Company's **Macbeth** in 1979, and more than 20 years later there's no reason to dispute that view.

This is a terrifying record of the production originally directed by Trevor Nunn at The Other Place in Stratford-upon-Avon in 1976, on a bare stage and with a budget of just £250, and the television version amplifies that stark simplicity. The actors perform against a blacked-out background and Nunn concentrates relentlessly on troubled voices and pale, often feverish, faces illuminated by harsh spotlight.

With Griffith Jones's meek, aged Duncan more like a pope than a king, Bob Peck's pious Macduff dressed in priestly black, and a mighty church organ dominating Guy Woolfenden's score, we witness a battle not unlike the one less convincingly depicted in Orson Welles's *Macbeth* (*see* page 72), between deeply religious souls and a man whose only god is ambition, Ian McKellen's intimidating Macbeth.

McKellen soars and plummets from swaggering confidence to breathless terror and back again. He forms an astonishing partnership with Judi Dench's black-clad Lady Macbeth, and the fluctuating balance of power in their relationship has never seemed clearer. He is as shocked by her initial resolve as she is by his foaming delirium at the 'sight' of Banquo's ghost. When she goes mad with guilt, his indifference is chilling.

The pair had won awards for their stage portrayals in 1976 and they provide most of **Macbeth**'s many unforgettable moments: McKellen grasping the grotesque puppets that represent the witches' apparitions; Dench's prolonged, screeching howl in the sleepwalking scene that, said *The Scotsman*, 'will be remembered as long as acting is honoured'.

There isn't a weak link in the cast. A naive-looking Roger Rees manages to bring off the notoriously difficult and, on screen, usually omitted speech in which Malcolm pretends to be even more wicked than Macbeth. Peck endows Macduff with profound love of God, Scotland and his family. His dazed, rather than triumphant, response after killing Macbeth leads into the production's suitably numbing final image: a freeze-frame showing Macduff's bloody hands clutching twin daggers, alongside the Scottish crown that has been the object of so much slaughter.

THE TAMING OF THE SHREW (1980)

UK/US 125 MINS COLOUR

CAST	JOHN CLEESE (Petruchio), SARAH BADEL (Katharina), JOHN FRANKLYN-ROBBINS (Baptista), SUSAN PENHALIGON (Bianca), SIMON CHANDLER (Lucentio), DAVID KINCAID (Grumio), FRANK THORNTON (Gremio), JONATHAN CECIL (Hortensio), ANTHONY PEDLEY (Tranio)
DIRECTED BY	JONATHAN MILLER
PRODUCED BY	JONATHAN MILLER
MUSIC	STEPHEN OLIVER

Below: Sarah Badel as Katharina and John Cleese as Petruchio on the Paduan marketplace, one of just three sets used in Miller's sprightly production.

As Petruchio in this BBC production, John Cleese can't help evoking memories of his most famous television role. Early on, when he gives a withering look to his insubordinate servant, Grumio (a shabby looking David Kincaid), and viciously twists his ear, we could be watching Basil Fawlty torturing Manuel in *Fawlty Towers*.

It is an inspired piece of casting. Cleese's immense height and famously sardonic tone of voice are perfect for Petruchio's overbearing arrogance, while anyone who recalls Basil's hopeless failure to tame the poisonously shrewish Sybil will relish the irony of Cleese overcoming Sarah Badel's proud, buxom Katharina. He does so with wondrous comic timing and a restraint that reflects director Jonathan Miller's belief that the *Shrew* 'really is a more serious play than most people have taken it for'.

Cleese's sober Petruchio is a very distant relative of the oafish drunkard played by Richard Burton in Zeffirelli's *Shrew* (see page 140). He takes no delight in depriving Kate of food and sleep and is movingly surprised by his physical attraction to her. By the same token, Badel's Kate knows she has found a loving husband without having to sacrifice her individuality completely. Miller wants us to see the taming as a reasonable way for Elizabethan men and women to arrive at a mutual understanding that, as Petruchio says, should bring them 'peace ... love and quiet life'.

Miller's staging is sparsely effective, with just three principal sets (a narrow Paduan marketplace, a sitting room in Baptista's house and Petruchio's very modest dining room-cum-bedchamber). Miller's sprightly treatment of the sub-plot ensures that this **Shrew** is only slightly less enjoyable when the lead couple are off screen, with fine performances from Susan Penhaligon, as a feisty Bianca, and Jonathan Cecil, as a simpering Hortensio. Anthony Pedley turns Tranio into an engagingly chirpy cockney.

The omission of the *Shrew*'s Induction was out of keeping with the BBC Shakespeare's generally faithful treatment of the plays, and Miller permits a few unnecessary ad libs. Otherwise, in the words of *The Listener* magazine, this is 'as fresh and appealing as Shakespeare could possibly be'. Anyone watching it after seeing Zeffirelli's loud and extravagant *Shrew* might almost suspect that they were based on different plays.

17

KING LEAR (1983)
UK 159 MINS COLOUR

CAST	LAURENCE OLIVIER (King Lear), DOROTHY TUTIN (Goneril), ROBERT LANG (Albany), DIANA RIGG (Regan), JEREMY KEMP (Cornwall), ANNA CALDER-MARSHALL (Cordelia), JOHN HURT (Fool), COLIN BLAKELY (Kent), LEO MCKERN (Gloucester), DAVID THRELFALL (Edgar), ROBERT LINDSAY (Edmund)
DIRECTED BY	MICHAEL ELLIOTT
PRODUCTION COMPANY	GRANADA TELEVISION
MUSIC	GORDON CROSSE

Olivier is too mellow, too childlike to hurl forth Lear's imprecations and too cozy for the character's anguish. Wall Street Journal

Confronted by the cloudy eyes, frail body and strained voice of Laurence Olivier as Lear, the king's opening promise to 'crawl toward death' has never sounded so credible, or so poignant.

Olivier was 75 and in poor health when he filmed **King Lear** at Granada Television's Manchester studios and, whether from physical necessity, choice, or both, his white-bearded Lear is touchingly benevolent where many other actors have made him tyrannical.

Within the miniature Stonehenge that dominates a murkily lit, Iron-Age production design, Olivier banishes Anna Calder-Marshall's earthy Cordelia more in bewildered sorrow than rage. It's easy to understand why he inspires affectionate, rather than dutiful devotion from John Hurt's boyish, slightly camp, Fool, Colin Blakely's stocky, fearless Kent, and Leo McKern's genial, dignified Gloucester.

Olivier, said the *Wall Street Journal*, was 'too childlike to hurl forth [Lear's] imprecations and too cozy for the character's anguish', but its critic still acknowledged 'a rare and profound performance', that magnificently shows Lear's half-senile mind wandering distractedly from thought to thought. When, in his madness, he strips to the waist the sight of his pale, wrinkled flesh makes it impossible to separate the king from the actor's past screen glories. You think of Olivier's athletic Hamlet, or muscular Othello, and are shocked by what age has done to him.

As his elder daughters, Dorothy Tutin and Diana Rigg match one another in pitiless disdain. Robert Lindsay makes a seduc-tive Edmund and David Threlfall impressively transforms Edgar from wimp to warrior.

Michael Elliott's direction, although sometimes hampered by awkward editing and monotonous camerawork (overreliant on tight close-ups in group scenes), is always sensitive. He uses the stone circle to achieve a powerful symmetry at the climax, as Lear, now clean-shaven and dressed in a ghostly white shift, lays down to die beside Cordelia, on the plinth that bore his throne in the opening scene.

This final image in Olivier's last screen Shakespeare project would have an ironic postscript. For all his evident frailty, Olivier lived until 1989; Elliott, an outstanding director who co-founded Manchester's Royal Exchange Theatre, died in 1984, aged just 53.

Above: Pictured here in the division of the kingdom scene, Laurence Olivier was a magnificent Lear – his body all too frail but his talents absolutely intact.

OTHELLO (1990)
UK 204 MINS COLOUR

CAST	WILLARD WHITE (Othello), IAN MCKELLEN (Iago), IMOGEN STUBBS (Desdemona), ZOË WANAMAKER (Emilia), MICHAEL GRANDAGE (Roderigo), SEAN BAKER (Cassio), CLIVE SWIFT (Brabantio)
DIRECTED BY	TREVOR NUNN
PRODUCED BY	GREG SMITH
MUSIC	GUY WOOLFENDEN

Trevor Nunn's riveting, minimalist **Othello**, like his *Macbeth* (*see* page 192), began life at The Other Place, the Royal Shakespeare Company's 200-seat studio auditorium in Stratford-upon-Avon, and its claustrophobic intensity translates perfectly from small theatre to small screen.

The costumes place *Othello* in the19th century; subtle lighting and a few pieces of furniture are all that denote changes of location, since every scene takes place within Bob Crowley's simple, courtyard design, bordered on three sides by pine-panelled walls at ground level and a first-floor facade of slatted shutters.

It leaves the play's victims trebly confined: by the edges of the screen, the courtyard and Iago's scheming. Iago's genius lies in his precise assessment of everyone around him, and McKellen responds with the acting equivalent of perfect pitch: tone of voice and body language altering precisely, as characters and occasion demand.

This stiff-backed soldier, with a clipped moustache and no-nonsense, North-of-England accent, is alternately reassuring and contemptuous towards Roderigo (movingly played by Michael Grandage), chummy with Sean Baker's modest, good-natured Cassio, or insidiously deferential to Willard White's Othello. In soliloquy, however, the mask falls away and McKellen stares into the camera, trembling with deranged hatred for the Moor and making the audience feel awkwardly complicit.

His performance, which on stage in 1989 had earned the *Evening Standard* Award for Best Actor, dominates the production without eclipsing the always-excellent Zoë Wanamaker, as a melancholy but resilient Emilia, or Jamaican-born White, an internationally renowned opera singer rising impressively to the challenge of his first straight acting role.

Tall and dignified, with a beautiful bass voice, he appears to be both father and husband to Imogen Stubbs's disarmingly girlish Desdemona, and this combination of delicate concern and the passion of a newlywed makes the Moor's transformation and her murder particularly dreadful.

The devastating conclusion comes after three hours during which Nunn has skilfully built up the tension more gradually than in the theatre, introducing fade-outs to indicate that several hours have elapsed during scenes that are continuous on stage. His expert control of pace and superb eye for imaginative details, added to the performances, led *The Observer* to conclude that this was 'as near to perfect a piece of television drama as you could get'.

Above: Jamaican-born opera singer Willard White made an impressive straight acting debut as the Moor.

When future generations look back on the 20th century's enormously varied array of Shakespeare on film and television, the work of John Gielgud will provide one of the most important and consistent threads.

A Gielgud screen retrospective would cover more than 70 years. It would begin with a scratchy, silent snippet of his stage performance as a 20-year-old Romeo, filmed at a London theatre in 1924 for *Eve's Film Review*, a women's 'cinemagazine', and carry on through to a fleeting, silent appearance as King Priam in Kenneth Branagh's *Hamlet*, and the advice he offers to Al Pacino on Shakespearean acting in *Looking for Richard* (both 1996).

His appearances in the intervening decades, chiefly in *Julius Caesar*, *Richard III*, *Chimes at Midnight* and *Prospero's Books*, demonstrate his exquisite voice and deep affinity for the rhythms and textures of Shakespeare's language. No one brought greater intelligence or humanity to characters such as Cassius and Clarence, Henry IV and Prospero, and the close-up might have been invented for a man who, as the great drama critic Kenneth Tynan put it, was always 'an actor from the neck up'.

Gielgud's screen work could hardly be more different from the unbridled energy of the man who was his principal rival for the mantle of England's greatest Shakespearean actor: Laurence Olivier. Gielgud always envied Olivier's far greater physical authority, and Olivier suggested the pair were 'the reverse of the same coin'. If Gielgud represented spirituality and beauty, Olivier was the baser, earthier parts of humanity.

Gielgud was born the son of a wealthy stockbroker in London in April 1904. The theatre was in his blood (his great-aunt was the legendary Victorian actress, Ellen Terry) and it soon took hold of his life. He made his professional debut at London's Old Vic at 17 as the Herald who announces 'the number of the slaughter'd French' in *Henry V* and soon graduated to leading roles.

His greatest blessing was a voice that carried the music of Shakespeare's verse and the essence of his characters, and which Alec Guinness would later describe as 'a silver trumpet muffled in silk'. His lyrical, romantic performances at the Old Vic brought huge acclaim, and he would go on to play all the great Shakespearean roles, including Macbeth, Benedick, Othello, Lear and, in more than 500 performances, Hamlet. In the 1930s he began directing with comparable success, most famously with a 1935 *Romeo and Juliet* in which he and Olivier alternated as Romeo and Mercutio. His film career, however, took much longer to blossom.

In 1934, the great producer, Alexander Korda, had offered to finance a feature film of Gielgud's *Hamlet*, but Gielgud declined, suggesting that 'Shakespeare was not a good idea for the screen'. His antipathy to filming the plays soon deepened. He walked out after ten minutes of George Cukor's *Romeo and Juliet* and wrote to a friend that watching Max Reinhardt's *A Midsummer Night's Dream* was 'like having an operation'.

> I think it might be of interest to somebody in the future to see what my Shakespeare was like.
>
> John Gielgud

Left: Kenneth Branagh, left, directs Gielgud for his brief, silent appearance as King Priam in *Hamlet* (1996).

Hollywood breakthrough

Cinema audiences did see glimpses of his talent, in a couple of 1920s silents, and in Alfred Hitchcock's *The Secret Agent* (UK, 1936), but in the 1980s he would recall that these occasional forays into cinema were 'remarkably uninteresting, giving me no confidence in my adaptability'.

It was not until 1952, when Olivier's *Henry V* and *Hamlet* had established his pre-eminence in filmed Shakespeare, that Gielgud finally awoke to the opportunities that cinema brought to the Bard, thanks to MGM's *Julius Caesar*.

Playing Cassius in Hollywood taught him that 'gesticulation and shouting' – necessary 'evils' for an actor trying to make every line of *Julius Caesar* reach the back row of a theatre's Upper Circle – could be reduced to a minimum on screen, 'where every look, every subtlety of phrasing, can be caught by the camera in a flash'. Reassured by director Joseph L. Mankiewicz's fidelity to the text, Gielgud began to appreciate 'the fascinating subtleties of screen acting'. Back home in England after the end of shooting, Gielgud was required to re-record some of his dialogue and Mankiewicz told him a print of the picture would be sent over. Don't bother, said Gielgud, who promptly recorded his lines on to tape. Such was his feeling for Shakespearean rhythms that the tape perfectly matched his lip movements on screen. The release of *Julius Caesar* in 1953 coincided with the award of Gielgud's knighthood – an honour that came years later than expected, with some suggesting the delay had been caused by his homosexuality.

Left: Gielgud as Hamlet in a 1936 stage production. He turned down an offer to film the play because at the time he believed that Shakespeare 'was not a good idea for the screen'.

Further evidence of his formidable technique came when he went to Spain to work on Welles's *Chimes at Midnight* in 1966. He had just ten days in which to film all of King Henry's scenes and, to make matters worse, in most of them was obliged to act opposite a stand-in, as Keith Baxter (Prince Hal) and the other co-stars were not present. Yet he gave an impeccable performance, and the experience led Welles to place Gielgud alongside Charlton Heston as one of the two 'nicest actors I've ever worked with in my life ... They're two kinds of angels'.

Filming was much more straightforward when he had to dress like Shakespeare and deliver the Prologue in Renato Castellani's 1954 *Romeo and Juliet* (a role he repeated on television for the BBC in 1978), and a year later his and Olivier's contrasting styles could be viewed side-by-side in *Richard III*.

A below-par performance from Gielgud as Caesar in *Julius Caesar* (1970) might have been the result of what he felt was a lack of input from director Stuart Burge. 'I *like* being given ideas,' he told an interviewer. 'Unlike Larry [Olivier], who has it all worked out, I'm never certain.' He was his usual, impressive self as the Ghost opposite Richard Chamberlain's prince in a Napoleonic-era *Hamlet* for American television in 1970 and as John of Gaunt for the BBC's *Richard II* (1978).

Every one of these parts confirms Gielgud's self-assessment, that he was 'quite unable to act without suggesting good breeding'. He was never an Olivier-like chameleon, who could master characters of every class and nationality. When he played Sherlock Holmes for the BBC and the great detective had to disguise

himself as a coalseller, Gielgud's attempt at a cockney accent was, by his own admission, laughable.

This lack of versatility never prevented him from winning well-bred roles in good movies: Lord Raglan in *The Charge of The Light Brigade* (UK, 1968), a butler in *Murder on the Orient Express* (US, 1974) and a surgeon in *The Elephant Man* (US, 1980). Then came the role of Hobson, Dudley Moore's long-suffering, sarcastic and surprisingly foul-mouthed butler in the comedy, *Arthur* (US, 1981).

Gielgud had turned the job down twice, believing that 'it would be rather cheap to say those four-letter words', but ended by earning the Golden Globe and Oscar for Best Supporting Actor. *Arthur* was a major international hit and, in his late seventies, Gielgud was suddenly 'discovered' by millions of people who had never seen or perhaps even heard of his Shakespeare work.

Waiting for Prospero

Throughout these years, he clung on to his dream of playing Prospero on screen. He had starred in *The Tempest* four times on stage, in 1930, 1940, 1957 and 1974, and believed that the play 'could make a marvellous film, if one could capture the strange and magical atmosphere of the island'.

He once talked to Benjamin Britten about composing a *Tempest* film score and at various points approached three great directors about the project – Ingmar Bergman, Akira Kurosawa and Alain Resnais, the Frenchman for whom Gielgud had given

one of his finest performances, as a sleepless, dying novelist in *Providence* (France, 1977).

His chance finally came after he narrated Peter Greenaway's adaptation of Dante's *Inferno* for Britain's Channel 4 television. He put the *Tempest* idea to Greenaway and it became *Prospero's Books*.

Before filming began, he worried that having played Prospero so often on stage, he would sound 'very hammy and old-fashioned and declamatory'. During filming he endured sitting in freezing water for days at a time, and wearing a robe so heavy that it had to be lifted on by four wardrobe assistants. Yet he still managed to give a performance of which he was immensely proud. It was only six years after the film's release that his true feelings about what Greenaway had done to *The Tempest* turned out to be the same as those of most critics; Greenaway, Gielgud told *The Sunday Times*, 'didn't know the point of the play'.

The years since *Prospero's Books* saw him collect many honours: he was made a fellow of BAFTA in 1992, the Globe theatre on Shaftesbury Avenue was renamed the Gielgud in 1994 and two years later the Queen presented him with the Order of Merit. In May 2000 he died peacefully at home in Buckinghamshire, aged 96.

· 'I think it might be of interest to somebody in the future to see what my Shakespeare was like', he said at the time of *Prospero's Books*. That remark is like a Gielgud performance – understated and absolutely true.

CHRONOLOGY OF FILMS

This chronology of Shakespeare films and their directors from 1929 to 2000 featured in this book illustrates distinct phases of production: the initial burst of activity in the US and Britain, in 1935–36; what might be called 'the Olivier/Welles era' from 1944 to 1966; the fairly random spate of films between 1967 and 1972; the very lean spell during the rest of the 1970s and through the 1980s and, finally, the renaissance inspired by Kenneth Branagh's *Henry V* in 1989 that shows no signs of ending.

1929   *The Taming of the Shrew* (US) **Sam Taylor**

1935   *A Midsummer Night's Dream* (US) **Max Reinhardt/William Dieterle**

1936   *As You Like It* (UK) **Paul Czinner**
      Romeo and Juliet (US) **George Cukor**

1944   *Henry V* (UK) **Laurence Olivier**

1947   *A Double Life* (US) **George Cukor**

1948   *Hamlet* (UK) **Laurence Olivier**
      Macbeth (US) **Orson Welles**

1952   *Othello* (Morocco) **Orson Welles**

1953   *Julius Caesar* (US) **Joseph L. Mankiewicz**
      Kiss Me Kate (US) **George Sidney**

1954   *Romeo and Juliet* (Italy/UK) **Renato Castellani**

1955   *Othello* (USSR) **Sergei Yutkevich**
      Richard III (UK) **Laurence Olivier**
      Joe Macbeth (UK) **Ken Hughes**

1956   *Forbidden Planet* (US) **Fred McLeod Wilcox**

1957   *Throne of Blood* (Japan) **Akira Kurosawa**

1961   *West Side Story* (US) **Robert Wise/Jerome Robbins**

1964   *Hamlet* (USSR) **Grigori Kozintsev**
      Hamlet (US) **John Gielgud/Bill Colleran**

1965   *Othello* (UK) **Stuart Burge**

1966   *Chimes at Midnight* (Spain/Switzerland) **Orson Welles**

1967   *The Taming of the Shrew* (UK/Italy) **Franco Zeffirelli**

1968   *Romeo and Juliet* (Italy/UK) **Franco Zeffirelli**

1969   *Hamlet* (UK) **Tony Richardson**
      A Midsummer Night's Dream (UK) **Peter Hall**

1970   *Julius Caesar* (UK) **Stuart Burge**

1971   *King Lear* (UK/Denmark) **Peter Brook**
      King Lear (USSR) **Grigori Kozintsev**
      Macbeth (UK) **Roman Polanski**

1972   *Antony and Cleopatra* (Spain/Switzerland/UK) **Charlton Heston**

1979   *The Tempest* (UK) **Derek Jarman**

1982   *Tempest* (US) **Paul Mazursky**

1985   *Ran* (Japan/France) **Akira Kurosawa**

1987   *King Lear* (US/Switzerland) **Jean-Luc Godard**

1989   *Henry V* (UK) **Kenneth Branagh**

1990   *Hamlet* (US) **Franco Zeffirelli**

1991   *Men of Respect* (US) **William Reilly**
      Prospero's Books (UK/Netherlands/France/Italy) **Peter Greenaway**

1992   *As You Like It* (UK) **Christine Edzard**

1993   *Much Ado About Nothing* (UK/US) **Kenneth Branagh**

1995   *Othello* (US/UK) **Oliver Parker**

1996   *Hamlet* (US/UK) **Kenneth Branagh**
      Richard III (UK) **Richard Loncraine**
      William Shakespeare's Romeo + Juliet (US) **Baz Luhrmann**
      Twelfth Night (UK/US) **Trevor Nunn**
      Looking for Richard (US) **Al Pacino**

1997   *A Thousand Acres* (US) **Jocelyn Moorhouse**

1999   *10 Things I Hate About You* (US) **Gil Junger**
      William Shakespeare's A Midsummer Night's Dream (US/Germany) **Michael Hoffman**
      Titus (US) **Julie Taymor**

2000   *Love's Labour's Lost* (UK/France/US) **Kenneth Branagh**
      Hamlet (US) **Michael Almereyda**

The shortage of concrete information about Shakespeare's career means that the dates of composition of most of his plays remain notoriously difficult to pin down. Scholars have used documentary evidence and intelligent guess-work to arrive at what they consider to be the most accurate dates, but sometimes this is still only within a period of two or three years, and the dates continue to fuel considerable debate.

The chronology below cannot, therefore, be definitive, but is designed to give an indication of where the most- and least-filmed plays fall within Shakespeare's career. Within the 25-year spread, the astonishing period between 1599 and 1606 has proved the most fertile for film-makers.

1588–91	*King Henry VI, Parts 1–3*
1588–93	*The Comedy of Errors*
1588–94	*Love's Labour's Lost*
1592–93	*The Tragedy of Richard III*
1592–94	*Titus Andronicus*
1593–94	*The Taming of the Shrew*
1592–93	*The Two Gentlemen of Verona*
1594–95	*The Life and Death of King John*
1594–96	*Romeo and Juliet*
1595	*The Tragedy of King Richard II*
1595–96	*A Midsummer Night's Dream*
1596–97	*The Merchant of Venice*
1596–97	*King Henry IV, Part 1*
1597–98	*King Henry IV, Part 2*

1598–99	*Much Ado About Nothing*
1598–99	*The Life of King Henry V*
1599–1600	*Julius Caesar*
1599–1600	*As You Like It*
1599–1600	*The Merry Wives of Windsor*
1600–01	*Hamlet, Prince of Denmark*
1601–02	*Twelfth Night; or, What You Will*
1601–02	*Troilus and Cressida*
1602–03	*All's Well That Ends Well*
1603–04	*Othello, the Moor of Venice*
1604–05	*Measure for Measure*
1605–06	*King Lear*
1605–06	*Macbeth*
1606–07	*Antony and Cleopatra*
1607–08	*Timon of Athens*
1607–08	*Coriolanus*
1607–08	*Pericles, Prince of Tyre*
1609–10	*Cymbeline*
1610–11	*The Winter's Tale*
1611–12	*The Tempest*
1612–13	*The Famous History of King Henry VIII*

INDEX OF PERSONNEL

INDEX OF FILMS

BIBLIOGRAPHY

Bragg, Melvyn – *Rich: The Life of Richard Burton*, London 1988

Branagh, Kenneth – *Beginning*, London 1989; *Much Ado About Nothing*, London 1993; *In The Bleak Midwinter*, London 1995; *Hamlet*, London 1996

Bulman, J.C. and Coursen, H.R. (eds.) – *Shakespeare on Television*, Hanover/London, 1988

Carey, Gary – *Doug and Mary*, Toronto and Vancouver 1977

Davies, Anthony and Wells, Stanley (eds.) – *Shakespeare and the Moving Image*, Cambridge 1994

Callow, Simon – *Orson Welles – The Road to Xanadu*, London 1995; *The National*, London 1997

Greenaway, Peter – *Prospero's Books: A film of Shakespeare's The Tempest* , London 1991

Hardy, Phil (ed.) – *The Aurum Horror Film Encyclopedia*, London 1995

Heston, Charlton – *In The Arena*, London, 1995

Hoffman, Michael – *A Midsummer Night's Dream*, London 1999

Holderness, Graham – *The Taming of the Shrew*, Manchester 1989

Holden, Anthony – *Laurence Olivier: A Biography*, London 1988

Jarman, Derek – *Dancing Ledge*, London 1984

Kozintsev, Grigori – *King Lear: The Space of Tragedy*, London 1977

Kurosawa, Akira – *Something Like an Autobiography*, New York 1982

Lambert, Gavin – *On Cukor*, London 1973

Leaming, Barbara – *Polanski: His Life And Films*, London 1982

Lippard, Chris (ed.) – *By Angels Driven – The Films of Derek Jarman*, Trowbridge 1996

Leemann, Sergio – *Robert Wise on his Films*, Los Angeles 1995

McKernan, Luke and Terris, Olwen, (eds.) – *Walking Shadows – Shakespeare in the National Film and Television Archive*, London 1994

Manso, Peter – *Brando*, London 1995

Marx, Arthur – *The Nine Lives of Mickey Rooney*, London 1986

Mazursky, Paul – *Show Me The Magic*, New York 1999

McGilligan, Patrick – *George Cukor: A Double Life*, New York 1991

Nunn, Trevor – *Twelfth Night*, London 1996

Olivier, Laurence – *Confessions of an Actor*, London 1982

Osborne, Robert – *70 Years of the Oscar – The Official History of the Academy Awards*, Los Angeles 1999

Parker, John – *Polanski*, London 1993

Powell, Michael – *Million-Dollar Movie*, London 1992

Richie, Donald – *The Films of Akira Kurosawa*, Los Angeles 1965

Rosenbaum, Jonathan (ed.) – *Orson Welles and Peter Bogdanovich: This is Orson Welles*, London 1993

Rothwell, Kenneth S. and Melzer, Annabel Henkin (eds.) – *An International Filmography and Videography*, New York and London 1990

Rothwell, Kenneth S. – *A History of Shakespeare on Screen*, Cambridge 1999

Thomas, Bob – *Thalberg: Life and Legend*, New York 1969

Thomson, David – *Rosebud: The Story of Orson Welles*, London 1996

Van Sant, Gus – *My Own Private Idaho/Even Cowgirls Get The Blues*, London 1993

Zeffirelli, Franco – *Zeffirelli: The Autobiography of Franco Zeffirelli*, New York 1986

ACKNOWLEDGEMENTS

Cover: Front Cover top The Ronald Grant Archive/ Royal Films International
Front Cover bottom The Ronald Grant Archive/ Britannia Films Limited
Back Cover top Kobal Collection/Fims Marceau/ Mercury Prods.
Back Cover bottom The Ronald Grant Archive/Mirisch Pictures

British Broadcasting Corporation 40 Top Right, /Thanks to Derek Jacobi for giving permission to use this image 170 Top, /Thanks to Helen Mirren for giving permission to use this image 169 Bottom, /Thanks to Sarah Badel & John Cleese for giving permission to use this image 193.
British Film Institute Stills, Posters & Designs 12, 111, 120, 169 Top, 171 Top Right, 191.
British Film Institute/Filmmuseum, Amsterdam 9 Top Left, /Frame stills from the following films are taken from the British Film Instituteís video release Silent Shakespeare. (For further details tel: 0207 957 8957) 61, 87, 148 Bottom Right, 170 Bottom.
Corbis UK Ltd/Bettmann 8, 198 Top Left, /Jerry Cooke 107, /Everett 20 Top Right, 28, 53, 81 Top, 81 Bottom, 82, 86, 92-93, 98 left, 136, 137, 142, 156, 173 Top, 175, 186-187, 196, 197, /Hulton-Deutsch Collection 106, 108, 198 Top Right, /Robbie Jack 174, /David Lee 146.
A Fox Searchlight Picture. 'TM & Copyright 2000 20th Century Fox' 164 left, 164 right, 165.
Kinema Collection 44, 59 Bottom Right, 66, 75, 138.
Kobal Collection 48, 51, 64, 65, 91 right, /Boyd's Co. 148 Top, 153 Bottom Centre, /BR Home,

Entertainment/ Warner Bros 50 Top, 103, /Castle Rock Entertainment 6, 7, /Columbia 141 Top Right, /Columbia/ Nautilus 149, /Filmways/ Athena/ Lanterna 62-63 Top, 63 Bottom Right, /Fine Line/ Renaissance 167 Top, 167 Centre Left, /20th Century Fox 50 Bottom, 116 Top, 130-131 Centre, /Hepworth 19 Bottom, /Herald Ace-Nippon-Herald-Greenwich 67 Top, 84-85, /Int Films Espanola - Alpine Prods 36, /LenFilm 21 Top, /MGM 57 Top, 57 Bottom, 122 Bottom, 123, /Midwinter Films 185, /Odyssey 183, /Olivier Prods/ London Films/ Big Ben Films 199, /Rank/ Castle Rock-Turner 33 Top Right, /Renaissance Films/ BBC/ Curzon Films 40 Centre, /Republic Films 72-73 Bottom, /Republic 109 /Sand Films 16-17, /TOHO 70, 76, 77, /Touchstone 69, 177, /Two cities 45, /Two Cities/ Rank 22, 49, /United Artists 176, /Unitel/ EMI 147 Bottom, /Universal 96-97 Bottom, /Vilealfa Film Productions 20 Top Left
/Warner Bros 88, Last Productions Ltd Front Cover.
Miramax/©Miramax Film Corp./ photographer Larry Riley 34-35.
Pearson Television 190, 192.
The Ronald Grant Archive 85 Top Right, 92 Bottom Left, 124, 125, 194, 195, /B.I.P. 135 Bottom Right, /Boyd's Co. 152-153 Bottom, 153 Top Left, /Cannon Films 68, /Cannon Italia 94 Bottom Left, /Capitol Film Corp. 135 Bottom Left, /Carollo 30, 31, 144, /Castle Rock 32-33 Top, 94 Top, 104-105 Top, 105 Bottom Right, /Cineman 180, 181, /Columbia Pictures Corp. 18 Top, 95, 154, 155, /Commonwealth United Productions 52, 58-59, /Entertainment Film 166, /Entertainment Films/ Sam Goldwyn Pictures 162-163 Bottom, 163 Top

Right, /Film Locations 74, /Folio Films 159 Top, 159 Bottom, /20th Century Fox 4-5, 60 Bottom, 116-117 Bottom, 117, 118, 131 Top Right, 132, 133, /Goldcrest Films/ Columbia Pictures Corp. 60 Top, /Greenwich Film Productions 67 Bottom, 83, /Guild 110 Top, 112, 114-115 Bottom, 115 Top Right /HOBO 182, /Inter Allied Film Productions 14, 14 Top, 15 Bottom, /Internacional Films Espanola/ Alpine Films 38-39 Top Left, /Internacional Films Espanola/ Alpine Films 39 Top Right, 39 Bottom Right, /Dino de Laurentis, Cinematografica 121, 128-129, 129 Bottom Right, 147 Top, /LenFilm 26, 27, /London Film Productions 113 Top, 113 Bottom, /Merchant Ivory 178 Bottom Left, 178-179 Top Right, /Mercury Productions 98-99 Centre, 100, 101, /MGM 54-55, 56, 122 Top, 139, 150, 151 /MGM/ Warner Bros. 110 Bottom Left, /©1999 Miramax Films & Universal Studios/ photographer Laurie Sparham 10-11, /©Miramax Films & Universal Studios 187 Top Right, 119, 126, 127, /Mosfilm 102, /Nelo Line 37, /Palace Pictures 157 Top, 157 Bottom, /Playboy Productions 78-79, /R.S.C. 90-91 Centre, /Rank Films/ photographer: David Appleby 184, /Renaisance Films 9 Top Right, 46-47 Centre, 47 right, 173 Bottom, /Republic Films Corp. 73 Top Right, /Republic Pictures Corp. 71, 134, 140-141 Bottom, 145, /Sands Films 13, /Touchstone 143, /Two Cities Films/ Rank 23, 24, 25 Top, 25 Bottom, 41, 42-43 Top Centre, 43 Bottom Right, /Universal Pictures 97 Top Right, /Warner Bros. 89, /Woodfall Film Productions 29.
The Shakespeare Film Co./ Intermedia/ photographer Laurie Sparham 160, 161 Top, 161 Bottom, 172.